MODERN STUDIES

The World Today

MODERN STUDIES

The World Today

Esmond Wright

 McGRAW-HILL · LONDON

New York · Sydney · Toronto · Mexico
Johannesburg · Panama

Published by
McGRAW-HILL Publishing Company Limited
MAIDENHEAD · BERKSHIRE · ENGLAND

First published 1961
Reprinted 1964
Revised edition 1968

9435²

PRINTED AND BOUND IN GREAT BRITAIN

Preface

Modern Studies, introduced into schools in 1962, is now being taught to secondary pupils following both certificate and non-certificate courses, and is examinable at Ordinary and Higher grades of the Scottish Certificate of Education. The subject has justified itself, and to meet its demands *The World Today*, first published in 1961, has been revised, expanded, newly illustrated, and in places completely rewritten to take account of the political and social changes since it was first planned.

This new edition has been prepared in the belief that Modern Studies has now established itself as a subject in the school curriculum. The book not only replaces the first edition but may be recommended also for classes studying aspects of modern history and international relations for Certificate of Secondary Education and General Certificate of Education examinations.

A number of new topic books are also being published. These, together with the other main text, *Britain Today*, by my former colleague Dr. J. J. Tumelty provide stimulating material for Modern Studies courses.

I am deeply indebted to Alasdair Nicolson of Jordanhill College of Education, Glasgow, for his advice and suggestions, and for arranging critical examination of the text by teachers and pupils involved in these courses.

Esmond Wright

Acknowledgements

The photographs on the following pages are reproduced by kind permission of:

Australian News and Information Bureau, *page* 18.
Camera Press Ltd., *pages* 5, 15, 111, 116, 145, 149, 154, 174, 176, 205, 211, 216.
Infoplan, *page* 44.
Keystone Press Agency, *pages* 2, 20, 82, 90, 93,128,180, 184, 189, 192, 243, 249, 259, 267, 276.
United States Information Service, *pages* 41, 48.

Contents

1. *The Geographical Background to International Affairs*

'Geography is about maps, biography is about chaps', but the connection between maps and chaps is very close. Climate and soil, natural products and pressure of population have always influenced history. Much of mankind's conflict, whether between tribes, city-states or nations, has been over geographical resources and boundaries, over control of minerals, raw materials and river valleys. 'The foreign policy of all the powers', said Napoleon, 'is shaped by their geography.'

The world Nature gave us

Highland and lowland

In mountain areas, with their more savage climate and poorer soil, both agriculture and human settlement are more difficult than in the plains. In all countries mountain people have developed differently from the people of the plains because they are more isolated. Often they even speak a different language.

Savage climate and poor soil limit human settlement in the mountainous areas of the world. In some regions mountains form protective barriers, preventing attack from neighbouring lands. Mountains also offer the chance of adventure or scientific and geographic exploration. The photograph shows members of an expedition climbing Cerro Cao, a mountain in the Andes.

In more highly developed parts of the world, mountain people are nowadays usually miners, lumberers or stock-raisers. In more backward areas, they are still organized in clans or tribes, often raiding the 'softer' and more settled people of the plains.

It is in the lowlands, especially in the river valleys, where settled agriculture and easy road-building are possible, that populations become dense and industry and trade develop, along with urban life. But many an old city still clusters and grows around the easily defended hill-fortress where the first settlement was made. Edinburgh, Stirling, Salzburg, Athens, Corinth are living illustrations of this.

The rivers

Water is one of the absolute necessities of life and that is why, in looking for places to settle and, later, to build their towns, men chose the banks and the mouths of rivers. The earliest civilizations in history grew up in the river valleys: the Nile, the Tigris-Euphrates, the Indus-Ganges, the Hwang-Ho. The rivers, with their periodic floods, provided a constantly fertilized soil and thus guaranteed a constant food supply; this made possible settled agriculture, and provided the stability essential to the growth of large political units; the surrounding deserts and mountains gave some protection from foreign invasion.

Rivers are important for other reasons, too. Originally they were the chief means of inland transport. The Chinese still speak of the roads as dry ways—an indication of the fact that to them the wet way—by river—is still the more natural method of travelling. Many railways, as well as roads, still follow the valleys, like the line from Perth via Pitlochry (along the Tummel) to Inverness and the North, or the Canadian Pacific Railway along the Fraser River to Vancouver.

Rivers allow access to the interior for ships—the Clyde, after it was deepened and widened, made Glasgow a great seaport: 'Glasgow made the Clyde, and the Clyde made Glasgow.' The Rhine reaches into the heart of Germany; and since 1959 the St Lawrence Seaway has been an ocean-route leading to Chicago and Duluth, a 2,000-mile highway. The early routes into the American interior were by water—the St Lawrence River, the Hudson, the Ohio, the Mississippi—although travellers had to carry their canoes (at the *portages*) from the headwaters of one river to the next or to avoid rapids and shallows. Indeed, the development of the United States has been largely shaped by the fact that the continent was approached from across the Atlantic, where explorers found a succession of rivers allowing easy access to the interior. Had they approached it from the Pacific it would have been much harder to find routes inland. Even as it was, the main river-system of North America (the Missouri-Mississippi) flowed from north to south, not from east to west. The pioneers were to move west by pony or by covered wagon, and later by road and rail, not by water. The development of Africa has been handicapped by the lack of such easy routes.

Rivers are important in other ways. 'Egypt is the Nile, the Nile is Egypt.' Desert areas depend on rivers as their one source of water. With adequate dams, barrages and ditches, they permit extensive irrigation. Rivers in upland areas like Northern Scotland or Switzerland, where the flow of water is rapid, are sources of hydro-electric power. The Italian railways are almost entirely run on hydro-electric power from the Italian Alps.

If rivers are blocked or diverted upstream, the life of the lowlands can be threatened. This is why Pakistan fears Indian control of Kashmir, from which the Indus flows, why Egypt fears the Sudan and why the Burmese fear the hill tribes controlling the Irrawaddy. Possession of the headstream can be a political or an economic weapon.

Moreover, rivers are not boundaries but centres of trade and traffic. It is easy to assume that a wide river is a natural frontier, as Louis XIV did in his view of the Rhine, or as the United States and Britain did in the 1840s when they sought to agree on the Columbia River, separating the Washington territory from Oregon, as the boundary between the United States and Canada.

3

But rivers in fact unite. The Mississippi in the United States, the Ganges in India, the Mekong in South-east Asia have brought great prosperity to all the peoples living on either bank. The Rhine is not so much a frontier between European countries as the source and index of their trading wealth.

Relief and the shape of the land

A country is permanently affected by its shape—Norway by its fjords, the Highlands of Scotland by its lochs, Greece by its islands. These features make land communication difficult, sea communication easy, and produce nations of seamen. To such nations the seas are at once a bridge and a protective moat.

Mountains protect also, as the Pyrenees have long cut off Spain from Europe, forming a perfect boundary line. The absence of mountains or rivers as defensive boundaries has always posed problems to Russia, Poland and France. Once an enemy has crossed the Bohemian Mountains the road to Moscow is wide open, although it is a long and cold road and runs across Poland. The only way to hold it, the Russians have found, is to have Generals January and February fighting on their side, as Napoleon discovered in 1812 and Hitler in 1942-43. Once the Germans have crossed the Scheldt, Paris has always been vulnerable; it was saved in 1914 by an army driven to the front line in Parisian taxi-cabs. The need for a defined northern frontier has been a French dream for at least three centuries. Not for nothing did Richelieu want the boundaries of France to be the 'natural' limits—the Rhine, the Alps and the Pyrenees.

Position on the map

The choice of the right place to grow is of vital importance in the birth and prosperity of towns. They are often sited at a river-mouth, river-junction or ford, at a point where a number of routes can converge, or on a natural harbour. Consider the position of Perth, of Panama, of Paris, meeting points of rivers, seas, roads and railways, or of Copenhagen, 'the merchants' harbour', at the entrance to the Baltic.

Trade and the resources of the surrounding area increase their importance. Many an industrial city is the product of a marriage between a river and its local iron or coal resources, like Glasgow or Newcastle. Lyons, Leipzig and Milan owed their prominence to their fairs, because each was the centre of a rich and fertile district. And towns today are becoming more and more important—and more and more alike—wherever they may be. Almost half the population of Britain lives in seven big areas (London, Birmingham, Manchester, Liverpool, the Sheffield-Leeds conurbation, Newcastle and Glasgow) and one-third of the population of Scotland lives or works within ten miles of Sauchiehall Street, Glasgow. One-third of the people of U.S.A. live in eighteen great urban regions. Two out of five Canadians live in the eleven big cities of

Vast deserts are a formidable barrier to travellers. This small group of people is approaching El Golea (in the Sahara), where massive sand dunes surround an oasis.

Canada and one in four in the two big conurbations, Montreal and Toronto. The town today is the economic 'growth point' in every country.

What is true of towns is also true of countries. Their position on the map affects their whole destiny. While the fact that Britain is an island gave reasonable security, Germany's position forced it to be a land power, building up an army to survive against strong neighbours like Russia, Austria and France.

Geographically, of course, a country's position is fixed and permanent, but the importance and strength of that position can be greatly changed in at least two ways.

New geographical discoveries, like those of Columbus, Magellan and all the great explorers of history, open up new routes and new lands. Until Columbus, the British Isles were on the fringe of the Western world, a remote outpost. As trade across the Atlantic developed, Britain became a centre of that trade, a great sea-power and commercial and banking centre. British ships and seamen gave the United Kingdom powerful protection, and its trading interests and desire for resources and ports of call led to the building up of a great overseas empire. The discovery of the Americas and of the Cape of Good

5

Hope route to India had a similar effect on Spain and Portugal, while exactly the same discoveries brought about the decline of Venice and Genoa and the cities of the Hanseatic League.

The other factor that can alter the importance of a country's position is scientific invention. Faster and bigger ships greatly increased both the power and the security of countries like Britain, U.S.A. and Japan, but the dawning of the air age—and now the nuclear age—have radically changed both traffic routes and strategy. The North Polar route, which no ship could ever use, is today one of the most important in the world, especially to U.S.A., Canada, Scandinavia and Russia. Today no country can rely on geographical remoteness to give it either protection or isolation from world problems, as even Tibet has discovered. Were a Channel Tunnel built between Britain and France, British isolation would cease and whether or not Britain joined the Common Market, its economy would become part of a vast trading area, stretching from Glasgow to Milan.

The golden age of geographical discovery is over. Few areas are still unmapped and the resources of nearly all parts of the world are known. But scientific discovery and invention know no boundaries or limits, and will continue to affect the fate of nations as far into the future as we can see.

The mineral wealth of the earth and its distribution

The minerals of the earth are as necessary to civilized life as are food supplies. Let us consider the most important of them.

Coal is no longer the only essential fuel for power and heat, but it is still vitally important. The history of Europe in the nineteenth century was dominated by the location of coal. It appeared in rich seams in Britain, re-appeared in small quantities in north-east France but in great quantities in Belgium and the Ruhr; it continued through Saxony and Silesia to the Donbas coalfields of Russia. As a result, Scandinavia and the Mediterranean countries were largely by-passed by the major industrial developments of the nineteenth century. North America and Europe produce four-fifths of the world's supplies at present. But vast resources are still to be exploited in China and Russia. Africa's lack of coal has been a serious drawback for her.

Iron Ore. This is the basic metal in modern industry and is the main ingredient in steel, an alloy of iron and carbon. France, Russia, Sweden, U.S.A. and Britain produce 75 per cent of the world's iron ore. U.S.A. has the advantage of having good coking coal, excellent for the processing of steel, and so is the world's leading steel producer. Germany is short of iron ore and imports from France, who is herself short of coal. Britain has good supplies of both coal and iron ore, but needs imports of the latter, which she gets from Sweden. There are considerable unworked deposits of iron ore in eastern Brazil and in central India and a good deal still not fully exploited in Russia.

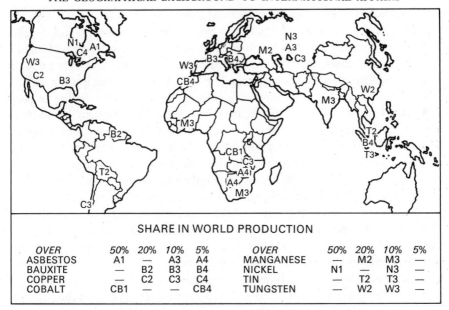

SHARE IN WORLD PRODUCTION

OVER	50%	20%	10%	5%	OVER	50%	20%	10%	5%
ASBESTOS	A1	—	A3	A4	MANGANESE	—	M2	M3	—
BAUXITE	—	B2	B3	B4	NICKEL	N1	—	N3	—
COPPER	—	C2	C3	C4	TIN	—	T2	T3	—
COBALT	CB1	—	—	CB4	TUNGSTEN	—	W2	W3	—

Oil is of paramount importance in the modern world as a fuel. (See *Modern Studies Topic Books*, Esmond Wright, McGraw-Hill.)

Copper. Next to iron, this is the main industrial metal. It is valuable because it mixes readily with other metals; with tin to make bronze, with zinc to make brass. Eighty per cent of the world's supplies come from Chile, U.S.A., Canada and Zambia. The Congo also has large supplies. Copper is often found in difficult and inhospitable regions, like the Atacama Desert in Chile, or the arid mountain states of the American West, so it is expensive.

Tin. Two-thirds of the world's supplies come from Malaysia and the East Indies. There are not large supplies and it is normally used as a thin coating on other metals, or as one ingredient in an alloy. It is very resistant to corrosion.

Nickel. Canada has 70 per cent of the world's supplies.

Aluminium. This is a very important metal since it combines strength, lightness and resistance to rust. It is widely used in modern engineering, especially for aircraft, motor-car, cable and rocket components. U.S.A. and France have large deposits of bauxite, the mineral source of aluminium.

Gold. This is the beautiful, untarnishable, imperishable metal that has been desired by all peoples, in all ages. This metal has long been the measure of value and the standard of wealth. Over one-third of the world's supply comes from South Africa, but it is also found in North and South America, Russia, Australia and New Zealand.

Silver is also extremely valuable. One-third of the world's supply comes from Mexico and one-third from U.S.A.

Uranium has become vastly important during the last few years with the coming of the nuclear age. Already it is one of the most valuable and sought-after of all minerals and has led to growing American investment in Canada. Some African states, like the Congo, also have deposits, and this helps to explain the interest of outside powers, like U.S.A. and Russia, in their future.

Obviously it is very important to a country to have good supplies of such raw materials within its own boundaries, but Nature has not distributed them evenly. Only the United States, China and Russia are really well supplied and they are the only countries which could be more or less self-sufficient. Of the three, only the United States has as yet developed its resources on a very large scale. China has hardly begun. The only other highly industrialized area in the world is Western Europe, where a Common Market has been formed to pool resources for greater efficiency both in producing and selling goods.

Nor should *water supply* be forgotten. To produce a loaf of bread—to grow the grain, make the flour and bake the loaf—calls for 500 gallons of water; a ton of rolled steel needs 110,000 gallons, a ton of synthetic rubber 660,000 gallons. For industrial and human needs the United States uses 320 billion gallons of water a day—over 1,600 gallons a day for every person in the country. Even in a Britain that seems never short of rain, few cities are as fortunate as Glasgow which has steady supplies of water from Loch Katrine. In the English Midlands the need for new sources of water is already an urgent matter, and when Manchester plans to 'raid' the English Lakes or Liverpool to 'raid' North Wales, bitterness can be aroused.

The world's main industrial power belt still remains the North Atlantic area—Eastern U.S.A., Britain, Western Germany, Belgium and Northern France.

The Power of the Powers:
their resources as % of world total

	Area	Population	Coal production	Output of Steel
U.S.A.	7	6	16	40
U.S.S.R.	16	7	19	17
U.K.	0.1	1.8	7	8
W. Germany	0.1	1.8	9	7
France	0.4	1.5	2	6
Benelux	0.05	0.7	2	4
Italy	0.2	1.7	—	2
Japan	0.3	3.2	2	3
China	8	22	1	1
India	2	14	2.5	1
Canada	7	0.6	0.5	2
Brazil	6	2	0.5	—
Australia	6	0.3	2	1

Some countries are poor in mineral wealth but have become great as 'middle-men'. Holland did so, in the seventeenth century, as shippers of other people's goods and as bankers and insurance agents. These roles Britain inherited after Holland lost control of the seas, and although rich in coal and iron, and leader of the eighteenth-century Industrial Revolution, Britain has lived ever since by trade. It must import large quantities of food and raw materials, and export large quantities of goods and machinery to support its large population.

Italy has very little coal, iron or copper, so could not develop as quickly as Germany in the second half of the nineteenth century. It has now caught up by using skill and inventiveness, especially in design. Italy has developed hydro-electric power from streams in the Alps and Apennines and has recently found deposits of oil and natural gas, especially in the Po valley. As a member of the Common Market Italy is able to get supplies of steel from the other members for its industries, especially for the cars, scooters, typewriters and coffee-machines which the world buys in large numbers. Shortage of raw materials, however, as of food, is dangerous to such countries in the event of war.

Many smaller countries, especially in tropical areas, are 'one-product' countries. Their main product may be either vegetable or mineral. Some countries of the Middle East produce little but oil; Egypt, cotton; North Africa, dates; Burma and Thailand, rice; Malaya, rubber, with some tea and tin; Cuba, sugar; Bolivia, tin; the Caribbean states, bananas; Venezuela, oil. They must import large quantities of finished goods and food. Their own products are apt to be sold exclusively to one particular industrialized state, for they need a guaranteed market. On this state they thus become dependent, even if they are otherwise 'free'. They suffer drastically if world prices fall, or if their chief buyer, often for political reasons, withdraws its custom. The United States has more than once used this weapon against the Caribbean states and Cuba. If they have to seek a new buyer, as Cuba and Egypt (since the Suez crisis in 1956) have sought Russia, single-product states often change their foreign policy too.

The need of industrialized states for raw materials has often been a cause of war in the past. As early as 1740 Frederick of Prussia invaded Silesia because of its coal supplies. Alsace-Lorraine and the Ruhr have frequently caused tension and conflict between France and Germany, also because of coal. Romanian oil and Germany's desire to secure African colonies rich in minerals were among the causes of the First World War.

We find ourselves now at the beginning of experiments with quite new materials for industry, clothing and power. The laboratory is taking the place of the mine as the centre of activity. It is possible now to make silk without silkworms, rubber without latex, wool without sheep and perfumes without flowers. Plastics have an infinite variety of uses and are constantly being

9

improved. Rayon, nylon and every other kind of synthetic fibre have become invaluable for every type and weight of cloth and carpeting; they can simulate fur as well as wool, silk, cotton and linen of every weave. Atomic power is being used for peaceful purposes and experiments are being made in U.S.A. and France in solar heating of water and space for houses and hotels. All this means that countries not very rich in natural resources can achieve a high standard of living through technical skill and scientific knowledge. Educated men and women are fast becoming the most valuable resources of all.

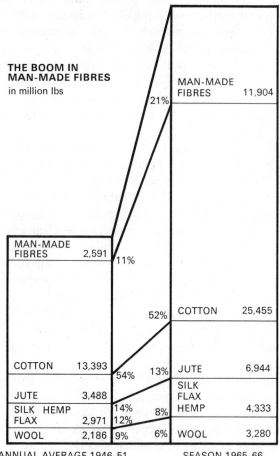

THE BOOM IN MAN-MADE FIBRES

in million lbs

ANNUAL AVERAGE 1946-51	SEASON 1965-66
MAN-MADE FIBRES 2,591 — 11%	21% MAN-MADE FIBRES 11,904
COTTON 13,393 — 54%	52% COTTON 25,455
JUTE 3,488	13% JUTE 6,944
SILK HEMP FLAX 2,971 — 14%	SILK FLAX 8% HEMP 4,333
WOOL 2,186 — 9% / 12%	6% WOOL 3,280

The sea and its importance

Seas are nurseries—of fish, fishermen, and sailors.

The economy of Europe has been greatly influenced by the fishing grounds of the North Sea and of the Baltic. The herring fisheries are as vital to Scotland as the cod fisheries have always been to countries who could reach the North Atlantic: America, Canada, Britain, France and Iceland in particular. Japan is the Pacific's greatest nation of fishermen. In parts of the Mediterranean the flesh of the tuna is a staple food, and Greece and Italy have been seafaring nations from the earliest times, Greece occupying innumerable islands, Sicily and Asia Minor, and Rome building an empire all round the shores of the Mediterranean.

Good fishermen make good naval men, and to those countries skilled in seamanship the seas are not a barrier, but a bridge. To them, sea routes are much easier than land routes. Vasco da Gama sailed round the Cape to India centuries before Speke and Livingstone penetrated the heart of Africa. Today these routes are easier than ever, since science has given us steam, oil and nuclear power, the magnetic compass, radio and radar. These things have made the seaman practically independent of the stars and much less affected by bad weather.

Easy routes mean easy trade; and they mean wealth to those who can control the seas, and even improve on Nature by cutting great canals like the Corinth, the Suez and the Panama. From the Phoenicians and Greeks, to Venice and Genoa and so to Spain, Portugal, Holland and Britain, sea-trading countries have been countries of merchants and prosperous middle classes, of cities and of empires. The change in Glasgow after the Union of 1707 is a good illustration of the benefits that sea power and trade can bring.

There is also a great deal of mineral and chemical wealth in the sea which man has hardly begun to exploit, although from earliest times he has dived for sponges, coral, pearls, mother-of-pearl and the sea-snail *murex* which yielded the dye loved by the ancient world, Tyrian purple. Today we have hardly added to this list, except for experiments with seaweed, from which we get iodine and other chemicals, and fertilizers. Yet every kind of mineral found in the earth is in suspension in the water, or in the sea-bed.

The Continents and their resources

EUROPE

Area: 3·8 million square miles. Population (including European Russia): 650 million.

Europe is the second smallest of the continents. Asia, the biggest, has five times its area. Yet Europe has 25 per cent of the world's population. Obviously it offers very favourable living conditions for man, and its importance is out of all proportion to its size. Since Greek and Roman times, right down to our own day, Europeans have been the most enterprising and inventive of all the world's peoples, both in thought and action. To the world they have given ideas of law and government, the Christian churches, the Italian Renaissance,

11

experimental science and the Industrial Revolution, and they have led the way in exploration and discovery of all kinds. What makes Europe so suitable a home for its energetic peoples?

First, geographical factors. Europe is a peninsula, jutting out from Asia and bounded on three sides by seas. It has many peninsulas of its own, including Greece, Italy, Spain, Scandinavia. It has, in fact, a 50,000-mile coast-line, and no part of Western or Southern Europe is very far from the sea. This meant opportunity for sea transport, which led to free movement from one part to another and the rapid spread of ideas.

As far as relief is concerned, the outstanding feature is the contrast between east and west. Eastern Europe is a vast monotonous plain which stretches without a break from the Urals to Romania, whereas Western Europe is a land of great diversity. The relief varies from (a) the high, folded Alpine ranges through (b) the mountains and plains of Central Europe to (c) the Germano-Polish lowlands, (d) the Caledonian mountains, and (e) Fennoscandia in the north. Nowhere, however, do these mountains form impassable barriers and, owing to the limited area of really high land and the generally good soils, much of Europe is suitable for agriculture. The rivers are numerous and generally navigable.

It is climate more than anything else which has made the continent so suitable for man. Most of Europe comes under the influence of the warm, moist south-west winds and, unlike the other continents, it has everywhere adequate rain and no real desert. Moreover, since it extends only to about 70°N and is greatly influenced by the warm Atlantic Gulf Stream, the summers, except north of 65°N and in the extreme east, are long and mild and permit cultivation to be carried on nearer the Pole than anywhere else in the world. Its temperature is ideal. The best temperature for physical activity is found around 64°, for mental, 38°. London, New York, Paris and Peking are in this range. The history of the world is largely the history of the temperate regions lying between 30° and 60°N. Europe has considerable mineral resources and it is particularly rich in iron ore (Sweden, Lorraine and Russia) and coal (Britain, Germany, Poland and Russia), salt (Austria), copper, lead, zinc, gold and silver. These have made possible steel and ships, railways and bridges, and a highly developed and complex industry.

On the basis of these rich natural resources Europeans have developed a civilization which, as far as material prosperity is concerned, surpasses all others, except today the North American.

Second, Europe is the Christian continent, pervaded—whether Catholic or Protestant—by Christian values, and with these have been incorporated that respect for the individual, for law, for justice and for intelligence that come not only from Christianity but from Greek, Roman and Jewish teaching.

Third, Europe has had the longest settled government, the longest continuous development of schools and universities, art and architecture, coupled with a belief in reason, in scientific enquiry and experiment, and the application of knowledge to the settlement of problems. The variety of peoples and languages has proved a source of conflict; it has also been a source of stimulus and inspiration.

Fourth, Europe did not stay self-contained or exclusive like Japan from 1650 to 1865, or China in its centuries-old scorn for the 'foreign devil'. It expanded. Other continents have been explored, developed and peopled by Europeans. The history of the world outside Europe from 1648 to 1914 can be described under the heading 'the expansion of Europe'. It expanded chiefly by using the highways of the Atlantic, that most important of the oceans, linking America and Africa with Europe. This expansion gave European nations close ties with all other parts of the world: Britain with U.S.A. and the Commonwealth including India and Australia; France with Algeria and Indo-China; Holland with the East Indies; Italy with North Africa; Portugal with Africa or India; Belgium with the Congo.

But today, while those ties have weakened, so has the position of Europe itself. It is, in the age of air travel and nuclear weapons like Polaris, no longer master of its fate, but a buffer between Russia and the United States. There are still two Europes—Western Europe, with its great cities and beautiful buildings, its highly skilled industries, its roads and the trade along them, and its middle class that lives by trade; and Eastern Europe, just beginning to develop most of these things.

ASIA

Area: 17½ million square miles. Population estimated at over 1,600 million.

Asia is the largest continent, one-third of the entire surface of the earth, with more than one-half of the world's population. China and Japan, which have for the most part a kindly and temperate climate, are very densely settled and so are India, Burma and Indo-China. In 1960 the population of China was 660 million, of India, 403 million, of Russia, 210 million. These people do not enjoy anything like as high a standard of living, or as varied a diet, as the Europeans.

Geographically, Asia has not been well served by Nature. Its coast-line of 35,000 miles is not long, relative to its size, and so much of the interior is removed from the influence of the sea. The northern shores are generally ice-bound. The surface of the land is extremely varied, from the Himalayas, the highest mountains in the world, to alluvial plains; from high plateaux to deserts. Until today communications in inner Asia have been far from easy; Tibet and Nepal have been the most remote countries in the whole world.

The rivers of Asiatic Russia—Ob, Yenisei and Lena—run north into the Arctic, so they are of little use to trade, and suffer from severe flooding because of melting ice and the flatness of the land. The rivers of China—Hwang-Ho (2,600 miles), Yangtse (3,200 miles) and Si-Kiang or Canton River (1,000 miles)—also flood badly; but the Yangtse, the greatest of them, is navigable for large ships for 1,300 miles from its mouth, and all could be developed and controlled. When this is done, they will be among the most important highways and trade routes of the world.

The rivers that drain the southern slopes of Asia's mountains and plateaux are the main centres of life. They are the Mekong (1,600 miles) in Indo-China; the Irrawaddy (1,200 miles) on which Burma depends; the Brahmaputra (1,600 miles) and the Ganges (1,500 miles) in India; the Indus (1,700 miles) running from the beautiful plateau of Kashmir through Pakistan into the Indian Ocean; and the two rivers of Mesopotamia or Iraq—the Euphrates (1,700 miles) and the Tigris (1,100 miles). They all suffer from floods, from rapids or from rocky defiles, but along their banks are packed many millions of people, and the river valleys of India, Iraq and the Near East were the cradles of most of the earliest civilizations of the ancient world.

Asia's climate is very varied. In the north the winters are long and severe, with the ground frozen solid to a depth of six feet. In the central mountain area the temperature is generally low and the soil poor. In the south, in India, Burma, Malaya and Indo-China, the temperature is very high and monsoon-like conditions give some areas great fertility. The dense populations, living here in hot and often steamy conditions, have in the past been weakened by tropical diseases and by the brazen heat of their summers, which makes long periods of hard work very difficult. Japan, and the great plains and river valleys of China, however, enjoy a temperate climate and in these countries the people are industrious, highly skilled and intelligent, with a long history of civilization behind them.

Asia is rich in valuable vegetable products, in tea, flax, hemp and jute, rubber, sugar-cane and cotton. Rice is the staple diet of millions of her people. Asia is also rich in minerals, as yet largely unworked except in the western part of Asiatic Russia. Gold and silver are found in the Urals and the Altai mountains, precious stones in India and Burma, tin in Malaya and oil all round the Caspian Sea and in the Near East. There are enormous coal deposits in China. Much of all this mineral wealth has still to be surveyed. The Industrial Revolution came very late to Asia—first to Japan at the turn of the century, then to Russia and only now to China and India.

AFRICA

Area: 12 million square miles. Population estimated at 275 million.

Africa is three times the size of all Europe and represents one-quarter of the land surface of the earth. Many of its peoples are tribal and primitive. Egypt and the coast of North Africa have always been part of the Mediterranean world, but the rest, cut off by the Sahara and the frightful swamps of the Sudd, remained for many centuries the 'Dark Continent'. Its outline and shores were known long before the interior was penetrated by the Dutch, Arabs and, in the second half of the nineteenth century, British, French and Belgians.

Africa's coast-line is short (about 15,000 miles) for so large a continent. For the most part Africa is a high tableland, dotted with enormous lakes, and surrounded by high mountain ranges. In the north are the Atlas mountains, fertile only on their northern slopes; in the east are the mountains of Ethiopia and of Kenya, where the White Highlands are very fertile and pleasant and make excellent farmland with a good climate, as do the slopes of the Drakensberg in South Africa. Even more formidable a barrier to the traveller and the explorer are the vast deserts—the Sahara, the Kalahari and the Great Karroo.

Africa's rivers drop from the central plateau to the sea through rapids and waterfalls. Most of them are of little use for navigation. Most important is the Nile—3,500 miles long—one of the great rivers of the world; but the ancient civilization it nourished, the oldest in history, was Mediterranean rather than African.

The Nile fertilizes a narrow belt of the desert, and floods every year. Today it is almost tamed by a system of dams and barrages. The Niger (2,300 miles) is navigable; the Congo (2,900 miles) drains Central Africa and is navigable

Workmen on the Nile near the site of Abu Simbel.

through its middle course, but at Leopoldville there begins a series of falls; the Zambezi (1,500 miles) is the largest river of East Africa and is hardly navigable at all. The greatest waterfall, the Victoria Falls, was discovered by Livingstone in 1850.

As Africa lies in the tropics it is very hot (except in the mountains) with a heat intensified by the deserts. The coasts and river valleys have abundant rainfall and very dense vegetation, especially near the Equator.

So far, Africa's vegetable wealth has been more exploited than its mineral wealth. It produces sago, coffee, ground-nuts, sugar-cane, and in the desert oases maize, coconuts and dates. Elephants provide ivory, the forests yield rich woods, like mahogany. South Africa and Rhodesia are rich in gold, copper and diamonds, and some lead and iron. The Congo may have big deposits of uranium as well as copper. There is said to be a great deal of oil beneath the Sahara. But, South Africa apart, the continent lacks industrial development and urgently needs the skills and knowledge of the West. It has been handicapped by its climate and the diseases it breeds.

NORTH AMERICA

Area: 9 million square miles. Population: 240 million.

This, consisting almost entirely of Canada, U.S.A. and Mexico, is the wealthiest of the continents. Its tremendous industrial development came later than that of Western Europe. Its machines and factories began by being up-to-date and efficient and, as with other industralized countries, are continuously modernized. Even its isolation, guarded by the Atlantic and Pacific oceans, has been a source of strength and prosperity, for until our own day of long-range missiles it has been free from the threats of invasion. Its natural resources are so great that the U.S.A. especially can be almost self-supporting.

Geographically it has some disadvantages. The northernmost coasts are ice-bound, the shores rocky. Even New England has a rough coast-line and a quite severe winter. The western coast is steep and has few good harbours, although two—Vancouver in Canada and San Francisco—are vast and splendid. From the Gulf of Mexico come hurricanes that sweep across the southern states.

But it has many advantages too. Only two mountain ranges hamper movement east to west—the Alleghenies, parallel to the east coast and rising to 6,000 feet, and the Rockies in the west. In the north-east and south are excellent and navigable rivers penetrating far into the interior, especially the Mississippi, including the Missouri (4,200 miles), and the St Lawrence draining the Great Lakes. The St Lawrence River itself is 1,000 miles long, even before it reaches Montreal. If we add to it the seaway and the lakes, we find that Duluth, at the western end of Lake Superior, is over 2,000 miles from the Atlantic.

The climate is very varied, because of the great extent of the continent, but most parts enjoy long, warm summers. And while the winters in the north are cold, often with blizzards, they are bracing because of the dry air.

Products and resources are equally varied. Maize, barley, wheat, oats, rice, tobacco, sugar-cane and cotton, and every kind of fruit and vegetable are grown. Vast prairies support tens of thousands of cattle, and hogs are fed on maize in the Middle West and on peaches in the South.

Gold, silver, iron, copper, coal and oil all exist abundantly in this continent and all have been extensively developed and exploited. The standard of living is the highest ever known.

SOUTH AMERICA

Area: 8 million square miles. Population (including Caribbean area): 240 million.

This continent, more than twice the size of Europe, is broken up into a number of independent countries most of them founded by Spain or Portugal. Their upper and ruling classes tend to be Latin; their peasants and workers are descendants of the original Indian inhabitants.

The coast-line is very regular, especially in the south-east, with some excellent harbours like Rio de Janeiro. In the north-east the land is flat and covered with tropical forest, especially in the Amazon basin. The centre is a great plain, flanked on the west by the lofty Andes. These spectacular mountains run from Panama to Cape Horn and rise to 22,000 feet. Many of the summits are active volcanoes.

From the Andes some shorter rivers drop steeply west into the Pacific, but the central fact of South American geography is the system of great rivers running across the continent to the Atlantic. There are three groups of these rivers:

(*a*) Those that drain the northern slopes, especially the Orinoco (1,500 miles) with its wide delta.

(*b*) Those draining the eastern slopes, especially the Amazon (4,000 miles), the greatest river in the world. It drains an area of three million square miles and the fresh water discharged by it can be traced 200 miles out to sea. It is tidal for 400 miles from its mouth. You can sail in luxury up it as far as Manaos, where there is an opera house. Beyond that point you enter a primitive, tropical world and might be welcomed with bows and arrows. Head-hunters still live in the almost unexplored forests.

(*c*) Those draining the south-eastern slopes, chief of them the Parana (2,200 miles) and the Uruguay (1,000 miles) which together form the Rio de la Plata, the Silver River.

The climate in South America is milder than its latitude in the northern parts might suggest, either because of altitude or the nearness of the sea. The

3

Amazon basin is tropical and has heavy rainfall. The west coast is generally hot and very dry.

South America is rich in resources. Maize, cocoa, coffee, tobacco, cinchona for quinine, potatoes, Brazil nuts and all varieties of fruits and vegetables are produced. All the valuable minerals are found there, especially gold and silver. But the South American states are not yet industrialized and most of the mineral wealth is still unexploited. Many of them are as yet one-commodity states and so are sensitive to world conditions. Venezuela depends on oil, Bolivia on tin, Chile on nitrates, Argentina on beef, Cuba on sugar.

OCEANIA

Australia

Area : 3 million square miles. Population : 12 million.

Australia is the 'island continent', as yet sparsely populated. Its coast-line, some 9,000 miles long, is generally uniform and unbroken. The Great Barrier

Books and bathers. A school swimming lesson on the beach near Perth, Western Australia.

Reef of coral, 1,200 miles long, forms a natural breakwater off the north-east coast. The Great Dividing Range, where opals are found, borders the coast on the east and divides the coastal plain from the Murray valley.

Australian rivers, chief of them the Murray (1,300 miles), are subject to serious flooding in the wet season.

18

The climate is very dry for most of the year. The northern rainy season is regulated by the monsoon. The south is more temperate and the most important cities and harbours are there. The centre of the continent, home of the Aborigines, is a huge near-desert with very high temperatures in the summer. Where water is available the soil is very fertile and cattle and sheep are raised in great numbers by the white stockmen of the 'outback'. Sometimes, in summer droughts, the cattle have to trek for many miles in search of water.

Especially in the south-east, and in Tasmania, Australia is rich in cereals and fruit, vegetables and dairy products. Copper is found in South Australia, tin in Queensland, lead in New South Wales, coal in Queensland and New South Wales, and gold is still obtainable.

New Zealand

Three islands—North Island, South Island and Stewart Island—make up New Zealand, with an area larger than that of Britain. Its population is 2,300,000.

The country has a long coast-line and excellent harbours. No part of it is very far from the sea. It also has beautiful mountains, with glaciers and alpine lakes, and in North Island volcanoes and hot springs.

The climate is like that of Britain, but warmer and more equable, making it a pleasant place to live.

The chief products of New Zealand are mutton, wool, butter and fruit and some gold, coal and copper.

South-East Asia   Population: 120 million

This includes Malaysia (British Commonwealth), the Philippine Islands (linked to U.S.A.), Celebes, Borneo, Java and Sumatra (ex-Dutch East Indies), all colonial or ex-colonial territories. They are very warm and fertile, densely populated, and produce sugar, hemp, coffee, cotton, tobacco, tea, tin, rubber, spices and precious stones. Singapore is a great port.

Micronesia

The name comes from the Greek *micro*, small, and *nesos*, an island. These are the islands south of the Equator and west of 180°E: New Guinea, the Solomons, the New Hebrides and Fiji. The Solomons were discovered by Captain Cook in 1774. Some of these islands were only fully explored during the Second World War. Fertile and well watered, they produce sugar, coffee, tea and cotton and tropical fruits.

Polynesia (from the Greek *polys*, many)

South of the Equator, and east of 180°E, these islands of the Pacific include Samoa, Tonga, the Cook Islands and Tahiti. They export coconuts, copra, cotton and mother-of-pearl.

19

Some of the islands of Micronesia were not fully explored until the Second World War. Above is shown part of West New Guinea.

Population

Until recent times the growth of population was curbed by natural disasters, by war, disease, drought and ignorance. The rat-borne Black Death carried off more than a third of Britain's population in the fourteenth century. The Thirty Years War (1618–48) did the same in Europe. Insect-borne malaria and sleeping-sickness for centuries kept the population of Africa low and drained of energy, and prevented penetration of the interior. Swarms of locusts brought periodical famine.

After 1700, with the coming of the Agricultural and Industrial Revolutions, and with tremendous advances in scientific and medical knowledge, the population of Europe began to grow, and has grown ever since at a rapidly increasing rate. In spite of wars, epidemics and quite large-scale emigration, especially to the U.S. and the British Commonwealth, it has increased fivefold in 250 years.

Four areas on the earth are especially densely peopled: South-east Asia, India, Western Europe and the north-eastern United States. In these four regions are no less than 35 cities each with a million or more inhabitants, and of which five are very large indeed: Tokyo (10 million), London and New York (each 8 million), Berlin and Moscow (each over 4 million). In the central plains of the American Midwest and on the Russian *steppes* the population is evenly spread. The central parts of Asia and Mongolia, and the great desert regions are all sparsely settled. Again, as we have seen, the growth of cities tends

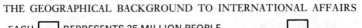

EACH ☐ REPRESENTS 25 MILLION PEOPLE

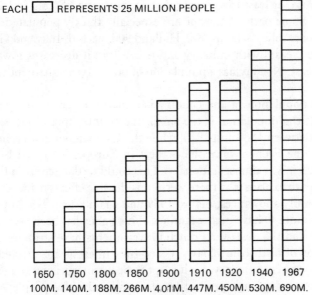

1650	1750	1800	1850	1900	1910	1920	1940	1967
100M.	140M.	188M.	266M.	401M.	447M.	450M.	530M.	690M.

The growth of Europe's population.

towards population concentration; but some large cities (Los Angeles, Rio de Janeiro, Mexico City) have thinly populated areas quite close to them. To them, air travel is of major importance. And the Australian cities, especially Sydney and Melbourne, are a reminder that large-scale urbanization is not solely a phenomenon of industrialization.

The present average density in Europe is 228 inhabitants per square mile,

EACH ■ REPRESENTS 500 MILLION PEOPLE

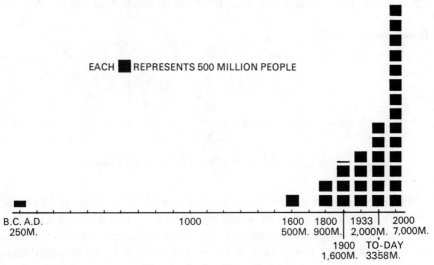

B.C. A.D.		1000	1600	1800	1933	2000
250M.			500M.	900M.	2,000M.	7,000M.

1900   TO-DAY
1,600M.   3358M.

The growth of world population.

21

twice that of Asia, at least three times that of the United States and 10 times that of Africa. Some parts of Europe are especially thickly populated: Britain has 500 per square mile, Belgium 700, Holland 900, parts of Italy and Germany 380. Density increases with industry and urban life; it decreases towards the north and the east. Norway has a population of only 23 per square mile, Russia only 20.

The size of population in any country is a matter of great concern to the government. If the population is too small, the country might not be able to defend itself. Between 1860 and 1910, while the German population increased by 27 million, the French, once the highest in Europe, increased by only 3 million; by 1935 it was almost stationary. This could be dangerous in the event of war and helps to explain why there were considerable efforts made, especially by means of family allowances, before 1939 and again after 1945, to persuade the people of France to have bigger families. This policy has been very success-ful since 1945, and the post-war French Governments have strongly opposed the introduction of birth-control laws. Peace-time interests are affected, too, if a population becomes stationary, for it is apt to be unenterprising and cautious. A Great Power needs a large proportion of young and active people.

Population policy can often cause international tensions. Hitler's propa-ganda drive to encourage large families in order to produce more Nazi soldiers caused fear and anxiety in all Germany's neighbours. The efforts of the U.S.A. since 1921 to curb the immigration of particular racial groups, like the Chinese and Japanese, and to impose quotas on others; the determination of Australia (four per square mile) to keep out the Japanese and other non-white peoples at a time when Japan's population density is 474 per square mile; the policy of Apartheid in South Africa—all these bring about dislike and controversy.

Population density

| Canada | U.S.A. | Europe |

Each oblong represents a square mile. Each dot represents three people.

The population of the whole earth now is over 3,000 million. And 85 babies are born every minute (ten of whom are Chinese). Since 1945 especially, the population has been increasing phenomenally in the more backward areas; they are benefiting from Western aid in the form of drugs and medicines, scientific and technical education, pest control and improved methods of food production and irrigation, as well as the beginnings of industrialization. All over the world, we must remember, increasing population is not the result of more births, but of fewer deaths and longer lives. There has been a sharp rise in the average span of life and a fall in the number of deaths of babies.

Is the world overpopulated? This question has long vexed mankind. In 1798, an English clergyman named Thomas R. Malthus wrote his famous *Essay on Population*. He predicted that there always would be poverty and misery in the world because the world's population tends to increase more rapidly than the supply of food. The only way in which population was held within the means of subsistence, he believed, was by the 'checks' of war, pestilence and famine.

Average length of life.

Malthus' ideas had a profound influence on the thinking of social scientists, political leaders and even biologists. About a century after the publication of his essay, however, it became clear that he had failed to foresee the great improvements in agricultural methods, the opening up of new food-producing regions and advances in transportation. These made it possible for the world to feed its rapidly increasing population without difficulty.

Since 1920, however, the pendulum has swung back closer to the position taken by Malthus. Despite the effects of world wars, the population of the world has increased at an unprecedented rate. Modern medical science has worked miracles in reducing infant mortality and in combating epidemics that formerly carried off millions of lives every year.

In various parts of the world, such as India, Japan and parts of China, famine, or the threat of famine, is today all too real a danger. These regions must draw on other areas in order to meet even the bare minimum food needs of their people. The situation is admittedly serious now; it is estimated that

23

four-fifths of the people in the world are not getting enough to eat. As Lord Ritchie-Calder has said:

'The litany of hunger is expressed in a saying in the East:

> Better to walk than to run:
> Better to sit than to walk:
> Better to sleep than to sit:
> Better to die than to wake.'

This tragedy is heightened by the gap between the 'have' and 'have-not' nations. Ten per cent of the human race have 60 per cent of the world's income while 60 per cent of the people have only 10 per cent of the world's income. Most of these unfortunates are in the Far East and they compare very unfavourably with those in North America (7 per cent of the world's population) who enjoy 40 per cent of the world's income. If population outstrips food supplies, this gap may widen even further at a time when newly emerging

Population Growth and Food Intake

COMPARISON OF THE DAILY INTAKE OF CALORIES BY REGIONS*

Region	Calorie Supplies	Calorie Requirements
Far East	2,070	2,300
Africa	2,360	2,400
Latin America	2,470	2,400
Europe	3,040	2,600
North America	3,120	2,600
Oceania	3,250	2,600

ESTIMATED PERCENTAGE POPULATION INCREASES IN EACH CONTINENT*

Years	World	Africa	North America	Latin America	Asia	Europe incl. U.S.S.R.	Oceania
1900–25	23	22	56	57	19	19	57
1925–50	31	35	33	65	35	14	36
1950–75	53	52	43	86	60	31	59
1975–2000	64	71	30	95	75	26	40

* Third World Food Survey, F.A.O., 1963.
Note: The calorie requirement represents the average need in calories of a healthy person.

states are casting hungry eyes on their more fortunate neighbours. Hunger can be the springboard of war which can be averted only by a more even distribution of the world's income. Despite this, many of our basic resources, including the soil itself, are being used up or destroyed at an alarming rate. Even in Britain, some estimates suggest a population increase of 20 million by the year 2000: with, as consequence, housing and land shortage, increasing chaos on the roads, and the continuous destruction of the countryside. Thus, it is believed in some quarters that Malthus' predictions may be borne out in our own generation.

Others, however, regard the future more optimistically. They emphasize the effects of such advances as improved farming techniques, hybrid grains, conquest of insect pests and plant diseases, the development of synthetic foods, better breeding of livestock, development of new sources of energy, progress in transportation, and the opening up of extensive areas to agriculture (for example, in the arid regions of the world). It is argued that if we really utilize the scientific and technological knowledge at our disposal, we can support not only the present population of the world but even a much larger population.

And they add that in some advanced countries the so-called 'baby boom' of the immediate post-war years is over. In the United States a quarter of a million fewer babies were born in 1965 than in 1964, half a million fewer than in the all-time peak year of 1957. The chief reason for this change has been the decision of parents to forgo a third and a fourth child, substituting perhaps a second car and colour television. Large families were fashionable in the years after 1945; now birth control is more acceptable both socially and ethically. And in the last 20 years Japan has been following a path different from that of the rest of the world: it has halved the size of its average family which is now down from four children to two. Its population is now fairly constant at 97 million. (And teenage Japanese are often twice the height of their parents, because they are now better fed.) Sweden and Denmark have been, through the United Nations, urging on the rest of the world the need for a policy of population restraint.

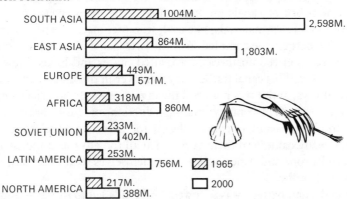

SOUTH ASIA 1004M. 2,598M.
EAST ASIA 864M. 1,803M.
EUROPE 449M. 571M.
AFRICA 318M. 860M.
SOVIET UNION 233M. 402M.
LATIN AMERICA 253M. 756M.
NORTH AMERICA 217M. 388M.
1965
2000

The populations of Asia, Africa and Latin America are expanding much more rapidly than those of Europe or North America. They will be the dominant groups by the year 2000.

Rapid increase of population brings other problems, of course, as well as food supply. There is a growing demand for homes and cars, for raw materials and manufactured goods, for schools, universities, hospitals and services of

25

every kind. As more old people and more newly-born survive, the working population has to maintain a larger proportion of non-workers. And changes in population mean changes in the balance of power. Look at the figures. By the year 2000 the world population is likely to be 7,000 million. There will be by that time, if the trend does not alter, 1,000 million Chinese, at least 700 million Indians and possibly 500 million Latin Americans who, with an annual rate of increase of 2.8 per cent, are multiplying most rapidly. Europe's rate of population increase is low (0.9 per cent). It is easy to see that, by that year, Europe will no longer be the most important continent.

Transport and communications

The land

One of the great legacies left to us by the Romans was their system of roads, knitting together their empire. Many of the main roads of England, and of Europe south of the Rhine, are built on Roman foundations. The Roman highway was strongly paved, with good bridges spanning the rivers. The routes, following the river valleys, or striding magnificently straight over hill and dale to link important towns, were carefully planned.

For centuries after the collapse of Rome, very little was done to extend, or even maintain, their road system. Ordinary people rarely moved outside their own villages, and traffic that could not be taken by river or sea was horse-drawn or carried. The cart, the litter, the pack-horse, the stage-coach, these were the ways of getting about until the early nineteenth century, and very slow and uncomfortable ways they were, especially in winter.

In the early stages of the Industrial Revolution in eighteenth-century Britain, a network of canals gradually linked the main rivers, and heavy or fragile goods and raw materials, like coal, iron ore, machines or pottery, could be carried by barge. The completion of the Erie Canal in 1826 transformed the trading patterns of the north-eastern United States and linked New York to the Great Lakes. This canal traffic was taken over in the nineteenth century by the new railways, and it was not until the invention of the internal combustion engine and twentieth-century mass-production of cars, heavy transport vehicles and buses—and, of course, the oil and petrol on which to run them— that roads really came into their own. Then all the advanced industrial states of Western Europe and America provided themselves with wide, well-surfaced roads for fast traffic.

Still the Roman pattern was followed. 'All roads led to Rome'—and still do. So, in France, all roads lead to Paris, and in England, to London. When Hitler came to power in Germany one of his first achievements was to build a network of great *autobahnen* centred on Berlin, along which speedy traffic, and later tanks, could move. So with Mussolini and his *autostrade*. Such road systems increase the importance and domination of the big cities and speed up both business and trade. In the extent and quality of its roads, Europe is far ahead of the rest of the world, except North America.

The United States needed good communications if the continent was to become a nation. Often its roads and railways appeared before the towns, and so were the chief reason for the siting of many towns. The U.S.A. has a magnificent series of Federal highways crossing the continent. Some of the earliest transcontinental roads, like U.S.30, the Lincoln Highway, have been replaced by toll roads, or turnpikes which by-pass towns, permitting cruising speeds of 60–70 m.p.h., and in places demanding minimum speed limits to clear town areas quickly. Roads such as these connect New York City and Chicago, the only necessary stops being for petrol or the payment of the tolls.

Railways were perhaps the greatest technical achievement of the nineteenth century. Britain pioneered in their development with its brilliant engineer, George Stephenson—they have been described as 'a child of the English North-East'. The President of the Board of Trade, Huskisson, was the first victim, fatally injured when he opened one of the earliest passenger lines in 1830. Before the age of the internal combustion engine, railways were the hallmark of a great industrial power. They became the makers of states like Germany and India and they were often the instruments of victory. It was largely because of its railways that the North was able to defeat the South in the American Civil War. The German victories over Austria in 1866, and over France in 1870, were largely due to the speedy movement of men by rail, just as their initial victories in 1940, over Holland, Belgium and France, owed much to their wonderful roads.

Railways affected the foreign policy and strategy of states too. The German plan to build the Berlin-Baghdad Railway, in the later nineteenth century, added to Britain's mounting fear and suspicion of Germany and caused it to draw close to France. Britain kept a wary eye, too, on the building of the Pilgrim Railway to Mecca. This railway was intended to enable good Moslems to visit their Holy City and also to link up the Arab parts of the Ottoman Empire with Turkey and with the Berlin-Baghdad line. But Turkey was an ally of Germany in the First World War and the whole project would have linked Hamburg to the Persian Gulf. The completed section of the line, Damascus to Mecca, was destroyed by Lawrence of Arabia and his Bedouin allies during the First World War. Its ruins can still be seen across the sands of Northern Arabia.

Railways have helped to build peaceful states as well as war-like. The union of eastern Canada with British Columbia in the west was made possible only by the building of a 3,000-mile railway, the Canadian Pacific. The United States first became aware of its real size and greatness when in 1869 a golden stake was driven into the ground on the Utah salt-flats to mark the junction of the two halves of the Union Pacific Railway, linking California with the east coast. The Trans-Siberian Railway, 4,600 miles in length to its terminal in Vladivostok, was completed in 1905. It shortened the journey from St Petersburg to Vladivostok from two months to less than two weeks. All these, in themselves tremendous achievements, brought about the settlement and development of the vast spaces they crossed. They practically created the modern, federal nations of Canada, U.S.A. and U.S.S.R.

The greatest dreams of all were never realized. In the late nineteenth century Cecil Rhodes had hopes of a Cape-to-Cairo railway. And early in the twentieth century the American millionaire, E. H. Harriman, hoped to build a railway from Ostend across Europe and Asia to the Pacific. But the war came too soon for work to start on his plans. By 1914 road and rail seemed, however, to be wonder-working agents, conquering space and time. Jules Verne's dream of going round the world in 80 days was on the point of realization. It can now be done comfortably by air in much less than 80 hours.

The sea

The first great explorers were those who, like the Phoenicians, Carthaginians or Greeks, were ready to adventure beyond the sight of land. One of their captains must have been the first to sail through the Pillars of Hercules, out of the sheltered Mediterranean into the stormy and uncharted Atlantic.

But it was the voyages of the great discoverers, using the compass and the telescope, that made the seas channels of commerce in both goods and ideas and highways to great empires. Diaz and Vasco da Gama, Columbus and Magellan, Cabot and Amerigo Vespucci, Drake and Hawkins, brought wealth and power to the countries looking westward across the Atlantic—Spain and Portugal, Britain, and later Holland.

Britain's Industrial Revolution enabled it to build ships of iron, powered by steam, and throughout the nineteenth century the country remained unrivalled at sea. By 1840 the Cunard Steamship Company was operating a regular service across the Atlantic, the Peninsular and Oriental to the East. This easier line of communication transformed the character of the Empire. In the eighteenth century, to take service in the East India Company was to accept the gamble of never again seeing Britain. After 1870 regular 'leaves' became possible, wives and families could move overseas easily, and life abroad became a would-be replica of that in the Old Country, except that there were native servants, the climate (and sometimes the food) was hotter than at home and one slept in the middle of the day. The British Empire of the nineteenth century, on which the sun never set, was built on a navy in command of the Seven Seas.

The power of Britain was envied, and imitated, by other nations; especially by Germany, which began in the 1890s a naval building programme to enable it to catch up with Britain and build an African Empire, and by the United

States. Under the direction of Admiral von Tirpitz, the German naval building programme was one of the causes of the First World War. In the United States views like those of Tirpitz came to be held by President Theodore Roosevelt and Admiral A. T. Mahan. Japan, fast becoming industrialized, challenged Russian naval power in the East.

Navies, and merchant ships too, demanded large supplies of coal and, after 1908, oil, for fuel. They needed ports of call at suitable sailing distances for bunker facilities and food and fresh-water supplies, and wherever they went they opened up the way to trade and to every kind of westernizing influence. Gibraltar, Malta, Port Said and Alexandria, Aden, Colombo, Hong Kong, Singapore, Fremantle, the Cape, St Helena, the Falkland Islands, Fiji, and Samoa all were, or became, British ports of call, dotted all over the world. This role greatly increased their importance and prosperity and in war-time gave Britain great strategic advantages.

At two points the navies were vulnerable. There were two important land bridges, one linking Egypt to the Levant, the other linking North and South America. Until 1870 travellers to the East left their ships at Alexandria and crossed Egypt by land, often taking in a conducted tour of the Pyramids en route to Suez, where they continued their journey by another ship. It was the foresight of a French engineer, De Lesseps, that led to the construction of the Suez Canal, opened with great pomp by the Empress Eugenie of France in 1869. It was Disraeli's foresight in buying up the Khedive's shares in the Canal that made it, and Egypt, from 1876 to 1956 a major British interest. It is an 80-mile highway of enormous importance to all naval and trading powers. In 1956 it was taken over by the Egyptian Government.

Similarly, until 1903, world shipping had to sail round Cape Horn on its voyages between the Atlantic and the Pacific. The American War with Spain in 1898, a war fought to free Cuba from Spanish control, and during which U.S.A. gained both the Philippine Islands and the Hawaiian Islands, drove home the need for a Panama Canal. During that war it had taken the U.S.S. *Oregon* 66 days to sail from its Pacific station to Cuban waters. The American administration of Theodore Roosevelt built a canal across Panama—and staged a revolution in Panama to do it—to ensure speedier communications in future. These two man-made waterways, and the Straits at the entrance to the Black Sea, have great strategic importance, are very profitable to the controlling countries and cause constant international tensions.

For the seas produce conflict as well as easy movement. Germany and Britain were bitter naval rivals in the years from 1900 to 1914, the years of the 'iron-clad', the heavily armoured battleship. Russia and U.S.A. are rivals today, seeking to outdo each other in building rocket-carrying or nuclear-powered submarines, or aircraft carriers, or in establishing new routes and bases, especially in the North Polar regions.

Naval rivalry was less striking in the years after 1918. For one thing, a defeated Germany was out of the race for a number of years, and when it resumed building, after Hitler came to power, it concentrated largely on submarines. For another, it was recognized in the 'thirties that air power was coming to equal, and might in the end replace, sea power. Lastly, the Washington Conference of 1922 had brought a temporary easing of the tension by laying down the so-called 5:5:3 ratio. In this ratio Britain, U.S.A. and Japan were to fix their relative strength in capital ships, that is, battleships and heavy cruisers, even destroying some that were then in process of construction. This conference was part of a genuine attempt to seek peace through gradual disarmament, but it did not satisfy other countries like France and Italy, whose ratio was only 1.75 in each case, and it caused a good deal of unemployment in shipyards. It turned out to be a great advantage to Japan, who, unlike Britain and U.S.A., did not have to police all the oceans, and for whom therefore it meant real mastery of its own home waters.

The air

The idea, or dream, of flight is older than history. According to Greek legend the first man to fly was Icarus, whose father Daedalus fashioned wings of feathers, held together by wax, on which he and his son sought escape from the island of Crete. But Icarus, in elation, flew too near the sun and his wings fell apart, plummeting him into the sea. Leonardo da Vinci, an Italian of the Renaissance, also took birds as his model, minutely studied their flight, and designed aircraft on the same principles of flight as theirs. But man was not yet on the right lines—he was far too heavy ever to fly like a bird.

Experiments were made with balloons in the late eighteenth and nineteenth centuries, and with airships in the twentieth, both kept aloft by lighter-than-air gases. The first flight made in Britain in any kind of heavier-than-air piloted craft was near Dumbarton in 1895. The pilot was Percy Pilcher, a lecturer at Glasgow University, who designed gliders and an undercarriage for aircraft; he was, in fact, the first to use landing wheels for take-off and landing. He was killed in 1899 while he was experimenting with a glider to which he had attached a petrol-driven engine. At last man was thinking along the right lines.

The honour of flying the first powered aircraft therefore went, not to Britain, but to the United States. In 1903 the brothers Wilbur and Orville Wright made the first real aeroplane flight, at Kitty Hawk, North Carolina—and very few newspapers even noticed the event! But in 1909, when Blériot flew the Channel, he made headline news. Towards the end of the First World War, the Royal Flying Corps performed with great valour in primitive machines. In 1927 Colonel Lindbergh made the first solo flight across the Atlantic, and now everyone could understand that a new air age had arrived. Large-scale commercial aviation could now begin.

Air travel is speedy and direct. It is revolutionizing the maps of the world. Mercator's flat charts are relics of the age of sea travel; now we must use globes. It is revolutionizing strategy and routes. As we have already seen, air power has practically destroyed the importance of the old naval bases. In the Second World War, Atlantic convoys were protected by air patrols based on Newfoundland, Greenland, Iceland and the Soviet Arctic—all areas of minor importance until then. The direct air route from Chicago to Berlin is over Labrador; from Chicago to Tokyo, or from Moscow to San Francisco it is over the North Pole; from Chicago to Shanghai it is over Alaska. And Chicago, and the American Middle West, are vulnerable in an air age when they were not in the age of the steamship. Dakar, on the West African bulge, has gained new importance, for it is the nearest point to America in either Africa or Europe.

Air routes over the North Pole.

Air power has transformed military strategy. Not only are places formerly safe now vulnerable to attack—few in fact are safe. The strategic value of the buffer state, of the *cordon sanitaire* and of so-called 'narrow seas' has been greatly reduced. Command of so-called 'strategic' resources like coal, iron ore and aluminium has become essential to the Great Powers.

The Strategic Air Command guards American security by patrols based on East Anglia, Germany, Wheelus Field in Tripoli, Dahran in Arabia and Okinawa in the North Pacific; it can put a girdle round Russia in four, not forty minutes. America's whole system of alliances and its diplomacy are based on the desire to have the use of airfields in places as close to the Russian border as possible, like Norway, Turkey and Pakistan as well as those already mentioned.

Before 1970, regular air travel at supersonic speeds is likely. It will be possible to fly from Prestwick to New York in two hours—you would, that is, leave Britain at 11 a.m. and arrive in New York at 8 a.m., ready for a second breakfast and a day's hard work.

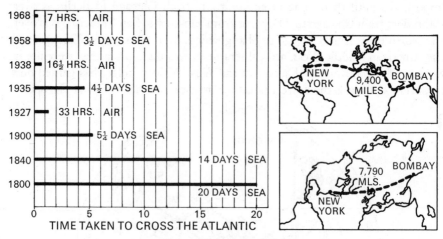

Sea and air routes compared.

The air carries messages as well as men and goods. Through radio and television, telephone and telegraph go the messages of fun and laughter, of propaganda and peace, of information and of S.O.S. Telephone and telegraph have transformed business, eliminated the need for lengthy letters, and lengthy waiting periods, too, and have eased the task of diplomacy. Indeed, diplomacy is no longer the work chiefly of ambassadors and the men on the spot, for the foreign minister or secretary of state, even prime ministers and presidents can fly quickly to any part of the world, to carry on negotiations at the highest level. As a cynical American diplomat put it, 'Why should they talk to the monkey when the organ-grinder is here?'

Air communication has defeated not only distance but ice. In 1911 Captain Scott, the father of the naturalist and TV personality Peter Scott, tried to reach and return from the South Pole. He made his way across the ice-shelf from McMurdo Sound by using sledges and Siberian ponies; 400 miles to the east, the Norwegian, Roald Amundsen, set up his base and set off for the Pole with sledges and dogs in a race with Scott to be the first to reach the Pole. As Scott and his men trudged over the flat, frozen wasteland, they did not know for certain that Amundsen had won. When Scott reached the Pole he found a flag and tent left by Amundsen, and his suspicions were confirmed. On the return journey one crew member died; another walked off and sacrificed himself to prolong the dwindling supplies for Scott and the remaining two members of the party. But to no purpose. Unable to go any farther, and caught by a blizzard, they lay in a tent and died, unaware that they were only ten miles from a supply camp they had set up to make the return easier.

Yet today there is an underground community at the South Pole and a radio station (K 4 WDB). Ever since 1955 the United States and other governments have maintained a scientific research team in the Antarctic, supported by the United States Navy in what it calls Operation Deep Freeze. Access to it is now relatively easy, by Hercules transports and helicopters, and there is even a nuclear station at McMurdo Sound. Soon the Antarctic stations will be covered with huge plastic domes to provide safety and temperate climates for scientists and explorers and even for tourists. The Antarctic has been conquered.

Space

The next assignment is the mastery of outer space. In April 1961 Major Yuri Gagarin of the Soviet Air Force was the first man to journey through outer space. He was hailed as the Columbus of the next age of discovery but he was killed in an air crash in March 1968.

Since 1961 both the United States and Russia have each regularly sent manned rockets into space. The United States Gemini programme is designed to have rockets manoeuvre and meet in space. In August 1964 their *Ranger 7* moon probe hit the moon after radioing back 4,000 excellent photographs of the moon's surface. In 1965 the Russians successfully photographed the hidden side of the moon, and in February 1966 the Russians achieved a soft landing on the moon. Their *Luna 9* spacecraft immediately began relaying pictures, which showed that the surface of the moon is hard and not covered by a deep layer of dust, as some had believed.

The Russian Lieutenant-Colonel Leonov was the first astronaut to leave an orbiting spaceship and to float or 'walk' in space attached to his craft by a lifeline. In December 1954 the United States successfully accomplished the first manned rendezvous in space. *Gemini 7* (Lieut.-Colonel Frank Borman and Commander James Lovell) was joined 185 miles above the earth by *Gemini 6* (Air Force Major Thomas Stafford and Command Pilot Wally Schirra). Together they continued to orbit in formation for $5\frac{1}{2}$ hours, their distance apart varying from 10 feet to 100 feet. This was not only an amazing technical but a great human achievement, for Lovell and Borman stayed in space for 330 hours in all and covered $5\frac{1}{2}$ million miles. In doing so, they surpassed the total number of Russian man-hours in space and equalled what will be the duration of a successful return trip to the moon.

The American objective is for the first astronauts to explore the moon by 1970. This will necessitate a station (code-name Apollo) in orbit round the moon from which crewmen will climb into a LEM (Lunar Excursion Module) and head for the moon. After exploring it they will blast off and rendezvous with the orbiting Apollo for the return trip to earth, using these Gemini techniques. Both a laboratory in space and planned meetings in space are now realities; a visit to the moon is now no longer a piece of science fiction but a practical possibility.

This is only the more dramatic aspect of the space age. Already the Americans and the Russians can photograph remote areas from high-flying aircraft. Alongside the space platforms, the United States hope to launch in 1969 'broadcasting satellites', with built-in nuclear power supplies designed to transmit programmes direct to domestic receivers in all countries—with many implications for global advertising, political propaganda and for the further 'Americanization' of all who see and hear them. World investment in telecommunications is expected to reach £20,000 million in the next five years.

QUESTIONS TO CONSIDER

1. What is the chief importance for a state of (*a*) its rivers and (*b*) its mountains? Give examples.
2. Estimate the advantages and disadvantages to Britain of its position on the map.
3. Why may the Arctic Ocean be called 'The Mediterranean Sea' of the twentieth century?
4. Why does the flag of the U.N. carry a polar projection of the world?
5. How important to a country is the possession of supplies of the chief minerals? Which are the most important?
6. What is meant by a one-product country? Give examples.
7. Why did population increase so slowly until the beginning of the nineteenth century?
8. Why and in what ways is a government concerned over the size of the country's population?
9. In what ways have discovery and invention altered methods of travel and communications in the twentieth century?

WORDS TO NOTE

Autobahn (Germany), *Autostrada* (Italy): main highway. In the U.S., these are sometimes described as Federal highways, since they were often built from Federal not state funds; sometimes they are *Turnpikes*, financed by the payment of tolls (as the new Forth Road Bridge).

Common Market: name given to the group of European states (France, Belgium, Netherlands, Luxembourg, German Federal Republic and Italy) which, in 1957, agreed to establish a common market for all their goods and to impose a common external tariff on the goods of all other countries. They have since then gradually reduced their tariffs on trade with each other. This economic union provides a market of 160 million people—almost as large and productive as that of the U.S.A. (200 million) or the U.S.S.R. (230 million).

Conurbation: a very large urban area, often consisting of a collection of towns, e.g. Clydeside, the Birmingham area or Greater New York City.

Delta: a triangular area at the mouth of a river, covered by the silt, sand and mud brought down by the river. This causes the river to divide into a number of distributaries, but it also produces fertile soil. Deltas are usually densely populated areas—e.g. the Mississippi, the Nile, the Po Delta in Italy or the Ganges Delta.

Turnpikes: Highways in U.S.A. which are financed by a fee (or toll) levied on all users. The Forth Road and Tay Road Bridges use a similar system of charges.

FOR FURTHER READING

Boyd, A.: *An Atlas of World Affairs*, Methuen, 1960.

Cole, J. P.: *Geography of World Affairs*, Penguin, 1959.

David, Sir J. Thomas: *The Motor Revolution*, Longmans' Then and There Series, 1961.

Gibbs-Smith, C. H.: *The Aeroplane, an Historical Survey* (H.M.S.O., 1960).

Pounds, N.: *An Historical and Political Geography of Europe*, Harrap, 1949.

Pounds and Kingsbury: *An Atlas of European Affairs*, Methuen, 1964.

Robbins, Michael: *The Railway Age*, Penguin Books, 1965.

Macdonald, R. S.: *Arctic Frontier*, University of Toronto Press, 1966.

2. The United States of America

The land and the people

One of the first things we have to realize is that the United States of America is not only a nation, but that it is at the same time both a continent and also 50 separate states, each with its own government. Accustomed to Europe and to countries that are small and compact, it is not easy for us to understand the size and problems of a 'continental' and a 'federal' country.

Take a look at the map. The picturesquely-named states stretch across the vast North American continent, from Cape Cod on the Atlantic to the Golden Gate of San Francisco, for 3,000 miles, the distance to London from Baghdad. It would take a train, travelling a mile a minute, 48 hours to cross the country. From Maine, on the Canadian border, south to the Florida Keys is another 1,600 miles. Along the 49th Parallel and through the Great Lakes, America has a 3,000-mile frontier with Canada, the longest undefended frontier in the world. Along the Rio Grande is the border with Mexico; the United States is a vast area.

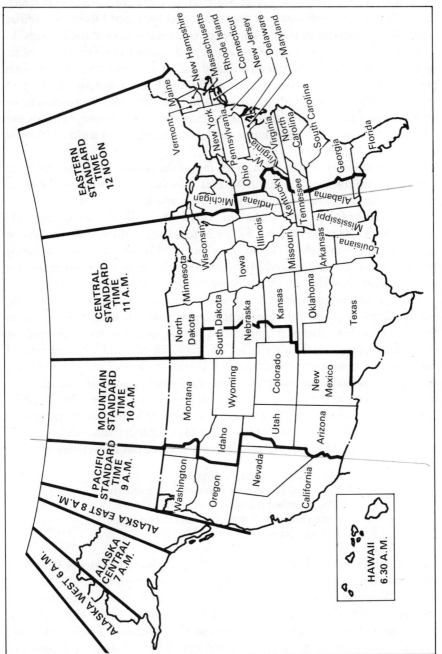

The Time Zones of the United States.

So it is with the different states themselves; Texas, no longer the largest in the Union, is eight times the size of Scotland. In it are great plains over which the cattle roam, though cowboys now ride a high-powered Dodge or Cadillac rather than a bucking bronco. In it are the southern fringes of the Rockies. In it is the oil belt—30 per cent of the world's oil comes from Texas. One of its ranches alone is larger than Scotland, and has its own post office and its own police. California, five times the size of Scotland, has a similar diversity of scenery. With its long coastline, its forests of great trees like the redwoods, its orchards and vineyards, its fruit farms, its deserts and its sunshine, a Hollywood director can make films with almost any kind of background within 100 miles or so of Los Angeles.

This fact of size is written plain on the face of the land. It is obvious in Grand Canyon, in Yellowstone Park or in Niagara. The largeness and grandeur of the American landscape has inspired many novels and films.

These are the things that 'make' the American. He lives in a continent. He tends to travel far more than we do, 'to go to school' (which means college or university as well as 'school' in our sense) outside his own state, to be as happy in sunny Florida as in forested Michigan. The history of the frontier, the size of the land, the limitless opportunities make him restless and ambitious.

America then is continental in its extent, in its climatic variations, its crops and products. It is not only continental but world-wide in its people. For in this vast area there live over 200 million people, drawn from all the ends of the earth. Hardly a nationality fails to be represented—and we must remind ourselves that at least one-third are not of British stock at all and many of them are still only partially Americanized. They have come in great tides of immigration from every country in the world, although since 1924 new Immigration Acts have reduced the flood to a trickle. For a time at least, many of them tend to think of America less as a 'home'—their old country remains that—than as a refuge, personified in the Statue of Liberty holding out its welcoming hand:

> Give me your tired, your poor,
> Your huddled masses yearning to breathe free,
> The wretched refuse of your teeming shore.
> Send these, the homeless, tempest-tost to me,
> I lift my lamp beside the golden door.

Such immigrants will often marry people from their own part of Europe or Asia, and so we can find little foreign-speaking communities dotted about the Middle West and in most of the great cities, preserving their original outlook and speech and way of life for quite a few generations. In the end, however, education in American schools, and the constant influence of radio, television and advertising, make their children and grandchildren more and more like other Americans.

This racial intermixture of the American people is an important aspect of American politics, for many of the 'foreign' peoples are settled in particular regions—Jews in New York, Irish in Boston, Swedes in Wisconsin and Minnesota. There are the prominent Italian colonies in Chicago and New York, German groups in St Louis, old French families in New Orleans or Charleston; all have a very strong character of their own, and are likely to have

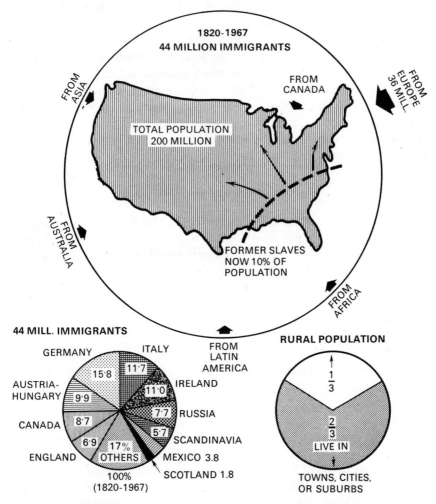

From 1968, the pattern of immigration to the United States will alter totally. The system in operation since 1924 (the national origins quota system) will disappear. It favoured British and Northern European immigrants and discriminated against Southern Europeans and Asiatics. Under the new law, immigrant visas will be issued on a first-come, first-served basis. Each country will be limited to 20,000. The total for Asia, Europe and Africa will be not more than 170,000; and for the Americas 120,000. The brain-drain from Britain will be curbed.

their own points of view about American foreign policy. Scattered through the Far West are the close-knit communities of Chinese and Japanese.

One area only the normal tide of foreign immigration failed to touch. South of the Mason-Dixon line that separates Pennsylvania from Maryland, the character of the people has remained more akin to that of the British, for the presence there of a large minority of coloured people always tended to discourage other immigrants. The Southern whites—some 60–70 per cent of the population of the South—are therefore basically Anglo-Saxon in background, name and outlook.

It is not so much the 50 states—the legal divisions—as some five or six great regions that make America. Not that the legal divisions are unimportant. One has only to drive from Mississippi into Louisiana to know that there is a change—the roads are so much better. If one wants to commit murder, it is better to do it in Maine—where the maximum penalty is life imprisonment—than in New Hampshire, next door, where it is hanging, or California, where it is the death chamber. In Utah a murderer can choose between hanging and shooting. The laws of the states do differ.

The regions or sections

But it is the regional differences that are striking. An American greeting is apt to be not 'what state are you from?' but 'what section are you from?' There is some controversy among Americans about the exact number of regions, since they shade into one another. But all would agree that there are six areas that are quite distinct—*New England*, the *Middle Atlantic States*, the *South*, the *Middle West* (including the upper reaches of the Mississippi, and the Great Lakes) the *Great Plains* and the *West*.

New England

States: Maine, New Hampshire, Vermont, Rhode Island, Massachusetts and Connecticut.
Chief city: Boston.
A region of light industries, fisheries, dairying, crafts and tourist trade.

This is the smallest of the regions, the longest settled, and in many ways the nearest, in geography and spirit, to the Old World. With rocky, stony soil, cliffs and many bays and inlets, New England is a land of mountains, lakes and rocky headlands. It has few natural resources; its rugged surface and short rivers have hindered movement; the winters are severe, the summer pleasant and the autumn (the 'fall') golden and glorious.

This area was first settled by the Pilgrim Fathers who landed from England in 1620, at Plymouth Rock, and in the 1630s by the Company of New England that founded the colony of Massachusetts Bay. Connecticut and Rhode Island

Townspeople of Plymouth, Massachusetts, dressed in seventeenth-century style, hold a Thanksgiving service at the site of the First Fort.

were colonized by religious dissenters from Massachusetts. New England was settled by Puritans, seeking religious and political freedom, a tough, vigorous and very moral people. Its local government is still that of the 'town meeting', its most characteristic scene still the church on the green.

The ideals and high standards of the Yankees—their ideas on government, religion, literature and education—have influenced the whole country. They built the first schools and colleges—Harvard University was founded, as Harvard College, in 1636, sixteen years after the first landing. Almost all the great American writers of the nineteenth century were New Englanders—Emerson, Melville, Henry James. For long their political leaders led the whole country. New Englanders were thrifty and hard-working.

They began as farmers on a rocky soil. In 1826, however, the completion of the Erie Canal, running from Lake Erie to the Hudson River at Albany, brought to New York the trade and the wheat of the Middle West. So they turned to dairy products, to fruit and potatoes—and to the sea. Even before 1620 the Grand Banks off Newfoundland had attracted the British and French fleets seeking cod and mackerel, hake and flounder. In the nineteenth century,

41

THE WEST	THE GREAT PLAINS	THE MIDDLE WEST	THE SOUTH	MIDDLE ATLANTIC STATES	NEW ENGLAND
Alaska	Colorado	Illinois	Alabama	Delaware	Maine
Arizona	N. Dakota	Indiana	Arkansas	New Jersey	New Hampshire
California	S. Dakota	Iowa	N. Carolina	New York	Vermont
Hawaii	Kansas	Michigan	S. Carolina	Ohio	Massachusetts
Idaho	Montana	Minnesota	Florida	Pennsylvania	Rhode Island
Nevada	Nebraska	Missouri	Georgia	W. Virginia	Connecticut
Oregon	New Mexico	Wisconsin	Kentucky		
Utah	Oklahoma		Louisiana		
Washington	Wyoming		Maryland		
			Mississippi		
			Tennessee		
			Texas		
			Virginia		

Alaska

Hawaii

ALASKA AND HAWAII ARE NOT SHOWN ON THE SAME SCALE AS THE REST OF USA: ALASKA IS SHOWN SMALLER, HAWAII LARGER.

needing whale oil for lamps, they became great whalers. They built the graceful, swift clipper ships that dominated world trade just before the coming of the age of steam. Today Boston, Gloucester and Portsmouth are fishing ports; Maine is famous for its lobsters and clams. And from the end of the eighteenth century they were also developing crafts and manufactures. They used the water power of their turbulent streams to set up mills and they became textile-, paper- and shoe-manufacturers, clock- and watch-makers and gunsmiths.

The growth of manufactures brought changes in population. The towns grew; today three out of every four New Englanders live in urban centres. The towns attracted the immigrant—French-Canadians and Irish, Italians, Poles and Central Europeans, nearly all of them Roman Catholic. These immigrants had to be educated, employed and Americanized. They were welcomed by the Democratic Party as a source of voting strength, and that party sought to find jobs for them in return for votes. The Irish among them flocked into the police force or into politics in Boston and New York. The Jews moved into the garment trades, and into business. New England is now an inaccurate name. Less than 40 per cent of the people are of old Yankee stock.

Middle Atlantic states

States: New York, Pennsylvania, New Jersey, Delaware, Ohio and West Virginia.
Chief cities: New York, Philadelphia, Cleveland, Pittsburgh.
Products: Diversified industry, mining, commerce, farming, steel, textiles.

These states are the heart of the great American manufacturing belt. It is one of the most populous regions, with two of the largest cities—New York and Philadelphia (12 and 4 million respectively)—and many others. The region has vast supplies of coal and water power. Its canals, roads and railways link it with the Great Lakes and along these routes, the Hudson-Mohawk route from New York to the Lakes, and the roads to Pittsburgh and the Ohio, towns and industry have grown. Its harbours give it easy access to world markets and have been the first ports of arrival for millions of immigrants. Its large population offers a market for all kinds of consumer goods. In western Pennsylvania and eastern Ohio are the steel towns (Pittsburgh and Bethlehem, Akron and Cleveland) but south-eastern Pennsylvania is excellent farming country; the Middle Atlantic area was, in colonial times, the granary of America.

It is, next to New England and the South, the longest-settled region. Manhattan Island was won by the British from the Dutch in 1664 and named after James, Duke of York (the later James II and VII). The earliest settlements in Pennsylvania and on the Delaware River were made by Swedes. But in 1681 what became Pennsylvania was granted by Charles II to William Penn, and Quaker influence became strong. Under it there was great freedom of religion and opinion, and Philadelphia flourished as The City of Brotherly Love, with a secular university, the first fire service and the first city pavements and street lighting in North America. For a decade (1790–1800) it was the capital of the recently formed United States, until Washington was built. To Pennsylvania immigrants flocked, especially the Scots-Irish from Ulster and the 'Pennsylvania Dutch' from the Rhineland. The Quaker, the Scot and the German has each made his distinctive contribution to the creation of America.

This region has continued to attract the immigrant. And New York City is now the largest city and the greatest port in the country. It is not the New York State capital, which is at Albany, and it was the capital of the whole country only for a few months in 1790. It has, however, long been the financial and commercial heart of the United States. It has always been a city dedicated to trade, finance and commerce. It is geographically very small—Manhattan Island is only some ten street blocks wide, flanked on each side by the Hudson and East Rivers. But in it work each day some 8 million people, and, since there is not room for them to sleep, they commute daily to the Bronx, to Brooklyn, to Queen's and Long Island or over the Hudson to the Jersey shore—New York is a vast conurbation, really a collection of cities. And even more than any other American city, it is a mixture of races. On the eve of the Second World War, there were more Negroes in New York (concentrated in Harlem) than in any other American city, more Irish than in Dublin, more Puerto Ricans than in any city in Puerto Rico, more Italians than in Rome, and more Jews than in the whole of Palestine.

The voting powers of New York State (16 million people), of Pennsylvania and of Ohio are considerable factors in American politics; the Governorship of any one of them is a possible stepping-stone to the White House. Two of the greatest presidents of the twentieth century served their apprenticeship, one as Governor of New Jersey (Woodrow Wilson), the other as Governor of New York (F. D. Roosevelt).

The South

States: All those stretching south from Maryland down to Florida, and across to the Mississippi, and including Texas—some 900,000 square miles and some 56 million people, of whom approximately one-quarter are Negroes. *Chief cities:* Washington, Baltimore, St Louis, Charleston, Richmond

Camping in the great National Parks is popular in the United States. This family is breakfasting in a Kentucky state park.

(Virginia), New Orleans, Birmingham, Houston, Galveston, Dallas and Fort Worth.

Products: Cotton, tobacco, sugar, citrus and other fruits, oil and cattle in Texas; manufactures of increasing importance, especially textiles and synthetic fibres like nylon.

The South is the most 'different' of all the regions—the one with the strongest character of its own. Rich in natural resources, with a climate ranging from Mediterranean type to sub-tropical, it has been slow to industrialize itself. Many of its people were for long unfree. It is almost a one-party region. Its way of life is slower and calmer than elsewhere.

It was along the banks of its great tidal rivers (the Potomac, the Rappahannock, the York and the James in Virginia and the Santee in South Carolina) that there grew up areas of cotton and tobacco, rice and sugar cultivation. These were and are plantation crops produced by hard manual work in the fields in a hot and sticky climate (and, if rice, in wet ground); white workers found the conditions too hard. So Negro slaves were imported from Africa. They were carried on special 'slave ships' and the trade was extremely profitable in the seventeenth and eighteenth centuries. As settlement was pushed west across the mountains, the Negroes became settled over a large area, wherever 'Cotton was King'. Even today in some Southern states, Negroes are almost as numerous as whites; in some areas of Mississippi and Louisiana they outnumber them.

Dependent for its wealth on cotton and tobacco, and firmly believing that slave labour was necessary to work the plantations, the South refused to allow interference with slavery or with its right to carry slavery into western lands as they were opened up. Lincoln, elected President of the U.S.A. in 1860, promised not to interfere with the institution of slavery in states where it already existed, although he detested it, but refused to permit it to be extended any further. On this the South, from Virginia to Texas (Dixie), seceded from the Union, and in 1861 established its own confederacy. It fought a four-year fight (1861–65) and in the end its society was in ruins, its wealth gone, its plantation homes burned to the ground, and many of its men killed. The Civil War was to the Southerners the War Between the States, since they insisted that they had the right to withdraw from a union they no longer accepted. When its great leader, Robert E. Lee, surrendered in 1865 it was the end of a way of life in the South; it was also the end of legal slavery for Negroes, and the victory of the North and of the idea of one strong Union. The sense of unity of the South today is the result of war, defeat, and a long memory. Most people in the South still believe in 'States' rights'—they believe that their own state is as important as the Federal Government and the Union.

Yet, while Negroes were in law unfree until 1865 and there were no schools or services for them except on the plantation itself, they were often well looked after by their masters—they were, after all, an economic investment. It was only after the Civil War that race prejudice on any large scale appeared in the South. By the end of the nineteenth century the Jim Crow system was in force—the segregation of black from white in hotels, on trains and buses, in

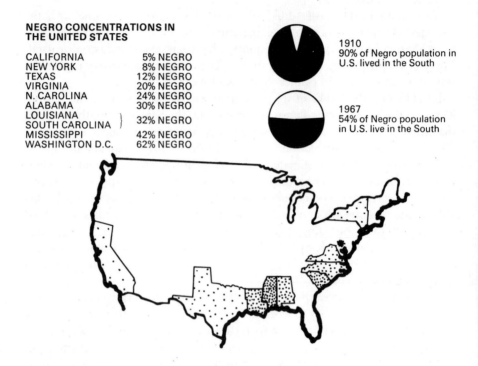

NEGRO CONCENTRATIONS IN THE UNITED STATES

CALIFORNIA	5% NEGRO
NEW YORK	8% NEGRO
TEXAS	12% NEGRO
VIRGINIA	20% NEGRO
N. CAROLINA	24% NEGRO
ALABAMA	30% NEGRO
LOUISIANA	
SOUTH CAROLINA	} 32% NEGRO
MISSISSIPPI	42% NEGRO
WASHINGTON D.C.	62% NEGRO

1910
90% of Negro population in U.S. lived in the South

1967
54% of Negro population in U.S. live in the South

theatres and schools. The South being now poor, the Negroes suffered acutely not only from segregation itself but from the poorer schools and housing they were allowed, and often from unemployment. In this century, the living conditions of Negroes have slowly improved; lynching is now happily extremely rare; almost all Southern states have abandoned the public segregation of the races, almost everywhere the same facilities are open to all. Yet here and there it is still possible to whip up public feeling against Negroes, and people can still be violent, especially where there is 'outside' interference from Federal troops or the Supreme Court or when marches are organized to protest against discrimination. There have been examples of this at Little Rock, Arkansas, in 1959, at Montgomery, Alabama, in 1961, and in Mississippi in 1966.

A feature of the years since 1890 has been the gradual industrialization of the South, since labour is cheaper there than in the North. Cotton mills were built, and later rayon and nylon were produced. Tobacco processing—particularly cigarette making—has steadily increased. Birmingham's steel industry has made it the Pittsburgh of the South; the mineral riches of the Gulf Coast are transforming Louisiana; and Texas is probably the wealthiest and most diverse state of all, from cattle to cotton, from oil to tin and zinc.

As well as the efforts of private enterprise there has been the aid of the Federal Government. In 1933 President F. D. Roosevelt declared that the South was the nation's 'economic problem number one', and that one-third of its people were ill-fed, ill-housed and ill-clothed; he set up the Tennessee Valley Authority to develop the seven states on the Tennessee River. The Authority's dams and power plants, its flood control system, soil conservation and housing schemes have made an immense improvement in the area. Land, sucked dry and eroded by cotton and tobacco, was saved by afforestation schemes. All this provided much employment.

Industries in the South also benefited from the Second World War. Ship-building became a Southern development; so did aircraft manufacture at Dallas and Fort Worth in Texas. Northern industries opened branches and assembly plants in the South. The improvement in Southern incomes brought an increased demand for manufactured goods, since the standard of living rose. Its prosperity in and after the Second World War has produced a 'New South'. But in the South, Old or New, a century after the Civil War, 'The War' is still not Hitler's War or the Kaiser's War but 'The War Between the States'.

The Middle West

States: Indiana, Illinois, Iowa, Michigan, Minnesota, Wisconsin, eastern edges of Kansas, Nebraska, North and South Dakota.
Cities: Chicago, Milwaukee, Minneapolis, St Paul, Detroit, Kansas City.
Products: Wheat, cattle, dairying, iron and coal, heavy industry.

The character of the Middle West is unmistakable: well-watered and practically treeless, its deep, rich soil gives a five- to six-month growing season; in the hot summers the corn (our maize) grows tall, far taller than a man. The corn belt covers some 250,000 square miles, west from the Alleghenies to eastern Kansas and Oklahoma, central Nebraska and eastern South Dakota. Two farmers out of every three, and one acre out of every four cultivated in the United States, grow corn. Its chief use is to feed pigs ('hogs' in American) or beef cattle—many of the cattle are bought as 'feeder' stock from western ranges and fattened by heavy grain feeding. But Wisconsin and Minnesota (the states with a thousand lakes each) are better suited to dairying than to grain; this is the butter and cream region.

But this area is also one of heavy industry. Its main contribution here is its iron-ore, especially in the Mesabi Range in Minnesota, from which 85 per cent of America's iron-ore comes. One must add to iron-ore, coal, oil and silica for glass (Illinois), gypsum, copper and limestone. This region is in fact richer

Part of the Ford factory at Detroit, U.S.A.

in mineral resources than the Middle Atlantic States. With the opening up of the St Lawrence Seaway, it is no longer as cut off as it was. With access to the Mississippi, to the Great Lakes and to the 1,000-mile-long seaway, it is now a major industrial area as well as a store-house and larder.

The capital of the Middle West is Chicago, second city in size in the United States and the greatest railway centre in the world. It is the distributing centre of the Middle West, the point where the Canadian traffic on the Lakes finds its quickest route to the Mississippi and Ohio. Its best-known industries are those that supply the farmers—like tractors and harvesters—or that use farm produce, especially slaughtering and meat-packing.

On the strait linking Lake Huron with Lake Erie stands Detroit, the other great city of the Middle West, scene in 1967 of bitter Negro riots. Along these cheap water routes it receives the steel and coal and ore for automobiles; it is surrounded by cities specializing in car components—Pontiac and Ann Arbor, Lansing and Toledo. The markets for their goods seem limitless—almost every American family has a car, many have more than one, and in Los Angeles, a city of over a million people, there are half as many cars as people.

Into this Middle West, a land of milk and money, people from every part of the world have moved. This is a thickly settled region—it has at least 27 cities of over 100,000 people each.

The Great Plains

States: The eastern edges of Montana, Colorado, New Mexico, the Dakotas, western Kansas and Nebraska, northern Texas and Oklahoma.
Cities: Denver.
Products: Cattle, some irrigated agriculture.

The Great Plains are really a continuation of the Middle West, but with less rainfall. They show how important are a few inches of rain each year. This area was described by the first explorers as 'The Great American Desert'. It stretches from the edge of the Middle West, at approximately the line where each year there are some 20 inches of rain, west to the Rockies, which rise sharp and sheer, a majestic wall of rock. The Plains are almost completely flat, and they present an awesome sight looking back from the 14,000-foot peaks of the Rockies. This is the land of sharp contrasts, of hot summers but freezing winters (as low as 50° below zero) and of strong winds. In the summer they blow from the south-west and are hot; in winter icy blizzards or 'northers' sweep as far south as Texas, and tornadoes occur too. Most homes have cyclone or storm-cellars, in case the whole house should be swept away.

The Plains are dry, treeless and open, but their grass is short and thick—so they are America's legendary cattle and cowboy country, the land of the big ranch and the tall tale. When the first-comers saw the Plains they saw no grass at all—all they could see were countless thousands of buffalo. On the buffalo the Plains Indians lived; theirs was in fact a buffalo culture—the skins for shirts, leggings and wigwam, the meat for food. The chief reason for the wars between white invaders and Indians was not the fight for land nor the fact that the white was a farmer and settler whereas the Indian was a nomad, but the fact that the white completely destroyed the buffalo herds and with them destroyed the Indians' capacity for survival. On the earliest rail journeys across the Plains the favourite place to ride was on the 'cowcatcher' in front of the engine, where you could slaughter buffalo as the train advanced. Millions of buffalo were killed within a few years, chiefly for their hides, and for the sake of quick money.

The buffalo have almost totally gone, and in parts of Montana and Wyoming sheep have replaced them. There is mineral wealth—gold and silver, phosphorus and phosphates, copper and lead and, in the Pecos highlands of west Texas, oil and coal and gypsum. Part of the region has become a 'dust-bowl' and the desert is slowly spreading. But the Plains are cattle country, not yet industrialized. The only large city is Denver and the population is thin and scattered. The White Sands in New Mexico are now a reserved zone belonging

5

to the Atomic Energy Commission. This is the place where the atom bomb was manufactured and tested in the Second World War.

The West

States: All those west of the Rockies.

Cities: Seattle, Portland, San Francisco, Los Angeles, San Diego, Salt Lake City.

Products: Citrus fruit, vineyards, cattle, mining, oil, films, aircraft manufacture, tourism.

By the West we mean all the states west of the Rockies. It falls into three sub-areas: the Rockies, the basins and plateaux between the Rockies and the Sierra Nevada, and the Pacific Coast.

The Rockies. Their richest treasures are minerals and scenery. Mining is still the leading occupation—not the gold prospecting of a century ago but the extraction of copper, lead, silver and zinc. Leadville, Colorado, at 10,000 feet, is one of the highest mining areas in the world. The world's largest open-air copper mine is at Bingham, Utah. Butte, Montana, is also the centre of much copper mining. Ranching and farming are, however, the main activities. There are no large towns; the population is scanty.

The Great Basin Country stretches from the Wasatch Mountains across most of Utah and Nevada. Here the scanty water disappears into the ground or flows into salt lakes that have no outlet to the sea. The Valley of the Great Salt Lake was discovered by Brigham Young in 1847, leading a colony of Mormons seeking escape from the United States of that time. They have irrigated the valley, and Salt Lake City, Provo and Ogden are prosperous and attractive Mormon towns. Mormons practised polygamy until 1890, and in 1896 their state, Utah, joined the United States.

South of the Great Basin is the great valley and gorge of the Colorado River which forms the Grand Canyon. This is perhaps the most impressive natural formation in U.S.A.—a gorge over a mile in depth, with canyons inside canyons, over 200 miles long and varying in width from 4 to 18 miles. The great river at the bottom can only be seen from three or four points. Visitors go down the canyon on muleback, if they have a head for heights. The canyon country of Arizona and New Mexico—with its flat-topped *mesas* on which the Navajo Indians live, its Indian pueblo architecture, its deserts so vivid in colour that they are called 'painted', its sagebrush, yucca and cactus plants—is a place of dramatic beauty, and attracts large numbers of tourists.

North of the Great Basin is the Columbia River Valley—the river that is the boundary between the States of Oregon and Washington, states rich in sugar-beet, vegetables and apples. The water power of both the Colorado and the Columbia has now been harnessed. The Hoover Dam (1936) supplies the power and light for southern California; and Grand Coulee in the north-west is the largest concrete structure in the world, providing electricity for an area that has little oil or coal for fuel.

The Coast

The Pacific Coast today has probably the highest standard of living in the world. A Mediterranean climate, great agricultural resources, the boost to industry provided by the Second World War, and the film and aircraft industries, have attracted many thousands of immigrants. To many Americans it is the Promised Land.

Its two chief cities are utterly different. San Francisco, the most beautiful of all American cities, has an exotic Chinese quarter, a magnificent harbour and a delightful climate—a city of steep hills, with little cable-cars moving up and down, of breath-taking views and of dramatic bridges, like the Golden Gate, sweeping across the bay. Vast Los Angeles, 450 miles to the south, sprawls across its seven hills. It is less gracious and much uglier than 'Frisco' and has a 'smog' problem, caused by the number of its car exhausts. Hollywood is one of its suburbs. The names of these two cities tell us that California was first settled by Spaniards.

Running from San Diego, through Los Angeles and San Francisco, north to Portland, Oregon, and to Seattle, Washington, and on to Vancouver, is the magnificent Coast Highway, a 1,000-mile road that takes the traveller from the purple bougainvillia and scarlet hibiscus of the sub-tropics to the giant redwood trees and the mountains, and on to the land of the North-West with its apple orchards and heavy rainfall, and its Indian and Anglo-Saxon names. This whole region, with its busy and rapidly growing cities, its great ports and trading centres, 3,000 miles from New York and 6,000 miles from London or Glasgow, looks out on the Pacific and on another world—the East.

How the U.S.A. is governed

The Union called the United States of America was born on 4 July 1776, with its Declaration of Independence. After the War of Independence was won, in 1783, the new Republic consisted of 13 states, all of which had been British colonies, on the eastern seaboard, stretching from the dripping pine-forests of rocky Maine, to the steamy swamps of Georgia, with its fireflies and magnolias. As the pioneers pushed west these were joined by new states, and today there are 50, including Hawaii and Alaska, the newest of all. 'Old Glory', the national flag, has had the number of its stars changed many times since first it flew.

State government

The 50 states vary a lot in size, population and wealth. Indeed one city in Illinois, Chicago, spends more on its police alone than Mississippi spends on its whole government. But each state has its own constitution and its own capital city, with a capitol building to house its congress. The state governor and the congress are elected every two years, and most state officials, from the sheriffs and judges down to the local dog-catchers, are also elected.

The states control their own affairs to a very great extent. They look after education, road-building, police, criminal justice, health services, and can raise money in all kinds of state taxes, on sales of goods, on property, on petrol, on income or houses—each one decides on its own methods. Since the New Deal the Federal Government has helped with the cost of such things as flood control, storm damage, road building and education, especially in the poorer states. We must remember too that many services in America are still provided by private firms and run as businesses for a profit—hospitals and medical services, rubbish removal, ambulances, telephones and telegrams, even, in many places, fire brigades.

Federal government and the nation

What holds this enormous Union, with its very different peoples and problems, together? What makes a continent, with 50 separate states, into one nation?

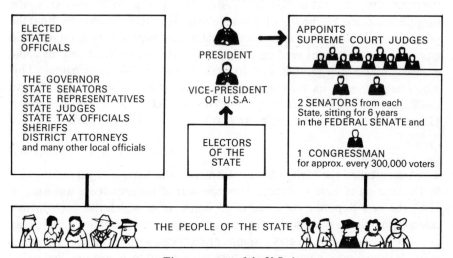

The government of the U.S.A.

Partly it is a single official language and a thorough system of education, with a lot of emphasis on patriotism. Partly it is the conquest of distance by science—railways, telegraphs, marvellous roads and airports. Partly it is the tremendous power of advertising, of press, radio, film, and the American skill in mass-production, coupled with a very high standard of living to produce uniformity in speech, manners and ambitions. But chiefly it is the Constitution of the

U.S.A. and the Federal Government which it established, the government, which, seated in Washington, the national capital, dwarfs the 50 states and welds the people together.

The Constitution of the U.S.A.

This is a written constitution, a document which has for the American the awe and majesty of our monarchy and Magna Carta rolled into one. It was adopted in 1787 and it is there, in black and white, that the sovereign power of the Republic is expressed—'We, the people of the United States . . . do ordain and establish this Constitution.'

The Constitution gives great powers to the Federal Government—the sole power of declaring war and making peace, of conducting foreign affairs, of maintaining and controlling the armed forces, of regulating commerce between the states, of running the Post Office, of collecting Federal taxes and minting money, of maintaining the Supreme Court and the Federal system of justice, among others. Powers not listed in the Constitution and its Amendments still belong to the separate states.

The Constitution lays down the actual form of government for the whole nation—a government of three branches: the Executive (President and Cabinet), the Legislature (Congress) and the Judiciary (the Supreme Court).

The Supreme Court

This Court, of nine justices appointed by the President for life (they cannot be dismissed), is the guardian of the Constitution—you might call it the watch-dog. It can, and does, hold up important new measures, or even reject them, if it thinks that they are unconstitutional. Reforming presidents, like F. D. Roosevelt, often have a great deal of trouble with it, but it does prevent a president from becoming over-powerful or tyrannical. The Supreme Court, with this great power of review of law-making, has no counterpart in Britain.

The President (or Executive)

The President of the U.S.A. is quite possibly the most important elected official in the whole world. He is a combination of king and prime minister, and has great powers.

He is commander-in-chief of the army and navy; he can make treaties—but they have to be agreed to by two-thirds of the Senate; he appoints ambassadors and Supreme Court Judges; he can call special sessions of Congress and he shares the law-making power of Congress. As head of the Executive, helped by an elected Vice-President, he appoints his own cabinet, from among his friends, party chiefs, businessmen and experts. These are not members of Congress, unlike Cabinet Ministers in Britain, who *do* have to be Members of Parliament (of either House), so there is no close link, as in Britain, between the executive and the legislative branches of government, although they do try to co-operate or control each other as much as they can.

Many of the new measures or laws in the U.S.A. are prepared by the President and his advisers and introduced by his party 'floor-leader' in one of the Houses of Congress. On passing both Houses they go back to the President for his signature before becoming law.

The election of a President is complicated. In November of election year there is an election in every state, in which people over 21 can vote. The President is, however, finally chosen by a special Electoral College, in December. Each state elects a number of Presidential Electors, equal to the number of its Senators and Representatives, so that the Electoral College for the whole country has $100 + 437$, or 537 members. Though legally free to choose any one of the candidates they like, these electors are bound by custom to choose the one who won a majority in their state in the November election. But it is the electoral vote, not the popular vote, that counts. Some Presidents, like President Hayes in 1876, have gained office with a majority of electoral votes, but without a majority of popular votes. President Kennedy was elected by a very narrow 'popular' vote in 1960—34,221,463 as against 34,168,582 for Mr Nixon. But in the Electoral College of 537 his majority over Mr Nixon was 81.

Until 1950 the President could be re-elected any number of times. In practice, until 1940, no President or Vice-President had held office for more than two terms—chiefly because of the refusal of the third term by Washington and Jefferson when they were begged to stand again. But F. D. Roosevelt overthrew this tradition by being re-elected in 1936, 1940 and 1944. In 1950 the Congress, fearful of over-mighty Presidents, passed the 22nd Amendment to the Constitution which now limits the President by law to two terms of office—eight years in all.

In addition to his other responsibilities a President is also leader of his party. He has to secure for it jobs and rewards, and force through Congress his party's policy. A defeated Presidential candidate, like Mr Nixon in 1960 or Mr Goldwater in 1964, is nominally the leader of his party until its next national convention, but this opposition leadership is very ineffective because he is not a member of Congress and so is little in the public eye.

The Congress (The Legislature)

The President has need of all his skill in dealing with the third branch of the Federal Government—the Congress—which is jealous of the President's power. Besides, it frequently happens that the President and the majority in Congress belong to different parties. And sometimes a large section of the President's party is opposed to him personally, as many conservative Democrats were opposed to F. D. Roosevelt and his reforms.

The President, especially in the 'honeymoon' period of his first few months in office, does have considerable influence over Congress. He has at his disposal many Federal and State offices, and by giving or withholding this patronage, he can 'persuade' Senators and Representatives to his point of view. He can send messages to Congress or, on special occasions, appear in person before a joint session of both Houses. The members of his cabinet can appear before Congressional Committees or talk to members privately. Above all, nowadays the President can appeal directly to the people, through press conferences, or a 'fireside chat' over radio or television, emphasizing to them that he is the real popular leader and shaper of national opinion.

	Head of State	Head of Government	Cabinet	Upper House	Lower House
U.S.A.	President	President	Chosen by President and reports to him alone.	Senate of 100 members, two from each state, elected for six years. Paid $22,500 (£9,350) per year, with free travel and very good office facilities.	437 Congressmen, one for approx. 300,000 voters, elected for two years. Same pay as Senators, and similar facilities.
U.K.	Queen	Prime Minister	Selected by Prime Minister from leading members of his own party in the House of Commons, or the House of Lords.	All hereditary peers of England and of Scotland, of Great Britain and of the U.K., plus two Archbishops and 24 Bishops, plus life peers. Paid 4½ guineas per day as expenses for each day's meeting.	630 M.P.s, one for approximately 70,000 voters. Paid £3,250 per year plus free rail travel (but no office or postage facilities).

Congress has two Houses—the Senate, and the House of Representatives. Members of both are elected in each state, by popular vote—two Senators, and a number of Representatives in proportion to the population. For example, Nevada has two Senators and only one Representative; Virginia has two Senators and ten Representatives; New York has two Senators and 43 Representatives. Senators are elected for a term of six years, one-third coming up for election every two years. The complete House of Representatives is elected every two years.

'Legislative' means 'law-making', and Congress shares with the President the power of drawing up and introducing new measures. Sometimes the President does not like Congress's new laws, or he does not like what they have done to his own in discussing and passing them, and so he refuses to sign them. If this happens, and two-thirds of both Houses agree to the new measures, then they become law in spite of the President's veto.

The House of Representatives, however, is not as powerful as the British House of Commons. It lasts only two years. Its members must be residents of the state they represent and so they are local rather than national figures, and worry less about international problems than about the politics of the corner drug store or the small town. The House is controlled by the Speaker, who is not an impartial chairman, but the leader of the majority party. Cabinet ministers are not members of the House, and so cannot be controlled by it.

The Senate is different, a smaller and much more respected institution. When Washington was asked by an intelligent Frenchman why there should be a Senate at all, the story goes that he poured some of his tea into his saucer and said, 'Just as I have cooled this tea, so we anticipate that the Senate will cool the hot measures passed by the more popular House.' Its 100 members, 2 per state, are normally men of great influence, sitting in Washington for six years, frequently re-elected. A Senatorship is, next to the Presidency, the great prize of American political life.

We get a most inaccurate picture of it when we imagine the Senate to be like the House of Lords. It can alter or reject financial measures; it confirms all major appointments; it must give its approval to treaties. Much of its work is done in special committees, to which most matters are referred before coming up for full debate. These committees are very powerful, and frequently have public hearings to which they summon important witnesses for evidence or cross-examination.

In these hearings they can cross-examine members of the Cabinet itself, and when such hearings are reported on television, as they often are, they can have considerable effect on public opinion—as did the investigations in 1966 into the conduct of the war in Vietnam.

The chairmanships of committees go to members of the majority party in order of seniority of service in the Senate, and the chairmen of really important committees, like Foreign Affairs or Finance, are often as important as the cabinet ministers themselves. The states, especially the smaller ones, look to this House, much more than to the House of Representatives, to protect their interests.

The parties in American politics

We have seen that elections are held very frequently in the United States and indeed more public officials at all levels are chosen by the votes of their fellow-citizens than in any other country in the world. These elections, like our own, are run on party lines, and the two biggest, and the only two important, parties are the Democratic and the Republican, highly organized in every state.

In many states there are held what are called 'primary elections' inside the parties, to select all their candidates, including Presidential candidates, for the big popular elections that follow. Every registered member of the party can vote in these 'primaries'.

Above the State Party—concerned with its own state elections for Governor,

Senators, Representatives and all the rest—is the National Party, run by a National Committee, and governed in their selection of candidates and 'platforms' by the National Convention, which meets every fourth year.

The Convention is the ultimate governing body of the party and consists of some 900 delegates representing the 50 states, the territories and the District of Columbia, roughly according to population. There will also be thousands of party notables, onlookers, newspapermen and television cameramen. If you think of the heat of Chicago, Philadelphia, Los Angeles or San Francisco in the summer and a mass of 6,000-odd people packed into an assembly hall, you can understand better the excitement and the temper of these great gatherings.

The Convention's task is threefold. First, it must adopt a 'platform', or, as we might say, shape a policy for the coming four years that will secure the party's success at the polls four months later. In America, as a wit put it, a platform is not so much something one stands on, as something one gets in on. Since neither party stands for any fixed belief or principle, there is frequently little to choose between the two platforms, and they tend to consist of pious promises, as high sounding, vague and inoffensive as possible.

Second, the Convention must elect a National Committee, whose job is to run the party for the next four years and to secure its success at the polls.

And third, it must nominate a candidate for President. This is its real business. Many names are submitted, except when the ruling President is a member of the party, and has served one term only, when his re-nomination is a practical certainty. The names are submitted to the Convention by each state in alphabetical order, beginning with Alabama and ending with Wyoming, and on being announced are greeted with tumultuous and well-planned applause. Nominating speeches are accompanied by bands, marching and the waving of banners; famous 'stars' like Frank Sinatra sing patriotic and campaign songs under the arc lights.

What do the Democratic and Republican Parties stand for—how exactly do they differ from one another? This is not an easy question to answer, for in so vast and varied a country no one political or economic idea can win enough support for one party to beat the other in national elections. Even the cause of labour is not political—the big trade unions prefer to act as pressure groups on both major parties rather than to back either one definitely or to form a party organization of their own.

Political parties in the U.S. have to be federal—that is, they have to be loose alliances of regional groups, without a fixed policy in common. What, then, holds them together? Again we can find at least three factors: history, jobs and the national situation.

The South is Democratic because it fought and lost the Civil War against Lincoln and the Republican North. The big cities, especially in the north and east, like Boston, New York and Philadelphia, are Democratic largely because of the big foreign-born vote—Italians, Irish, Jews—because in the past the Democratic Party helped the alien and the underdog. The rest of the North is Republican because of Lincoln, and because the Republicans in the past have been helpful towards 'Big Business' and commerce.

Some 250,000 Federal offices and an even larger number of state and local offices are the prize of success at the polls. In the old phrase, 'To the victor belong the spoils'. The different groups and interests in the parties stay united to hold on to, or to gain control over, these.

A further factor is the national situation at the time of the election. There might be a common problem, e.g., the land problem and the serious plight of the farmers kept South and West in an uneasy Democratic alliance for years. Or there might be a dynamic national leader. Mr Roosevelt in 1936 won not only South and West, but every state in the North except Maine and Vermont. In 1964 Mr Johnson won all but six states.

As a rough guide it may be said that the Democratic Party has its chief strength in the South, in the Mountain States, and in the great cities of the North and East. The Republican Party has its chief strength in the East, outside the big cities, and in the industrial and farming Middle West.

Again roughly, it may be said that the Democrats are readier to spend public money on social services and are less the party of 'Big Business' than the Republicans, and that until the growing power of Russia and China frightened both parties, the Republicans tended to be more 'isolationist' and less sympathetic towards Europe than the Democrats. But we must remember that changing circumstances can always change allegiances in any area of the U.S.A., even the 'Solid South'.

The New Deal

In the years between 1918 and 1941 the United States faced two major issues. At home there was a severe economic crisis, which had to be dealt with in bold, new ways; and in foreign policy there was a constant struggle between isolationists who wished to keep out of European affairs altogether, and the interventionists who believed in working with other countries, especially those in Europe, to keep the peace of the world.

It is hard for us today—and for many Americans—to realize that the United States knew widespread poverty not long ago. It did so in its pioneer days, of course, and when the settlers were moving west, but in the years from 1929 to 1934 it did so again. The American Depression of these years followed the fantastic extravagance and high spending and gambling of the 1920s, the Jazz Age.

But when prices began to fall, in 1929, after the collapse of a number of companies, some of them fraudulent, investors and businessmen lost confidence. The United States had become heavily dependent on the home market and on advertising and hire-purchase. High tariffs hampered trade with Europe; manufacturers stopped producing goods as world markets disappeared and this caused unemployment, a loss of spending power at home and a failure to meet hire-purchase agreements, with further cuts in production. Corn and cotton prices fell alarmingly, and the farmer, who had not shared in the ease of the 'twenties, was badly hit. By 1932 some 15 million Americans were out of work. There existed no government relief for them and no adequate social services. On the day the new President, F. D. Roosevelt, took office in January 1933, all American banks were closed.

To meet this crisis, Roosevelt carried through the New Deal Federal relief and reform measures. By a series of acts over the next three years, the banks were more strictly supervised; the *Securities and Exchange Act* was passed to control stock exchanges; the country abandoned the gold standard. The Civilian Conservation Corps (C.C.C.) was created to employ young men on road-building and afforestation in healthy surroundings, with their families at home receiving part of their pay. The Tennessee Valley Authority (T.V.A.) was set up to provide cheap power in some of the poorer states of the South, to provide work, and to control the flood water. By the *Agricultural Adjustment Act* (A.A.A.) farmers were given subsidies, and production, especially of corn and cotton, was controlled so that prices would artificially rise—by 1939 the farmer's income was twice that of 1932. The *National Recovery Act* (N.R.A.) shortened working hours, raised wages and recognized trade unions. The Works Progress Administration (W.P.A.) financed new building projects—and many of the splendid post offices one sees in American towns today are the result. The Federal Government even brought in social security benefits for unemployment and old age—always thought of before this as 'state' not 'federal' matters.

These measures set the country on the road to recovery—as did the contracts for arms and supplies for defence that poured in as the danger of war in Europe increased. Roosevelt's measures were not socialist, although many of his opponents described him as a 'Red', and worse. His job, as he saw it, was to revive the capitalist system—which had produced so high a standard of living in the past—by using Federal funds to 'prime the pump', and to start the economy moving again. He had to inspire in Americans a new faith in themselves—all that America had to fear, he said, was fear itself. In economic terms, what he did was to apply the principles of Lord Keynes; in hard times he believed there should be not economy and wage-cuts but a release of money (from, in this case, the Federal Government) to set going again the normal demands for goods.

He was successful; and he not only revived the economy but enormously extended the power and impact of the President. He also won over to the

Democratic Party many of the poorer groups, especially the Negroes. Next to Lincoln, who freed the slaves, F. D. Roosevelt was idolized by American Negroes and by many working-class people.

It is equally hard for us, accustomed to the important role played in the world by the United States since 1945, to realize that until 7 December 1941, when Japanese bombs were dropped on Pearl Harbour, the United States preferred isolation to intervention in European affairs.

Isolationism won its biggest victory in 1919–20 when the Senate refused to allow the United States to join the League of Nations. But the Depression increased isolationist feeling for a number of reasons.

For one reason, Americans had so many troubles at home, in unemployment, poverty, business and trade stagnation, that they felt that all their energies were required for domestic problems. For another, a wave of economic nationalism swept over the globe. The various nations set up currency controls, placed quotas on imports and exports and enacted tariff laws against each other's trade. Finally, the Depression brought Hitler into power in Germany, overthrew the last hopes of the liberal, anti-military party in Japan, and strengthened reaction in Fascist Italy. The whole atmosphere of the world became stormier and chillier. Americans, anxious to remain at peace, reacted to this change in atmosphere by retreating into their storm-cellars.

In all sections of the country, especially the Middle West, fervent isolationists could be found. They argued that the U.S. should stay aloof from European wars and tensions. And Neutrality Acts were passed to ensure it.

The majority of Americans took another view. The United States has repeatedly been ready, they said, to denounce tyrannies and dictatorships, and to take practical measures against them. Lincoln declared in 1863 that the Civil War was proving to the entire world the ability of 'government of the people, by the people, for the people' to survive. In 1898 McKinley led the United States to war on behalf of the Cubans, struggling for self-government against Spain. In 1917 Wilson headed his great crusade 'to make the world safe for democracy'. Franklin D. Roosevelt was simply following a long American tradition when in the years 1935–40 he made it plain that the United States had a vital interest in the survival of democratic freedoms abroad, in face of the threat from Hitler. He made his most vehement protest in his famous speech at Chicago on 5 October 1937. Here he declared that the peace-loving nations should unite to 'quarantine' the nations which behaved like gangsters and caused international disorder and fear.

The dramatic series of Axis aggressions in Europe and Africa and the threats from Japan rapidly convinced all far-sighted Americans that they could keep aloof from the common democratic cause only at their peril. If the peace-loving nations remained disunited they would be cut down one by one. In fact, they were being cut down.

First Austria, then Czechoslovakia, then Albania, lost independence; Ethiopia was conquered, and Spain controlled indirectly by the Fascist powers. It became plain that Roosevelt was right in criticizing the Neutrality Acts, which prevented the United States from assisting weak nations under attack.

The demonstration was complete when the Japanese struck at Pearl Harbour, the American base in the Hawaiian Islands, in 1941, two years after Hitler attacked Poland and started the Second World War. The United States found itself for the first time in its history assailed by powerful foes on both the Atlantic and the Pacific flanks. It was at last clear that the United States could remain peaceful and protected only if it joined other nations in setting up an organization to stop war at its source. The attack on Pearl Harbour ended isolation for any realist.

Since 1945, it has disappeared because of the Cold War; because Presidents and Senators have persuaded Americans to help countries poorer than themselves; and because a succession of international crises since 1947 has made it impossible for Americans to believe any longer that they can isolate themselves from the rest of the world.

World leadership for the United States

The Presidencies of H. S. Truman (1945–52) and
Dwight D. Eisenhower (1952–60)

For two years (1945–47) after the Second World War, glad to be out of it, the United States went swinging back to isolation. President Roosevelt died in April 1945, to be replaced by President Truman; Lend-Lease supplies to Britain ceased seven days after the surrender of Japan in August 1945; troops were called home.

But, with the inability of Britain, in 1947, to continue aid to Greece and Turkey, it became obvious that Europe needed a common plan for economic recovery, and help from the United States. Then, in 1948, the Communist *coup* in Czechoslovakia and the Russian 'siege' of Berlin raised fears that Communist power might spread westwards, and the United States moved fully into European affairs when she relieved Berlin by a dramatic 'airlift'.

With the victory of Mao Tse-tung in China, in 1949, and the outbreak of the Korean War in 1950, the United States became just as deeply involved in the affairs of Asia. Step by step, she has now become the leader of the 'free world', no longer a New World isolated from the complications and problems of the Old.

What were these steps towards world leadership? Here are the most important:

1947. The Truman Doctrine. U.S.A. offered help to Greece and Turkey, of loans and gifts of food and dollars.

1947. U.S.A. requested permission from U.N.O. to hold in trust some 98 Pacific islands.

1947. U.S.A. ratified the Rio Pact, which pledges armed support to any American republic in need of it.

1948. The Marshall Plan. The United States launched the European Recovery Programme, with large-scale loans and gifts to needy countries in Western Europe.

The U.S. helped to organize the Berlin Airlift in 1948–49, to ensure food supplies and freedom for the people of Berlin.

1949. U.S.A. organized and joined NATO, the North Atlantic Treaty Organization, for the first time committing itself permanently in peace-time to membership of a military alliance.

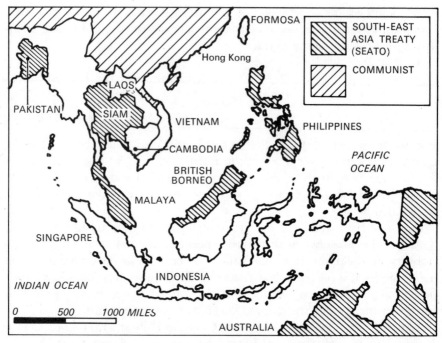

Member states of South-East Asia Treaty Organization.

The U.S. aided South Korea when it was invaded by North Korea (1950–53).

1952–59. John Foster Dulles, Secretary of State under President Eisenhower, sought to protect American security by arranging alliances and pacts like SEATO and CENTO, in different parts of the world, to halt the spread of

Communist power. Many American bases were established throughout the 'free world'.

Since 1959: a policy of 'interdependence'. The growing realization that Russia and the U.S. could destroy each other led to a new foreign policy. Each had nuclear power; so each returned to the use of more conventional diplomacy. When wars occurred they were 'small scale' wars, as in the Congo and in the Middle East.

What the United States has done

These military threats led the United States to help to form the North Atlantic Treaty Organization (NATO, 1949), the South-East Asia Treaty Organization (SEATO, 1954), the Pacific Security Treaty (1951) with Australia and New Zealand (usually known as the Anzus Pact) and the Baghdad Pact (1955), now the Central Treaty Organization or CENTO.

The U.S.A. has surrounded Russia with air bases, from Iceland through East Anglia and Germany, across North Africa and Arabia to Formosa and Okinawa, and equipped these fields with planes of the Strategic Air Command, some of which are always in the air, carrying nuclear weapons. Since 1960, submarines carrying the Polaris long-range missile have been on constant patrol, some of them from a Scottish base on the Holy Loch.

It has helped the economic development of backward areas, with schemes like the Colombo Plan.

It gathers information about the intentions of Russia and China. Among these has been the use of intelligence reports collected by the U.S. Central Intelligence Agency, which sometimes has sent high-flying aircraft on photographic missions over Russian territory. In 1960 the Russians shot down one of these planes (from a height, they claimed, of 68,000 feet) and tried and imprisoned the pilot.

The U.S.A. tries to impress the Russians with its scientific skill, by developing nuclear-powered submarines or by sending missiles into space or into orbit with the intention of equipping artificial satellites which can act as tracking, photographic, or even as military, stations in space. The Russians have been seeking to rival the Americans here in what has become a race for the moon.

The anxieties of world leadership

These developments since the end of the Second World War have also brought anxieties to Americans. At times, some say partly as a result of the freedom and frankness of their own newspaper, radio and television commentators, these anxieties have become crises. Among the causes of tension are:

First, rivalry and hostility between the United States and Russia. The United States did not recognize the Soviet Government until 1933 because, being an intensely democratic republic, the United States dislikes and fears

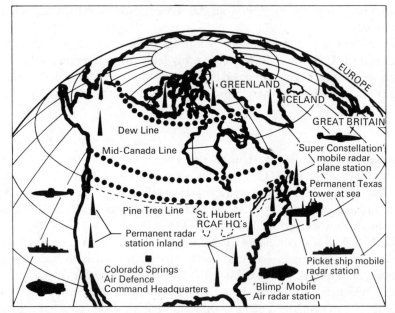

NORAD, the North American Air Defence Command, based on Colorado Springs, is an elaborate protective system of ships, planes and especially of radar. A key part of it is the D.E.W. line (Distant Early Warning), a series of semi-automatic radar stations stretching from the Aleutians across Alaska and Canada to Greenland and Iceland. They will set off an alarm if an enemy bomber appears.

Communist ideas and what it regards as tyrannical government. It takes pride in individual enterprise, believing that this alone has produced the high standard of living in the United States. Although American civilization is materially so impressive with its cars and refrigerators, its wealth and its gadgets, Americans are strongly religious—almost 100 million people go regularly to Sabbath services—and there is profound dislike for Russian and Chinese materialism and 'ungodliness'.

Russian activities since 1945 have increased the enmity, particularly Russia's growing control over the satellite states in Eastern Europe. The United States has shown itself since 1945 particularly sympathetic towards refugees. In 1948 it admitted thousands of Poles, and in 1956 thousands of Hungarians, in excess of their immigration quotas.

Second, the increasing power of Communist China. Since 1949 China has become as menacing as Soviet Russia and this to many Americans is more puzzling, since there was, until then, considerable contact between the two countries. Many American missionaries had served in Christian missions in China. The Americans had been generous to Chinese universities. And in the years from 1937, when China, led by Chiang Kai-Shek, was at war with Japan, the United States poured in supplies to Chiang. Madame Chiang, a very accomplished woman who was educated at one of the best American girls' colleges (Wellesley) and who converted Chiang to Christianity, was very popular in the United States and was a close friend of President Roosevelt. The collapse of the Chiang régime in 1949 and the victory of Mao Tse-tung were hard for Americans to grasp. The United States has not recognized as the legal government of mainland China the Communist régime of Mao Tse-tung and continues to recognize the régime of Chiang, although it is now confined to the island of Taiwan (Formosa).

Third, fear of military aggression from Russia and China. This springs largely from the size of the two countries, their enormous natural resources and their power to win 'converts' in Central Europe and in Asia. China has the world's largest population (700 million) and it is increasing rapidly; even if the country is still industrially backward, it can be a formidable threat in Asia.

Fourth, the fear of Communist penetration at home. There has not been a great deal of evidence of this, but enough to cause indignation and waves of alarm. In 1949 Alger Hiss, a former New Dealer, was convicted of perjury for denying that he had had contacts with Russian agents, and in 1953 the Rosenbergs were executed for treason. Joseph McCarthy, an ambitious Republican Senator for Wisconsin from 1946 until his death in 1957, built up a formidable but on the whole non-proven case that there were traitors in the State Department itself. The Korean War was frightening and cost many American lives. In the years 1950–55 particularly, the United States lived through a succession of domestic crises brought about by these charges and counter-charges. They ended with the downfall of Senator McCarthy, but since 1954 the Communist Party has been completely banned in the U.S.A.

In 1960, when President Eisenhower had completed his second term, the Republican candidate for the Presidency was Richard Nixon, who had been Vice-President for eight years. He was narrowly defeated by the young and glamorous Democratic candidate John F. Kennedy.

The Presidency of John F. Kennedy (1960–63)

On 22 November 1963, while driving in a motorcade through the streets of Dallas, Texas, on his way to a luncheon, President Kennedy was assassinated, and Governor Connally of Texas, who accompanied him, was seriously wounded. The rifle shots were fired by an unseen assassin, apparently from a building along the route. President Kennedy was the fourth President in American history to be assassinated (the others being Abraham Lincoln in 1865, James A. Garfield in 1881 and William McKinley in 1901; and attempts were also made to kill Andrew Jackson, Theodore Roosevelt—whose life was saved by the 50 pages of his speech in his pocket—Franklin D. Roosevelt and Harry S. Truman).

6

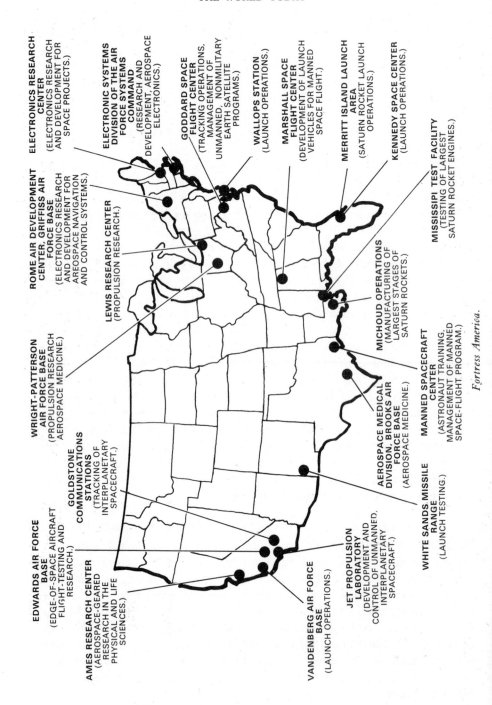

ELECTRONICS RESEARCH CENTER
(ELECTRONICS RESEARCH AND DEVELOPMENT FOR SPACE PROJECTS.)

ELECTRONIC SYSTEMS DIVISION OF THE AIR FORCE SYSTEMS COMMAND
(RESEARCH AND DEVELOPMENT, AEROSPACE ELECTRONICS.)

GODDARD SPACE FLIGHT CENTER
(TRACKING OPERATIONS, MANAGEMENT OF UNMANNED, NONMILITARY EARTH SATELLITE PROGRAMS.)

WALLOPS STATION
(LAUNCH OPERATIONS.)

MARSHALL SPACE FLIGHT CENTER
(DEVELOPMENT OF LAUNCH VEHICLES FOR MANNED SPACE FLIGHT.)

MERRITT ISLAND LAUNCH AREA
(SATURN ROCKET LAUNCH OPERATIONS.)

KENNEDY SPACE CENTER
(LAUNCH OPERATIONS.)

MISSISSIPI TEST FACILITY
(TESTING OF LARGEST SATURN ROCKET ENGINES.)

ROME AIR DEVELOPMENT CENTER, GRIFFISS AIR FORCE BASE
(ELECTRONICS RESEARCH AND DEVELOPMENT FOR AEROSPACE NAVIGATION AND CONTROL SYSTEMS.)

LEWIS RESEARCH CENTER
(PROPULSION RESEARCH.)

MICHOUD OPERATIONS
(MANUFACTURING OF LARGEST STAGES OF SATURN ROCKETS.)

WRIGHT-PATTERSON AIR FORCE BASE
(PROPULSION RESEARCH AEROSPACE MEDICINE.)

GOLDSTONE COMMUNICATIONS STATIONS
(TRACKING OF INTERPLANETARY SPACECRAFT.)

AEROSPACE MEDICAL DIVISION, BROOKS AIR FORCE BASE
(AEROSPACE MEDICINE.)

MANNED SPACECRAFT CENTER
(ASTRONAUT TRAINING, MANAGEMENT OF MANNED SPACE-FLIGHT PROGRAM.)

EDWARDS AIR FORCE BASE
(EDGE-OF-SPACE AIRCRAFT FLIGHT-TESTING AND RESEARCH.)

AMES RESEARCH CENTER
(AEROSPACE-GEARED RESEARCH IN THE PHYSICAL AND LIFE SCIENCES.)

WHITE SANDS MISSILE RANGE
(LAUNCH TESTING.)

JET PROPULSION LABORATORY
(DEVELOPMENT AND CONTROL OF UNMANNED, INTERPLANETARY SPACECRAFT.)

VANDENBERG AIR FORCE BASE
(LAUNCH OPERATIONS.)

Fortress America.

66

Lee Harvey Oswald, described as a one-time defector to the Soviet Union and a member of the 'Fair Play for Cuba' Committee, was arrested for the Kennedy crime; two days later, while being transferred to the county jail, Oswald was killed by a Dallas night-club owner, Jack Ruby (Rubinstein). Because television cameras were following the President's journey and covering the movement of Oswald, both murders were seen by millions of viewers. While awaiting trial Ruby was found to be mentally ill; he died in 1967. We will never be absolutely sure who killed President Kennedy.

John Fitzgerald Kennedy (1917–63) was not only the youngest President in American history and the first Roman Catholic to be elected President, but he promised to be one of the greatest. Harvard-educated, a liberal and a thinker as well as a man of action, and a member of a wealthy Irish-American family, he had a distinguished and courageous record during the Second World War when he served in torpedo-boats in the Pacific. From 1952 to 1960 he was a Senator for Massachusetts.

Civil Rights became the foremost part of his domestic programme as President, and he strove hard to ensure for the Negro equal rights and equal opportunities. In this he was assisted by his younger brother Robert, whom he appointed Attorney-General, and who is now Senator for New York. After compelling Premier Khrushchev to withdraw Soviet-supplied missiles from Cuba in October 1962, President Kennedy worked for a 'thaw' in the Cold War. Although on guard against further Soviet expansionism, he improved relations between the Soviet Union and the United States by setting up a 'hot line' between Washington and Moscow, by negotiating (and persuading Congress to accept) the treaty in 1963 banning the testing of nuclear devices in the atmosphere, and by easing the most acute tensions over Berlin. Young and friendly, he represented, as he said in his Inaugural Address, 'a new generation of Americans'. He surrounded himself with a brilliant group of cabinet officers (especially Robert McNamara at Defence and Dean Rusk as Secretary of State) and aides, and was very skilful in handling the Press. His weekly Press conferences were regularly televised. His wife, Jacqueline Lee Bouvier, whom he married in 1955, brought into the White House a new interest in the arts.

American foreign policy under Kennedy

The main themes of President Kennedy's foreign policy were:
1. *The Grand Design in Europe.* This was an attempt to extend the European Economic Community (or Common Market) by the adherence of Britain and the Scandinavian states, and to help it to become a political community. It was hoped that this would lead to the development of the Atlantic Alliance into a balanced partnership between two more or less equal elements—equal at least in population and economic potential—United Europe and the United States. The vision appealed to the idealism of Americans, and to their hopes that a

united Western Europe would bear a greater share of its own defence in men and money, and that this in turn would permit more money going as aid to underdeveloped countries. This policy was supported by the British Government led by Harold Macmillan which, observing the success of the European Economic Community, from which it had originally held aloof, took the decision in August 1961 to apply for membership.

The weakness of the 'equal partnership' theme of the Kennedy Administration was that the nuclear dominance of the United States made any real equality of rights and duties within the Atlantic Alliance impossible. In the event of aggression, it is one man—the President of the United States—who alone decides to launch, or not to launch, the inter-continental ballistic missiles (I.C.B.M.) and other strategic nuclear weapons, and authorizes the use of nuclear warheads—which are in American hands—in the tactical weapons of the Allies. Furthermore, the U.S. President is prohibited from sharing this nuclear monopoly with any foreign nation, with one exception. That exception is the United Kingdom, because of its wartime partnership with the U.S.A. Hence the British 'deterrent', which gives a measure of diplomatic and military independence to the British Government, though in fact the British have become increasingly dependent upon the United States for the means of delivery of their nuclear bombs or warheads.

In December 1962 President Kennedy announced the decision of his Government to abandon production of the Skybolt missile, on which the British Government was largely depending for the arming of its strategic bombers. The proposal was made to supply Britain with Polaris missiles, to which British warheads could be fitted, for use in submarines. These would form part of a strategic nuclear force within NATO; but it was agreed that they might be used independently in a national emergency not involving the Atlantic Alliance. The closeness of the links between the United States and Britain alarmed General de Gaulle and probably contributed to his opposition (January 1963; November 1967) to the British application to join the Common Market.

As conspicuous as his support for Britain was President Kennedy's support for West Germany. His visit to Berlin in 1963 and his famous speech (*Ich bin ein Berliner*) won him great goodwill in West Germany.

2. *Firmness towards Russia, especially over Cuba.* While trying, without much success, to strengthen the Western bloc in Europe, the President was seeking both to be firm and to be conciliatory towards Khrushchev. The Cuban crisis of October 1962 perhaps showed Kennedy at his most successful. Eighteen months earlier, in April 1961, when still new to office, President Kennedy had permitted an attack on Cuba (dominated by Dr Fidel Castro since 1959 when he overthrew the corrupt Batista régime, and an open ally of Russia since about 1961) by Cuban exiles and some American sympathizers. This 'Bay of Pigs' invasion was a disaster, and the President was among the first to admit it. By

October 1962 it became clear that Soviet planes and intermediate-range rockets were being installed in Cuba, 90 miles from Florida. Kennedy demanded their withdrawal, and supported his demand by mobilizing troops and by enforcing a blockade. Mr Khrushchev's compliance with this demand (28 October) was hailed throughout the Western world as a victory for firmness. The Cuban crisis also revealed the fact that the launching or prevention of a nuclear war, which could wipe out millions of people in a matter of minutes, lay absolutely in the hands of the two giants—the United States and the Soviet Union.

This firmness in 1962 has not halted Cuban attempts to influence the neighbouring Caribbean or Latin American states. One U.S. intelligence estimate is that 1,500 Latin American guerrillas are being trained each year in Cuba, with Venezuela, Colombia—where banditry is rife—and the Dominican Republic as obvious targets. In 1965 the American Government intervened in the Dominican Republic to protect American lives in the revolution of that year, and to prevent the success of a military *coup* that it saw as 'Communist and Castro-ist'.

That the U.S. Administration could also be conciliatory was proved by the signing in Moscow in August 1963 of the nuclear test-ban treaty, whereby the U.S.A., the U.S.S.R. and the U.K. agreed to abandon the testing of nuclear devices in the atmosphere.

3. *The Alliance for Progress in Latin America.* In the 20 republics south of the Rio Grande live at least 200 million people. Most of these countries are very poor (but potentially rich); they are cosmopolitan (Paraguay, Bolivia and Peru mainly Indian; Haiti African; Argentina, Uruguay, Chile and Costa Rica overwhelmingly European and Spanish-speaking; Brazil multi-racial and Portuguese-speaking); and they are remarkably addicted to political revolutions (in the 100 years from 1852 to 1952 Bolivia had 100 *coups d'état*). Today only 14 of the 20 republics can claim to have democratically elected governments; in only five of these—Chile, Costa Rica, Mexico, Panama and Uruguay—can political stability be assumed, and, in each case, power is in the hands of an oligarchy. The others—Argentina, Bolivia, Brazil, Colombia, Ecuador, El Salvador, Guatemala, Honduras and Venezuela—have democratically elected régimes that survive only as long as they are tolerated by the military, but they are apt from time to time to erupt into revolution: Guatemala's left-wing régime was overthrown (with United States help) in 1954, but the leader of this *coup* was murdered in 1957; in Argentina, General Perón was driven from power in 1955, Arturo Frondizi was forced from office by the Army in 1962, and Arturo Illia (who succeeded Frondizi) in 1966; in 1964 the liberal President of Brazil, Joao Goulart, was overthrown by the army and exiled. Of the other six republics, three remain old-fashioned dictatorships—Haiti (under Dr François Duvalier), Nicaragua (Colonel Luis Somoza) and Paraguay (General Alfredo Stroessner)—and the rest have essentially military régimes.

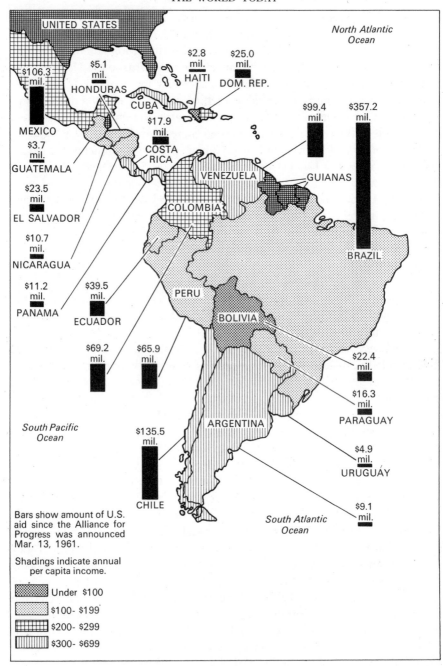

Latin America: aid, poverty and wealth.

Latin America : problems.

From the beginning of its history the United States has been concerned with South America. In 1823 the Monroe Doctrine, which forbids outside inter-ference in the affairs of North and South America, was proclaimed. (This was, in part, a consequence of the meddling of European Powers in the Latin American revolutions of the previous decade.) In 1898 the U.S.A. fought a war with Spain to free Cuba. At Chapultepec Palace in Mexico City in 1945 and at Bogotá, Colombia, in 1948 the United States promised military assistance

71

to Latin America in the event of attack; in 1948 it set up the Organization of American States and machinery for the peaceful settlement of disputes; and since 1948 it has provided well over $100,000 million in aid to Latin America.

In the years after 1945, at a time when the U.S.A., through the Marshall Plan, was being particularly generous to Europe, Latin Americans felt aggrieved. They frequently complained (in private, if not in public) that they, as reliable friends of the United States, received a much smaller proportion of U.S. aid than far less well-disposed nations elsewhere.

In 1961 President Kennedy committed his country to a ten-year plan of economic and social development of Latin America estimated to cost $13,000 million and known as the Alliance for Progress. This aid was made conditional on the willingness of the Latin American Governments to carry out social reforms—in particular, land reform and adequate taxation of the rich. While outwardly grateful, some Latin Americans resented these political strings; others doubted whether this attempt to impose social democracy from without could be successful.

A major fact in Central American affairs is the Panama Canal, constructed in the years from 1903 to 1914. The Canal links the Caribbean with the Pacific, and bisects the Republic of Panama, which had declared independence from Colombia in 1903, after a revolt in which it had American support and after which it promptly got American recognition. In the same year the United States and Panama signed a treaty giving the U.S.A. the right to construct the Canal, and granting to the United States in perpetuity the use of the Canal Zone and complete control of police, judiciary and health services. In return, the United States pays Panama an annual rent of $430,000. The Canal itself is entirely under American control.

The cities of Panama and Colón are enclaves within the Zone, and under Panamanian jurisdiction, but the United States has certain rights in them where shipping and health are concerned. Political parties in Panama and elsewhere in Latin America have long pressed for the control of the Canal to be vested in Panama or in an inter-American or international body. Some of these parties staged riots in January 1964.

The other major U.S. bases in the region are Chaguaramas (Trinidad) and Guantánamo (Cuba). The former was obtained in 1941 as part of the warships-for-bases deal with Britain, the latter by treaty in 1901 after the Spanish-American War. Dr Castro has asked the United States to leave Guantánamo and refuses to accept rent for it.

L.B.J.: the Man and his Policy

President Kennedy was succeeded by his Vice-President, Lyndon B. Johnson, who took the oath of office as President on board the Presidential jet plane *Air Force One* before it began the journey back from Love Airfield, Dallas, to

Washington with the body of the late President. He was elected easily in his own right in the November 1964 elections, when he carried 44 states and defeated Senator Barry Goldwater, the right-wing Republican candidate.

Lyndon Baines Johnson (b. 1908) is a Texan—the first Southerner to become President since his namesake, Vice-President Andrew Johnson, succeeded Lincoln in 1865. He is an experienced politician who believes strongly that problems can be settled if men will reason together. Very much an admirer of F. D. Roosevelt, he was in the House of Representatives from 1937 to 1948, a Senator for Texas from 1948 to 1960, and Senate majority leader from 1953. Less an 'intellectual' than Kennedy, President Johnson is less ready to surround himself with Harvard men and Nobel Prize winners; and he is, in manner at least, much less sophisticated. He is less skilful in handling the Press and much less appealing as a television performer; but he has been more successful in his dealings with Congress. His background is less wealthy than Kennedy's, although his wife is now a millionairess, and he has a genuine concern for the poor. He is not so much a 'New Frontiersman', the phrase used by the Kennedy group, as an 'Old New Dealer'—his style and his phrases are mindful of the 1930s. He is shrewd and patient; he promised cheaper and more frugal administration, and introduced in 1964 a number of tax cuts, to the extent of $11\frac{1}{2}$ billion dollars. His hopes for more of these economies have, however, been delayed by the costs of the Vietnam War and in 1967 taxes had to be sharply increased.

The Great Society: The Vision

He calls his hopes for America those of 'The Great Society' and he has been, until recently, mainly concerned with domestic affairs. He has already persuaded Congress to pass an impressive amount of legislation which in its scale recalls the New Deal legislation. The major measures were:

The Civil Rights Act. This prohibited racial discrimination in public places or under any federal aid programme.

The Appalachia Redevelopment Bill. Appalachia is a depressed hill region sprawling over West Virginia and parts of ten other states, where the poverty is alarming. In spite of Republican claims of 'boondoggle' and 'pork barrel'—political slang implying that the money is appropriated more for local patronage than for genuine reasons—grants were made for the construction of 3,350 miles of roads, health facilities and vocational schools, land improvement and the development of timber and water resources.

The Education Bill authorized for the first time federal funds ($1,300 million (£540 million) in the first year) for the general improvement of elementary and secondary schools, and extended aid for the first time to parochial schools, mainly Roman Catholic.

The Excise Tax Reduction Bill. This measure reduced or repealed the federal excise tax on diesel and special motor oils, luxury goods, cars and various appliances by an estimated $4,700 million (£1,950 million) over a 3½-year period. It was the third important reduction in federal tax liabilities since 1962, and was intended to maintain and increase the present high level of prosperity.

The Constitutional Amendment Bill. To ensure presidential continuity, it permits the Vice-President to become acting President if the President is unable to perform his duties, and also provides for the appointment of a Vice-President.

The Medical Care-Social Security Bill. This measure ended a 20-year struggle fought over the highly contentious topic, 'socialized medicine'. It will probably prove to be the thin end of the wedge for a more comprehensive national health service. The law provided for a health-care insurance programme under social security for persons aged 65 and over, and increased social security pensions.

The Voting Rights Bill. The second important civil rights law in two years, it directed the Attorney-General to take court action against the poll tax, suspended literacy tests and provided for the registration of voters by the federal Government whenever necessary.

The Department of Housing and Urban Development Bill. A new Cabinet post and federal department was established for the purpose of improving metropolitan areas.

The Immigration Bill provided for the gradual elimination of the national origins quota system which had made it difficult for Southern Europeans and Asian immigrants to enter the United States. Under the new proposals (1968 enforcement) visas will be issued on a first come, first served, basis, and each country will be limited to 20,000 (28,000 British immigrants were admitted in 1965). The total for Asia, Europe and Africa will be limited to 170,000. Thus the preference for British and Northern European immigrants is at an end.

The Great Society: the problems

Despite the fact that the United States is the richest country in the world, one in five of its people (39 million) falls below the poverty line. In his best-selling book, *The Other America*, author and social worker Michael Harrington has described this unfortunate fifth of the nation, a group that comprises those families with incomes lower than 3,000 dollars (£1,250) a year. Of these, more than half have less than 2,000 dollars (£832), and five million people have less than 1,500 dollars (£625) a year. In considering these figures it must be remembered that the cost of living in America is appreciably higher than in the United Kingdom. Rent, food and transport costs can be high. Americans aim at owning rather than renting property, and a very modest house will cost $20,000 (£8,300). There is no national health service; even a family with a comfortable income can be ruined by one serious illness. And even the middle class, who live very comfortably in suburban homes with modern cars, television, electrical appliances, and children in university, save relatively little of their incomes.

Particular groups and areas are especially vulnerable. Two-thirds of all farm workers earn less than $1,000 (£416) a year; and nearly 80 per cent of all Negro families live in poverty. About half a million Negroes under 21 are out of work—and many of them form the gangs of Chicago, Los Angeles and New York.

The Negro question

It is the Negro who is the main victim of American inequality. The Negro problem is a poverty problem and a 'ghetto' problem as well as a racial problem. The majority of Negroes are poor, ill-educated and denied the opportunities that are open to whites. It is calculated that, on average, by the time he retires, a Negro will earn less than half what a similarly educated white will earn; and this itself represents less than one-half what a well-educated white can earn. More than this, the Negro sees himself as the victim of race prejudice, and in particular has long sought to end the system of segregation of white and non-white in restaurants, hotels, cinemas and public services that, till recently, prevailed in some states of the Deep South.

A number of organizations, mainly Negro but supported by white sympathizers, came into existence in the 1950s to end segregation on buses, in hotels and eating-places, in schools or on 'white' bathing beaches. Alongside the National Association for the Advancement of Coloured People (N.A.A.C.P.), which is the oldest and most responsible, there are organizations like the Congress of Racial Equality (CORE), the Students' Non-violent Co-ordinating Committee (S.N.C.C., familiarly known as SNICK), the National Urban League, and the Southern Christian Leadership Conference (S.C.L.C.)—the best-known leader of which was Dr Martin Luther King, who was awarded the 1964 Nobel Peace Prize for his work and was murdered in April 1968.

In August 1963 a Freedom March on Washington was organized by Negro groups, to rally public opinion to their cause. It was followed by many marches into the Deep South, designed to encourage Negroes to register to vote. After a decade of agitation and protest, Negro opinion is now militant. Dr King was gentle and religious, a believer in passive resistance, but Mr Floyd McKissick of CORE is a militant radical who dreams of a day when Negroes will have political power. He was elected director of CORE in 1966, replacing the gradualist James Farmer, a friend of Dr King; after 23 years, CORE renounced its alliance with N.A.A.C.P., and sneered at the Civil Rights Act and the anti-poverty programme. Mr Stokely Carmichael, the bitter Trinidad-born chairman of SNICK, does not want any help at all from whites, since he sees all 'white racists' as his enemies. He preaches violence and has organized a group called 'Black Panthers'; their cry is for 'Black Power'. On the extreme Right of the Negro groups stand the Black Muslims, who claim an Islamic creed and want Negro segregation—even a separate state for themselves. Their dominant figure in recent years, Malcolm X (born Malcolm Little, but they refuse to use surnames because they see them as the badges of white rule) was killed in February 1965.

There have been counter-demonstrations by some whites in Alabama and other states, to prevent the admission of coloured students to schools and colleges which until 1963 had been segregated. Negro marches into the South have often been met by violent opposition. A prominent leader in these marches is James Meredith, the first Negro to be admitted as a student to the University of Mississippi in 1962. To secure his admission, Federal troops had to be called out to quell a 15-hour riot that cost two lives. When he led a march into Mississippi in 1966 to show Negroes that they had nothing to fear, he was shot at and wounded 26 miles after he crossed the State line.

In January 1964 President Johnson pledged the support of his Administration to a 'war against poverty' and to a policy of aid for 'the forgotten fifth'. He presented to Congress the Civil Rights Bill, initiated by President Kennedy, guaranteeing non-discrimination in jobs and in the use of public services and accommodation in the South as well as the North. A number of Southern Senators opposed the Bill by a filibuster—a sustained attempt to 'talk it out'— which lasted for three months. The Bill finally became law in July 1964. The racial disturbances that were expected to follow the passing of this Bill did not materialize to the extent feared; in fact, desegregation has, on the whole, proceeded quietly in the Southern states, despite the tensions produced by Negro marches.

It has been in Northern industrial cities (e.g., New York and Rochester) that serious eruptions have occurred; the summer heat produced ugly Negro riots in 1964 in Philadelphia, in 1965 in the Watts district of Los Angeles (28 deaths, 760 people injured, $100 million worth of property destroyed) in 1966 in Chicago's West Side, and in 1967 in Cleveland, Newark and Detroit.

Although the Negro problem has special American aspects, the situation is not, or soon will not be, peculiar to America. Similar problems are developing in other industrialized countries. On a smaller scale the interlocking of city, race and employment issues has already begun in Britain, and we are doing far less about its racial aspects than the Americans. There is also a terrifying similarity between the pattern inside America and the dangerously widening gap in the world at large between the rich, industrialized white societies and the poor, struggling rest of the globe.

Foreign policy

With Kennedy's death President Johnson faced a host of foreign policy problems. In two years he had to cope with riots in Panama, civil war in Cyprus, massacre in the Congo, a slump in the prestige of the Alliance for Progress, Gaullism in NATO, chaos in the Dominican Republic and, above all, the war in Vietnam.

Vietnam

Vietnam, the eastern coastal strip of what used to be known as Indo-China linking Tonking (Red River delta: port Hanoi) with Cochin China (the Mekong delta: port Saigon), has been the scene of civil and international conflict since long before the Second World War. Vietnam sought to free itself from the French long before that war and from the Japanese during it. In the years from 1947 to 1954, it again struggled to free itself from the French control re-imposed after the war ended. After the French disaster at Dien Bien Phu in 1954 and their consequent withdrawal, it was divided politically, at the 17th parallel, into two areas: in the north the 'Democratic Republic of Vietnam', a Communist régime with a population of about 17 million people, and in the south the 'Republic of Vietnam', with a population of about 16 million. It is not possible, however, to understand the present conflict without remembering that Vietnam has a long history as a single state, however divided at intervals it has been by dynastic rivalries, and that the populations of the two areas are similar in racial origin and understand the same language. But if it is a unity in race and thought, it is now the centre of a conflict between North and South which has been, in disguised fashion, a struggle of Communism (the North, led by Ho Chi Minh, aided by China and the U.S.S.R.) versus the Free World (the South, supported by the United States). In 1960 North Vietnam called for the liberation of South Vietnam. Many South Vietnamese rose to support the North as guerrilla fighters, and the National Liberation Front was formed, the political arm of the guerrillas.

Although the first American assistance to South Vietnam was promised by President Eisenhower in 1954, and the U.S. had aided the French régime financially, it was not until 1961 that this became a major U.S. military exercise.

The United States began by sending training teams to South Vietnam to train the forces of the strongly Catholic régime led by Ngo Dinh Diem. A Military Aid Command was set up early in 1962. By the end of 1962, 10,000 Americans were there. In November 1963 that régime was overthrown and Ngo was murdered; it was replaced, behind a civilian 'front', by a military junta (led since June 1965 by Air Marshal Ky). North Vietnamese forces have had much aid from the South Vietnamese guerrillas, the Vietcong, who control, in fact, much of the South Vietnamese countryside; the war has been not only military and political but religious, with frequent Buddhist demonstrations against the South Vietnamese government.

In August 1964 American warships in the Gulf of Tonking were attacked by North Vietnamese torpedo boats. Since then the amount of American intervention has steadily increased. The demand for this was one of the themes in

77

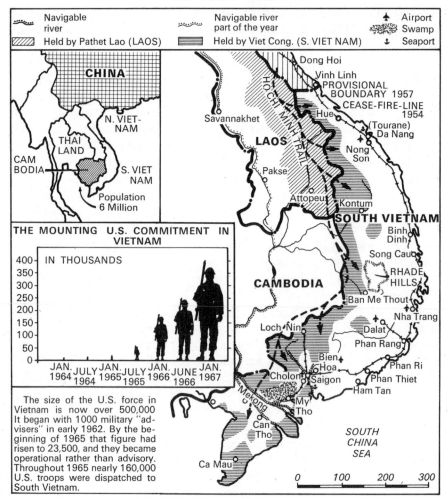

| Navigable river | Navigable river part of the year | ✈ Airport |
| Held by Pathet Lao (LAOS) | Held by Viet Cong. (S. VIET NAM) | Swamp / Seaport |

THE MOUNTING U.S. COMMITMENT IN VIETNAM

IN THOUSANDS

The size of the U.S. force in Vietnam is now over 500,000 It began with 1000 military "advisers" in early 1962. By the beginning of 1965 that figure had risen to 23,500, and they became operational rather than advisory. Throughout 1965 nearly 160,000 U.S. troops were dispatched to South Vietnam.

The mounting U.S. commitment in Vietnam.

Mr Goldwater's campaign in 1964. In February 1965 United States' air raids on North Vietnam began. In June 1965 United States forces began to give combat support to the South Vietnamese army, and it was announced that United States forces would be increased to 125,000. North Vietnam countered by sending in regular troops itself. By the end of 1965, 1,200 Americans had been killed in Vietnam; by May 1966 almost 200,000 American troops were stationed there; by the summer of 1967 half a million were involved. Australia and New Zealand have also sent forces to assist South Vietnam. Despite increases in the intensity of the fighting, and despite daily bombing of the

North, the South Vietnamese and United States forces have only been able to hold their own.

Popular support for the President's Vietnam policy remains high, but he has been under attack not only from right-wing Republicans demanding 'total victory' but from critics within the Democratic Party, notably Senator Fulbright, Chairman of the Senate Foreign Relations Committee, and the majority leader, Senator Mansfield, and from student groups, alarmed at the prospect of being drafted for a war that seems endless. The debate has been between the 'hawks' and the 'doves'. Nevertheless, the massive air raids in June 1966 on oil and fuel depots in the Hanoi-Haiphong area of North Vietnam, though criticized by the British Government, brought to President Johnson considerable popular support in the United States and in Australia.

The President sees the struggle as one to check a Communist advance in Asia. Communist control of the populous, rice-growing area of South Vietnam must be prevented, he believes, because it would threaten the whole of Southeast Asia, not only Laos and Cambodia, but also Thailand, Malaysia and Burma, besides turning the scales decisively in the Chinese favour in Indonesia. This strategy of containment is particularly directed against the People's Republic of China, the great Communist power of Asia, now in process of becoming a nuclear power. On the other hand, it is a major interest of the United States not to allow hostilities caused by this strategy of Asian containment to escalate into a world war, and in particular not to embroil America with Soviet Russia, with which, since the nuclear stalemate between the two giants has been accepted in Moscow, there now exists a kind of truce which it is always hoped may develop into something better than peaceful co-existence. President Johnson has consistently declared his readiness for peace talks but the South Vietnamese have been unwilling to hold discussions with representatives of North Vietnam.

The disturbing facts are that South Vietnam is disunited and contentious, scarred by political, religious and personal feuds; that the longer the American army remains, the more like a French and foreign imperialism it becomes; and that whatever they do is likely to be wrong. It is difficult to see how disengagement could now be effected without grave damage to the whole American strategy in Asia. It is also debatable whether a jungle war of subversion can be won by bombing military targets in the rear. In a situation which causes anxiety throughout the world the basic enigma is that, while the Western and unaligned countries want nothing better than peace in the area, there is no reason to suppose that Ho Chi Minh—supported in this by Peking and his 'National Front for the Liberation of Vietnam'—desires a settlement at all. For it is precisely a continuation and extension of disorder and disunity in the South which will best help the purpose to which he has been committed for over 30 years.

The U.S.S.R. and Britain have both sought to mediate as the joint chairmen of the Geneva Powers of 1954; so far without success.

QUESTIONS TO CONSIDER

1. What are the chief features of any two of the following regions? (*a*) New England, (*b*) Middle Atlantic States, (*c*) South, (*d*) Middle West, (*e*) Great Plains, (*f*) West.
2. With what matters does a State Government deal?
3. Outline the main features of the American Constitution.
4. Outline the powers of the President of the United States.
5. Distinguish between the Senate and the House of Representatives in the United States.
6. What was meant by the New Deal?
7. Summarize the arguments for and against American isolation in the years 1920–41.
8. Why does the United States fear Communism?
9. Trace the stages by which the U.S. came to play the role of world leader.
10. What were the main characteristics of the Presidency of John F. Kennedy?

WORDS TO NOTE

Axis: The alliance which centred on the capitals of Italy, Germany and, later, Japan, became known as the *Rome-Berlin-Tokyo Axis.*

Canyon: Deep, narrow valley or gorge caused by a river cutting through soft rock.

To commute: To travel by season ticket from suburbs to place of work.

Gold Standard: International monetary system in which gold was the currency. All countries had to maintain reserves of gold in order to meet possible demands for settlement of outstanding debts. Many countries abandoned the gold standard in the early 1930s.

Jim Crow: The 'Jim Crow' laws were passed by the Southern States after the Civil War to segregate Negroes from whites in all social contacts: separate hotels, cinemas, public conveniences, etc.

Keynes, J. M. (Lord): British economist who argued that governments should spend money to prevent slumps. Had great influence on President F. D. Roosevelt.

Keys: Islands off the coast of Florida, linking Miami with Key West 180 miles away.

Mesa (Spanish word for table)*:* Flat-topped blocks of land, characteristic of Southwestern states and the Indian country.

New Deal: Name given to F. D. Roosevelt's legislation of years 1933–36.

Patronage: In U.S.A., the right of the President, or ruling party, to distribute offices after elections.

Prime the Pump: A process of public expenditure by the Federal Government to bring about increased employment, thus stimulating economic growth.

BOOKS TO READ

Steel, R.: *Pax Americana*, Hamish Hamilton, 1968.

Pear, R. H.: *American Government*, MacGibbon & Kee, 1955.

Potter, A. M.: *American Government and Politics*, Faber & Faber, 1961.

White, T.: *The Making of the President, 1960*, Cape, 1962.

Ions, E.: *The Politics of John F. Kennedy*, Routledge, 1967.

Schlesinger, A. M., Jr.: *A Thousand Days: John F. Kennedy in The White House*, Deutsch, 1965.

3. *France*

The land and the people
Rural France

Apart from the area round Paris, the Lille-Calais region (producing cotton and woollen goods, coal and locomotives), the Lorraine ore field, Lyons (silk) and Marseilles (shipping, oil refining, soap), France is rural; hardly 20 towns have populations of more than 100,000; half its population of 50 million live in the countryside. This is a world remote from the boulevards and the fashion industry of Paris: the roads are cobbled, the farm houses look shabby, the dress is of workaday jackets and blouses. These appearances can be deceptive, for the money is invested in cattle and land and traditionally saved up and kept in the farm rather than invested in industry or houses or banks; and the people are well fed—food and wine are matters of importance in France.

The French peasant is renowned as thrifty, hard-working and an individualist. He owns his land and works it himself—or with his family. In France as a whole there are some two and a half million small estates. The peasant has often little capital equipment. He often has neither electricity nor piped water

Harvesting grapes in the Champagne district.

on his farm. But he cares for his land passionately. He can live off its produce and be indifferent to trade and industry. And he is not very sympathetic to 'government', or to officials. France values the idea of equality. 'Here everyone is Monsieur.'

This applies also to politics. Governments and ministers come and go in Paris, but the life of France, the local administration, the work in the fields and vineyards, goes on. Far more revolutionary than the new constitutions of 1946 or 1958 were the proposals of Mendès-France in 1954 to persuade the people of France to drink milk rather than wine. This was a real interference with their habits and with their economy, for there are two million wine-growers in France. There were riots and strikes in all the wine-growing areas at his proposals. Wine is not a luxury but a normal part of the diet. Normandy is well known for its calvados (apple brandy), and Burgundy for its wine. And wine is a major export, too.

Equally, since the 1830s there has been a tension between the farmers and the industrial workers; the small farmers have been interested in keeping food prices high and in having high tariffs on foreign food imports. Industrialists have favoured low tariffs to keep the price of food low. The farmers have usually won because the political system has favoured them. There are very few large towns and few great industrial centres able to influence Paris. British observers are apt to forget that France is rural, that she is self-supporting in agriculture and that she is protectionist. They are also apt to overestimate the importance of Paris and of its 'crises', which often leave quite unaffected the mass of the French people.

France, unlike Britain, produces most of its own food. Indeed, if one adds its overseas territories, almost all of it. These territories are far more closely linked to France than the British colonies ever have been to Britain, and they provide olive oil and phosphates, palm oils and bananas.

French industry

French industry developed more slowly than British. It was delayed by three main factors: the emphasis on and strength of agriculture; the absence of large quantities of coal and coke, on which the British Industrial Revolution was based; and the slow growth of her population. It was not until the 1850s that industrialism came to France, and in 1870 she lost Lorraine and its iron ore deposits to Germany. Two world wars have not helped. The first killed one million Frenchmen. In the second her territory was occupied, and over 600,000 people were killed and 800,000 sent to Germany. Moreover, most French industrial businesses are on a smaller scale than British, worked by a few men, and often run by one particular family. Before 1939 there was not enough investment in industry, and so one reason for the defeat of the army in the field in 1940 was the lack of adequate industrial equipment.

There are many small traders: France has one shop for every 32 inhabitants, Britain one for every 68. The French industrial workers, far fewer in number or proportion than the British, are less well organized in trade unions, and the unions are split between Catholic, Socialist and Communist. Many industrial workers are not French but foreigners: there is a large Polish colony working the coal-mines of the Pas-de-Calais, and perhaps one-quarter of the industrial workers of Marseilles or Nice are Italians.

France has an economy so strong in agriculture that it can ride out many storms—it was less hurt by the Depression of 1929 than were the industrialized countries. Its major lack is coal, and it has been keen to develop an economic link with the Saar coalfield, adjacent to the iron ore of Lorraine. Out of this, indeed, came the Coal and Steel Community and something of the spirit behind the proposals for a Common Market in Europe. France has always been noted for fine textiles and fabrics, for leather and lace, for porcelain and jewellery. Today, France is also noted for her motor-cars.

The French Republic

The central fact in French history is the Revolution of 1789, the greatest social and political upheaval any European country ever experienced. The old régime —of an absolute monarchy, a large court, an untaxed and over-privileged aristocracy, and a mass of poor and oppressed peasants—was then overthrown. In 1793 the King, Louis XVI, and his Queen, Marie Antoinette, were guillotined; the Church and aristocracy lost their estates; the peasants were given the land to which they now passionately cling; and all men were declared to be equal in law and in rights.

Under Napoleon as First Consul (1799) and finally as Emperor (1804) the ideas of liberty, equality and fraternity were exported to most parts of Europe. After Napoleon's final defeat at Waterloo, two Bourbon kings, brothers of Louis XVI, returned to France (Louis XVIII 1815–24 and Charles X 1824–30) but a second revolution occurred in 1830, and Charles X was replaced by a liberal middle-class king, Louis Philippe. In 1848 Louis Philippe in turn lost his throne, and there came the Second Republic (1848–51) succeeded by the Second Empire (1852–70) of Napoleon III, a nephew of the first Napoleon.

After the defeat of France in 1870 by the newly united Germany, when France lost Alsace-Lorraine, the Third Republic began. It lasted 70 years (1870–1940). During the Second World War, northern France was occupied by Germany, and southern France was ruled from Vichy by a pro-German puppet government of Marshal Philippe Pétain, First World War hero, and Pierre Laval. After the defeat of Germany, a Fourth Republic came into being in 1946. This was overthrown in 1958, and the Fifth then began under the presidency of General de Gaulle.

Since 1789 France has had four kings, two emperors, five republics and one puzzle (Vichy). The present constitution (of 1958) is the sixteenth since 1789.

Politically, then, France has been very unstable. Ever since 1789 important

THE STRUCTURE OF GOVERNMENT IN FRANCE

LEGISLATIVE BODY	GEOGRAPHIC UNIT	EXECUTIVE AGENCY
PARLIAMENT	CONTINENTAL FRANCE	MINISTRY
	Divided into	
GENERAL COUNCIL	90 DEPARTMENTS	PREFECT
	Divided into	
COUNCIL	170 ARRONDISSEMENTS	SUB-PREFECT
	Divided into	
COUNCIL	37,000 COMMUNES	MAYOR

groups have been opposed to the constitution under which they are governed. But, whatever this instability, the life of France itself has not been greatly affected by the crises in Paris. For life is local. France has been described as 'a tranquil country with agitated legislators'.

In Napoleon's time, the country was divided into 83 departments, now increased to 90. These are subdivided into arrondissements, into cantons and these into communes. At the head of each department is a prefect, a provincial governor with considerable power.

The regions of France

The word *pays* is untranslatable. It is something more than a region, and much more than countryside. It may be one's country as a whole, but normally that is too large and too remote an idea. The *pays* is that area you identify yourself with—soil and climate, home and kindred, the memories and experiences of your own childhood, and of those of your race. Each Frenchman, it is said, has two countries—his own, and France.

France is a country with distinct *pays* or regions inside itself—far more than England or Scotland. This is in part due to its size: it covers 212,000 square miles, larger than any other European country except Russia; it is a compact, square, well-defined country. Its boundaries are clear: in the east the Rhine separates it from Germany, and the range of the Jura from Switzerland; the Alps cut it off from Italy, the Pyrenees from Spain. But firm though the boundaries now seem, the fight to secure these boundaries was a persistent theme in medieval and early modern French history. The frontiers at the Pyrenees were not fixed until 1659, those at the Rhine and with Germany have been fought over twice this century. Indeed its natural frontiers have mattered to France extremely because where there are none—in the north-east—she has been invaded, from the dawn of her history.

Even where Nature helped, the frontier line is often of recent date. Nice and Savoy were only incorporated into France in 1860. France's weakest frontier has always been its point of closest contact with its neighbours—the frontier adjoining the Low Countries. From 1870 to 1914 France lost three of her northern departments to Germany; between 1914 and 1918 ten departments, five of them wealthy, were occupied by the enemy. And worse came in 1940 when two-thirds of France were under Nazi control.

The rivers of France help her unity. The Seine and its tributaries run north-westwards to drain the Ile de France. The Loire, rising in the Massif Central, runs north, then west, to enter the Bay of Biscay at Nantes and St Nazaire. Running directly westward from the Massif is the wide Garonne, with Bordeaux as its port and a broad estuary to the Bay of Biscay. And most splendid of all is the Rhône rising in the Alps, joined by the Saône from the Vosges, which runs through Provence to enter the Mediterranean.

Regionalism survives also because of the survival in France of other languages—and customs—than French. In the north, the Flemings still keep their own language. Much German is spoken in Alsace. In the south, the Midi,

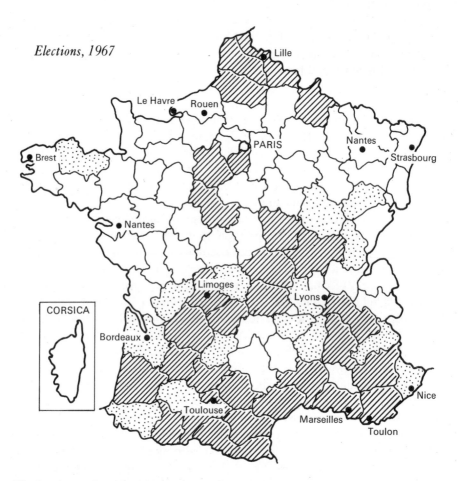

Elections, 1967

The departments shown by shading are those where the Left-wing parties together won more seats than the Gaullists; those unshaded are the Gaulist majorities; in the rest, the Left and the Gaullist were evenly divided.

Provençal is found; in western Brittany, Breton. And in the Pyrenees, the normal language is Catalan at the eastern extremity, but at the western end it is that most curious of all European languages—Basque. Algerians and Negroes are conspicuous in Marseilles and the South.

There are seven main regions in France.

Central France

Central France is itself varied. Much of it in the south is a high and lonely plateau, part granary, part vineyard—as names like Burgundy suggest. In the south, this plateau (the Massif Central) is rough and rugged, rising to 6,000 feet, but with an average height of 3,000 feet: its gorges require high viaducts for roads and railways. It is a land of granite moorland and bare limestone, like the Auvergne, the home of a canny and thrifty peasantry. In one or two places, however, there is industry—in Clermont-Ferrand (cars and tyres) and St Etienne (steel). But in the north the plateau is skirted by great rivers—the Meuse flowing northwards to Belgium, and the Seine flowing through the heart of Paris—and it is the source also of the Garonne, the Dordogne and the Loire, on whose banks stand the splendid châteaux that recall pre-revolutionary France, and the finest Gothic cathedrals of the thirteenth century. This north-central area was the cradle of the Kingdom of France, the centre from which the kings pushed out their grip on their neighbours' territory. Its centres include Rheims and Orleans and Chartres on its hilltop, and, most of all, Paris.

The Ile de France

Paris was founded by the Romans two thousand years ago. Its centre is still the Ile de la Cité, in the middle of the Seine, on which the Cathedral of Notre Dame and the Conciergerie, the palace of the medieval kings, stand. On the left bank is the University, older than Oxford or Cambridge, in one of the oldest parts of the city. Not far away is a much newer structure—the Eiffel Tower, relic of the exhibition of 1889. The history of Paris reflects, and indeed largely is, the history of France.

Twelve miles outside the city Louis XIV built Versailles, a palace whose splendour dazzled Europe and which, on a smaller scale, was imitated by many eighteenth-century German princes. In Paris, too, was the Bastille, the prison fortress, whose fall on 14 July 1789 marked the beginning of the Revolution, and the Arc de Triomphe built to celebrate Napoleon's victories. The nine-teenth-century history of Europe is bound up with events in Paris, for when Paris sneezes, it was said, Europe catches cold. The Revolution of 1789 and the Napoleonic drama unfolded there. The revolutions of 1848 were triggered off by Paris. The Fourth French Republic of 1946 and the Fifth, of 1958, were proclaimed in Paris.

The plan of Paris is striking. The centre—the Ile de la Cité—reflects a medieval world, but modern Paris is largely the work of Napoleon III (1852–70) and Baron Haussmann, who planned its great system of boulevards. Outside these boulevards industrial development has taken place, but beyond, in the Ile de France, are rich farmlands and market gardens, poplar-lined roads and orchards stretching north-west to the Channel ports.

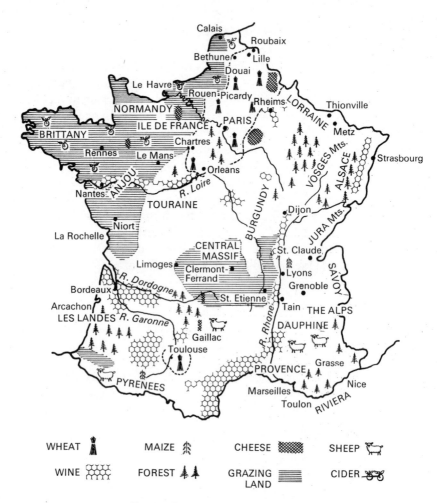

WHEAT   MAIZE   CHEESE   SHEEP

WINE   FOREST   GRAZING LAND   CIDER

France: the regions and their resources.

The Channel coast

The ports for Paris are Rouen and Le Havre, both badly damaged in the Second World War. Rouen is the capital of the province of Normandy, a land of dairy farms and cattle, and rich apple orchards; and to the east of Normandy is the plain of Picardy, where sugar-beet and flax are grown. This is the route of armies, both invading and liberating. Many battles were fought here in both World Wars. What is true of Picardy is true also of Flanders—a battlefield that is now one of the industrial areas of France. To the west of Normandy is the rocky peninsula of Brittany. The Breton language has links with Celtic,

88

and Breton fishermen and onion-sellers try to make themselves understood in Welsh and Irish ports. They are poor and hard-working, and are devout Catholics.

The South-west

The Loire almost cuts France into two. It flows through Touraine and Anjou, famed for their vineyards and their sheep and dairy farms. Further south the chief feature is the Garonne, with the rival towns of Bordeaux and Toulouse, the former a major port, home of claret and of some manufacturing, and the latter important for cereals. South of the Garonne, stretching to the Pyrenees and facing the Bay of Biscay, is the country known as Les Landes, a flat surface of sandy soil, with forests of pines. Facing the Atlantic and cut off by the Massif Central from the warmer and sheltered lands of the Midi, the South-west is mild and wet, with stormy winters.

The South

Next to the river of Paris, the River Rhône is the most important river and route in France. It forms one of the few easy passages through the belt of mountains that stretch across Southern Europe. It is the route of the great PLM railway express (Paris-Lyons-Marseilles). This, too, is a land of vineyards and orchards, although Lyons, where the Rhône and Saône meet, is the centre of the silk industry, and St Etienne, a steel town on the edge of the Massif, is now industrialized. Further south lies Provence, perhaps the most beautiful province in all France, with its tall cypresses and its olive and almond groves, its Roman aqueducts and buildings—a reminder that it was a province not of Paris but of Rome. Here are Avignon, with its forbidding Papal palace and the remains of its famous bridge, and Nîmes, Orange and Arles, with their temples and amphitheatres where bull-fights still recall the Roman games. In the west, in Languedoc and leading to the Pyrenees, are picturesque, ancient cities—like the walled hill town of Carcassonne. In the east is the French Riviera—St Tropez, Cannes and Nice, the fashionable tourist centres of the Mediterranean, with their fishing villages by a blue sea and wooded mountains as a backdrop—centres so popular with the British that the main street in Nice is still the Promenade des Anglais (The English Promenade).

The Rhône opens out into a wide and muddy delta, cutting off Marseilles from Provence. Part of this is the flat, low-lying Camargue, a strange region of sandy mud-flats and lagoons, of flamingos and egrets and especially of wild white horses. Quite a few 'Western' films have in fact been shot in the Camargue—with the difficulty that French cowboys ride standing up, with straight legs and long stirrups. And prominent on the delta is Marseilles, born long ago as a Greek colony. Today it is the next city in size to Paris, a polyglot and vigorous place, the port for North Africa and the Levant.

A crowded beach in the great holiday playground of the French Riviera.

Eastern France

The mountains that rise so sharply behind Nice are part of the French Alps, the barrier between France and Italy. In France they are almost 100 miles wide. From them, the rivers drop to the Rhône, providing hydro-electric power (the French 'white coal') for the small iron and steel industries clustered round Grenoble. The Alps run north-north-east to form part of the provinces of Dauphiné and Savoy, and to border Switzerland. With the Jura and the Vosges they constitute France's eastern frontier. They shelter the wine-growing province of Burgundy, once a powerful Duchy, and its capital, Dijon. And in the Jura valleys, clocks and watches, glassware and toys, butter and Gruyère cheese are produced. And, as almost everywhere, there are vines.

The North-east

Alsace-Lorraine is the eastern border province of France, lying between the Rhine and the Vosges. The principal towns are Strasbourg (pop. 200,000), Mulhouse, Colmar and Metz. During the Middle Ages the country, split into a number of petty principalities and free cities, belonged to the Holy Roman Empire. Most of Alsace was conquered by French armies during the Thirty Years War, and formally handed over to France by the Peace of Westphalia in 1648. Lorraine was added to France in 1766. The French kings respected local

90

rights and customs and so the German character of the country was largely preserved. The French Revolution marked a change. Local rights were abolished and the country was divided into three *departments*. Only the French language could be used in schools and courts. Nevertheless, the Alsatians heartily welcomed the Revolution, as it freed them from feudal bondage.

After the Franco-Prussian war of 1870–71 the newly established German Empire annexed the three departments, uniting them into the province of Alsace-Lorraine (German name: Elsass-Lothringen). By the Treaty of Versailles in 1919, the provinces were reunited with France.

In Alsace nearly the entire population speaks German, while in Lorraine about 70 per cent of the people speak German and 30 per cent French. On the whole, there are about 1,500,000 German speakers in Alsace-Lorraine, and while there are many people who do not know any French, or very little of it, there are others who are completely bi-lingual.

Post-war France

The Third Republic under which France was governed after 1870 was a parliamentary system: a Chamber of Deputies popularly elected for four years, a Senate, elected largely by the municipal councils, and a President, with very limited powers, elected for seven years by both Chamber and Senate. Elections were by a system of proportional representation reflecting the wishes of the voters but giving no one party a clear majority. In the years from 1918 to 1940 no one party ever had a majority of the 618 Deputies—all governments were therefore coalitions, and hardly one could carry through a consistent programme.

In both the Third Republic and the Fourth there were quite large numbers of Deputies who sought not just to overthrow the government of the day but to overthrow the Constitution with it. The Fascists attempted this in the 1930s, the Communists in the late 1940s. On the fall of a government, however, there was no general election—as would be the case in Britain—unless the four-year term had expired. A new government would be formed from the same 618 Deputies, often indeed of the same men, in an endless game of musical chairs. France in 70 years had 108 governments. By 1939 there were many Frenchmen—and some of her allies—who despaired of the Constitution. By 1939 there were some Frenchmen—and all of her enemies—who profited by the despair.

France has never forgotten the shock of its defeat at the hands of the Germans in 1871, when they occupied Paris and proclaimed the new German Empire in Versailles itself. After that date France no longer dominated Europe, and feared and distrusted Germany in particular. In the First World War it was invaded and laid waste again, and, on the failure of the Guarantee Treaty of 1919, it took care to build up, between 1922 and 1927, a system of alliances against Germany.

Pacts were made with Poland, Yugoslavia, Romania, Czechoslovakia and Belgium.

Efforts were also directed to reaching an understanding with Germany which appeared at that time to be liberal and genuinely anti-war. Under the influence of Briand in 1925, France joined in the Locarno Pact with Britain, Germany and Italy, all promising to maintain the existing frontiers and not to use force against each other. In 1928 France agreed—as did Germany—to outlaw war in the Kellogg-Briand Pact. France agreed in 1930 to the withdrawal of troops from the Rhineland, and in 1932 to the abolition of reparations. Even after 1933, with Hitler in power, France at first acted liberally. But its position gradually weakened: its allies in Central Europe were lost as German power and aggression grew. Many at home saw in Nazism a bulwark against Communism. The abandonment of Czechoslovakia at Munich in 1938 was a sign of bewilderment and loss of spirit.

Yet the quest failed—the quest for reliable allies against Germany, or for a satisfactory and lasting agreement with Germany. So did the quest fail for a line of defence. Although an impressive system of fortifications was built in eastern France between 1927 and 1935 by Maginot, the French War Minister, it had not been extended as far as the Channel on the outbreak of war. France's population in 1939 (42 millions) had been static for 40 years. Germany had twice these numbers.

The defeat of 1940: Vichy, occupation and their results

The first nine months of the Second World War was the period of the 'phony war'. Then in May 1940 Germany struck at the Low Countries and invaded France through Belgium. France held out only for six weeks; Paris fell to the Germans; the French Government retreated to Bordeaux; the British army at Dunkirk was rescued.

In June 1940, Paul Reynaud, the last Prime Minister of the Third Republic, called on Marshal Pétain, a veteran of the First World War (he was 84 years of age in 1940) to see if he could save the situation. The Marshal, believing further resistance to be useless, decided to sue for peace and accepted Hitler's armistice terms, under which he became leader of a new, German-controlled French Government. These terms divided France into two areas, occupied and unoccupied, the French Government having, at least nominally, full powers in the latter area. The new government set up its headquarters at Vichy in central France, just inside the unoccupied zone. Paris remained in German hands.

Most of the politicians rallied to Pétain but to many Frenchmen the new régime smacked of defeat and shame. One such man was a general of the French army—Charles de Gaulle—then relatively unknown outside military circles, although, in fact, a junior minister in the French Government. In June 1940, he made his way to London and from there broadcast to France and the world

The Maginot Line was constructed as an impenetrable part of France's defence system. The machine-gunner is on watch at Thionville.

that he was continuing the fight against Germany and invited all like-thinking Frenchmen to do the same. Gradually many came to join him, and the Free French Movement was founded.

In 1942, the Allies liberated French North Africa and de Gaulle created in Algeria a Free French Provisional Government.

By this time, in France itself, difficulties multiplied for the 'Vichy Régime'. Marshal Pétain found himself more and more the prisoner of unscrupulous politicians, notably Pierre Laval, who, long disliking the republican system, thought they saw their best chance of success by siding with the Germans. In 1942, the Germans, hoping to prevent Allied invasion and the escape of the French fleet, occupied the whole country. The Vichy Government still claimed, however, to be the legitimate government of France. The ineffectiveness of the Marshal to protect his people from the demands of the Germans, in particular the drafting of all able-bodied Frenchmen to labour camps in Germany, caused many people to flee to the countryside and to join the various resistance movements which were being created. Borrowing the Corsican word for a large part of the countryside of that island, the resistance groups were called the *maquis*.

In 1944, the Allies invaded France, which was finally liberated later that year. By the end of the war most of France's communications, notably the railway system, had been rendered completely useless, most of its factories razed to the ground and a number of towns virtually wiped from the map. Industrial production was almost at a standstill. Serious as were these physical effects, however, the moral effect of the occupation on the French nation was even more serious.

General de Gaulle headed the Provisional Government, whose main task was to restore order and reconstruct the country. This Provisional Government remained in power until the first government of the Fourth Republic was elected under a new constitution in 1946.

The Fourth Republic, 1946–58

By a referendum held in October 1945, the Constitution of the Third Republic, whose weakness was held to be responsible for France's shame and defeat, was abandoned. It took a year to work out a form of government for the Fourth Republic. It was not agreed upon until October 1946, when nine million voted for it, eight million voted against it, and another eight million did not vote at all. General de Gaulle resigned in January 1946, saying that the main task of liberation and reconstruction was over, and the work of the Provisional Government finished. In 1947 he organized a new party, the R.P.F. (The Rally of the French People) advocating a stronger executive, a nationalist foreign policy and opposing self-government for the French African territories.

The Constitution of the Fourth Republic was very similar to that of the Third. The parliament consisted of a popularly elected National Assembly of 626 deputies and an indirectly elected Council of the Republic of 320 members. Together they chose the President who held office for a seven-year term (Vincent Auriol 1946–53, René Côty 1953–58). The President chose the President of the Council of Ministers (Prime Minister), who had to submit his cabinet and his programme to the Assembly; the Assembly sat for five years. Since in 1946 there was much fear of the power and popularity of the large Communist Party—who had played a major role in the French Resistance—it was made especially difficult to pass legislation. For some bills, majorities of two-thirds or three-fifths were needed. There was much lobbying, especially by Algerian settlers. And in the Assembly, as in the Third Republic, there was the customary mixture of groups and parties.

Why the Fourth Republic failed

There are three main reasons for the failure of the Fourth Republic: constitutional, economic and overseas.

As in the years 1870–1940, legislation was difficult to agree on; all governments were formed by precarious alliances of groups; in the 12 years' existence of the Fourth Republic there were 26 governments; and two of the groups, the Communists and the *Poujadistes* (small traders' party), sought throughout to overthrow the Constitution. When the 52 Poujadistes joined the 150 Communists in opposition to the Constitution (a favourite Communist device being to bang the lids of their desks to drown the voice of any speaker they did not want to be heard), government could only be carried on by an unnatural coalition between the Radicals, the Socialists and the right-wing groups, who had little in common except dislike of the sort of authoritarian government that they believed the opposition would have established.

The French economy, at the end of the war, had not been adjusted to the twentieth century. To the stagnation of industry in the 1930s was added the destruction and dislocation caused by war on French soil. In spite of governmental weakness, however, the two Monnet Plans were successful. The first (1947–53) successfully dealt with basic industries, most of which have been nationalized (e.g. coal, electricity, iron, steel, oil and transport); while the second plan (1953–58) endeavoured to stimulate the producer-goods industries (e.g. agriculture, housing and construction).

But France is not yet fully industrialized. About 25 per cent of the labour force in 1956 was in firms with over 500 workers, compared with 45 per cent in Britain, while small craftsmen had increased from the pre-war figure of 180,000 to 400,000; there are over 7 million in agriculture compared with 1 million in Britain, and, of the 7 million, 6 million are farmers and $1\frac{1}{4}$ million labourers. Nine departments, or one-tenth of the country, produce over half of its income.

There were questions that even the wisest government would have found it hard to solve: the future of France overseas, especially in the colony of Indo-China (Cochin China, Annam, Cambodia and Laos), and the cost of the war there (1948–54); the future of the North African territories; the role in Europe; the attitude to Germany. Only a strong government could solve such questions —if they could be solved at all.

France overseas

France is, along with Portugal, the last of the great empires, and its difficulties in Algeria may well have been the last example of colonialism. The French Empire in 1939 consisted of French Indo-China; Syria and the Lebanon; the tiny area of French Guiana in South America (where there was the penal colony of Devil's Island); French West Africa (eight territories), French Equatorial Africa (four), French North Africa (part of Morocco, Algeria, conquered in 1830, and Tunis, conquered in 1881); and a number of tiny islands in the Caribbean and the Pacific.

While socially France was more liberal than was Britain, especially in matters of race and colour, it governed these territories more autocratically than Britain did its colonies. The French aim was to develop the overseas territories so that their inhabitants would ultimately become full French citizens, irrespective of race, colour or creed. The aim was assimilation. It failed to reckon with the force of nationalism, and a succession of weak governments at home prevented anything being done to link the territories with Paris, unlike what was being done by Britain.

In 1945 Syria and the Lebanon became independent. In 1954 the former French posts in India joined the Republic of India. In 1954, after a six years war and a major battle at Dien Bien Phu, France lost Indo-China, which became independent. All the former territories in Equatorial and West Africa are now independent states after years of unrest. In 1956 France recognized Morocco and Tunisia as independent states. Algeria was another problem.

The French moved into Algeria in 1830 and found that there was no central native government or authority through which they could rule, as was to be the case later in their Protectorates of Morocco and Tunisia. It took a long time to subdue the country, but finally the French succeeded and annexed the territory, later declaring it to be a part of France. Algeria (approximately 850,000 square miles) is four times the size of metropolitan France and nine times the size of Britain. Most of it is in the Saharan zone, where oil has recently been found. The three northern departments were developed as part of France and have a total population, European and others, of about ten million, of whom more than one-quarter live in the cities. Of these, over one million were Europeans. The Algerian economy was largely integrated with that of metropolitan France.

There are some big landowners, but the majority of the *colons* (French settlers) have only small holdings, averaging, in the coastal area, 17 acres in size. The majority of the European population consisted of artisans, workers, technicians, employers, and small business people—strongly pro-French and on the whole anti-Arab. They wanted to retain the link with France, and opposed Algerian independence. Since the northern departments were represented in the French Chamber they formed a strong and conservative pressure group.

From 1954 an Algerian independence movement, mainly non-European and Moslem, the Front de Libération Nationale (F.L.N.), fought the French army in Algeria with considerable success. The F.L.N. had much assistance from Tunisia and Morocco. In May 1958 the French troops in Algeria under General Salan, with the support of the French settlers and of a former Resident-Minister, Jacques Soustelle, who was a friend of de Gaulle, refused to recognize the French Government, believing it to be ready to negotiate with the F.L.N. A Committee of Public Safety for Algeria was set up which demanded that de Gaulle assume full power in France. This led to the downfall of the Fourth Republic.

De Gaulle: the man and his policy

Charles de Gaulle was born in Lille in 1890. He fought in the First World War, and in 1939 he became France's youngest general and was appointed Under-Secretary of Defence in the Reynaud Cabinet.

On the fall of France in June 1940 he flew to London and called on French troops to continue the war at Britain's side. Until 1944 de Gaulle commanded the Fighting French, and on the liberation of France he became head of the Provisional Government.

In 1946, however, the war hero turned his back on party politics in disgust. In 1947 he organized his Rally of the French People but then withdrew again from active politics in 1951. He spent the next seven years in retirement, writing his *Mémoires*.

De Gaulle's return to power was the result of a military-colonial rising in Algeria which a weak government made no serious attempt to control, so that it was the revolutionaries who chose the head of the new government in Paris. He was imposed by French Algeria on Paris. The French army had suffered heavy casualties in Indo-China (1948–54) and felt let down by the politicians. It did not want another Indo-China in Algeria. It distrusted politicians like Mendès-France, who had ended the hostilities in Indo-China in 1954 and granted independence to Tunisia in 1956. Their choice of de Gaulle was satisfactory to the right-wing in view of de Gaulle's anti-Communist record, his military background and the right-wing state he was expected to introduce; it was acceptable to the left-wing because of his leadership in the Resistance during the War.

De Gaulle: the President

In January 1959 Charles de Gaulle became President of the French Republic for a seven-year term. He was elected under the terms of the Constitution of the Fifth Republic, which had been approved by an overwhelming majority (80 per cent) of the French people in a popular referendum the previous September. This Constitution gives the President greater powers than did earlier constitutions: he nominates the Prime Minister; he can dissolve Parliament within a year of its being elected; he presides over the Council of Ministers, is Chief of the Armed Forces, and can, in a crisis, rule autocratically. President de Gaulle has used the device of seeking popular approval by plebiscite for his actions (notably to win approval for his Algerian settlement and to amend the Constitution in 1962 so that in future the President will be elected directly by the people), so that his form of government is closer to dictatorship than to democracy; it has been described as dictatorship by plebiscite.

Nevertheless, de Gaulle's form of government is in the French tradition—witness the dictatorships of Napoleon I and of Napoleon III, the attempted *coup* by Boulanger in 1889, the Vichy system of 1940. De Gaulle clearly has considerable popular support. The French people, especially in the provinces, are proud to have a leader subservient to no other Power, who has brought them peace and increased prosperity—and saved them the inconvenience of bothering about politics. The Parliaments elected during de Gaulle's 'reign' have so far had substantial majorities of the *Union pour la Nouvelle République* (a 'party' that transcends normal political parties) and other members who support him. Denounced by the spokesmen of all the other conventional parties—Socialists, M.R.P., Radicals and Communists—and by politicians of the Right for his 'abdication' in Algeria, President de Gaulle still clearly retains the support of the majority of people. The developments of 1958 were the first peaceful revolution in France since 1789.

De Gaulle's achievements

The settlement of Algeria. There is no evidence that when de Gaulle returned to power he foresaw the complete independence of Algeria. Indeed, the fact that the General had come to power because of a threatened military revolt against the very idea of treating with the Nationalists laid him open to the charge of treachery and double-dealing when, within a year, he proposed self-determination for Algeria through a referendum, if only the Nationalists would lay down their arms. It is not difficult to understand the exasperation of the French settlers and officers in Algeria, which led to a series of ever more violent revolts: the rising of Joseph Ortiz and the *pieds noirs* in January 1960, the mutiny of Generals Challe, Zeller, Jouhaud and Salan in April 1961, and the blind terrorism of the *Organisation de l'Armée Secrete* (O.A.S.) which continued until June 1962. However, de Gaulle was realist enough to see that a free vote for independence in Algeria was the only alternative to an endless and increasingly bitter war, and this was quickly appreciated by the bulk of the French people. When the cease-fire was eventually signed at Evian in 1962, it was received with immense relief, and a subsequent referendum confirmed it. Algeria is now free and independent. Brought back to power in 1958 in order to keep Algeria French, he used his power in fact to set Algeria free.

But the price of peace was the bitter resentment of the European population of Algeria, 750,000 of whom took refuge in France, leaving behind houses, cars, and often household goods; doctors left hospitals unstaffed, and other key workers left their posts without any trained replacements. The lasting hatred of a small minority made it necessary to retain emergency powers. But the General survived a number of attempts at assassination.

The French Community. There have been three stages in De Gaulle's policy here. First in 1944, at Brazzaville in French Equatorial Africa, de Gaulle proposed that whites and blacks should be regarded as enjoying common citizenship, but that colonial administration should be centralized on Paris (i.e. 'centralization' and 'assimilation'). Accordingly in 1946 French citizenship was conferred on all French subjects; a fund was set up to promote capital investment; Deputies were elected to the French National Assembly in Paris (though not as many proportionately as in France), and territorial Assemblies set up.

The second stage evolved because the 'winds of change' were too strong for this system to last. On his return to power in 1958, de Gaulle promulgated a new constitution, under which French territories had to choose, in a referendum, between membership of a French Community of self-governing peoples or total secession from the French Colonial Empire. For members, federal machinery (an Executive Council, a Senate and a Court of Arbitration) would deal with foreign policy, defence, currency, and common economic and financial policy. Secession, however, involved the loss of all French co-operation and aid. In the event, only Guinea broke away; and the eight French territories in West Africa, the four territories in Equatorial Africa, Madagascar and French Somaliland all joined the Community.

Even so, these measures, too, soon proved insufficient and so the third stage was set. In December 1959 President de Gaulle proposed negotiations with those countries that wanted independence—which proved to be, in the end, all of them. The Executive Council of the French Community therefore disappeared, to be replaced by a periodical conference of Heads of Government (which can be joined for economic discussions by non-members in the franc area). The Community Senate was replaced by an 'interparliamentary consultative Senate', to which delegates are sent by the respective Parliaments; while the Arbitration Court was replaced by a non-permanent Court of Arbitration, along the lines of the International Court of Justice at the Hague. To provide for defence, national armies are being created with the assistance of France.

Economic aid. French economic aid to overseas areas since the war, despite its own post-war situation, has been on a much greater scale than that of Britain, and in 1959 accounted for 1.5 per cent of the national income. For the period 1956 to 1959, French aid—official and private—amounted to $4,921 million (Britain's to $3,149 million). A third of France's overseas aid goes to its former territories in Africa. Now, as a member of the Common Market, France helps to provide £180 million a year to help overseas territories.

Ex-French Africa now consists of:

Ex-French West Africa. This area, with a total population of about 20 million, comprises eight territories—Mauritania, Mali (Sudan), Niger, Senegal, Guinea, Ivory Coast, Dahomey and Upper Volta. The first three are largely desert, while the rest, except the last, possess a coast-line.

In 1958–59, aware of the danger of the 'Balkanization' of Africa, several of the territories considered joining the Community as federated units. Senegal and Sudan united to form the Fedération of Mali, a union which soon broke down. Senegal joined the French Community; but the Republic of Mali decided against membership and, in 1961, with Guinea and Ghana, formed the Union of African States. In 1960, Dahomey, Ivory Coast, Upper Volta and Niger formed the *Conseil de l'Entente* ('Council of the Entente'), and decided to seek independence outside the Community. However, despite their independence, all these former French territories except Guinea retain some links with France.

Equatorial Africa and Madagascar. The four territories—Chad, Gabon, the Congo Republic and the Central African Republic—have a population of five million and, having each voted to join the Community, announced in January 1959 the formation of a customs union, since the richest territory, Gabon, was unwilling to share its wealth by a political federation. The other three then formed the Union of Central African Republics and recently became independent but remained within the French Community.

Madagascar also chose independence within the Community under the name of Malagasy.

The present position

The present composition of the Community, in which the status of each territory has been determined by free choice, can be summarized as follows:

The French Republic consisting of (*a*) Metropolitan France, (*b*) the Overseas Departments, (*c*) the Overseas Territories;

The Republic of Senegal;

The *Malagasy* Republic;

The *Gabon* Republic;

The Union of African Republics (the republics of Chad, Congo and Central Africa);

'Special relations' or 'special links' have been established by agreements between France and the following states:

The Council of the Entente (the republics of the Ivory Coast, Upper Volta, Niger and Dahomey); *The Islamic Republic of Mauritania*; *The Federal Republic of Cameroon.*

The republics of *Mali, Guinea and Togo* have agreed to co-operate with France in certain fields.

The total population of all ex-French Africa is 40 millions, scattered through some fifteen territories. If the links with Paris are still close, they are now economic and cultural rather than political. The pole of attraction is now not so much Paris as Lagos, the capital of a country, Nigeria, with a population greater than that of all combined. Despite the signing of defensive treaties, French troops have not in fact intervened in local crises: neither in January 1963, when President Olympio of Togo was assassinated; nor in August 1963, when the Abbé Youlou, President of the former French Congo, was deposed; nor in October 1963, when President Maga of Dahomey was overthrown. Only in February 1964 did French forces intervene—to restore a President, Léon M'Ba of Gabon. But despite this evidence of restraint, Black Africa is now looking increasingly to itself, and to the Organization of African Unity. In conceding independence and treating the former colonies with great financial generosity, de Gaulle has lost control of the former French Empire in Africa but won its goodwill. There is little anti-French feeling and great respect for de Gaulle. He has his hands free of colonial or ex-colonial controversies, and he can pose as the friend of independence and neutrality against the encroachments of imperialism, whether American or Communist.

The economic recovery of France. National planning in France goes back to the Monnet Plan, prepared during General de Gaulle's tenure of office as President of the Provisional Government in 1946. It failed, however, to be fully effective under the Fourth Republic, due partly to the undermining of business confidence by the political instability of those years, and partly to the effect on the economy of the fact that France had been continuously at war since 1939. But since 1958 the French economy has been expanding dramatically and undoubtedly it is the strong government provided by de Gaulle that has made planning really work.

The de Gaulle Government introduced a drastic financial programme: devaluation, a new currency and, for a time, an austerity programme. He converted a deficit of 300 million francs into a surplus of 600 million in eighteen months. As a result, French expansion became the fastest in the Western world. It has been especially fast in the 'newer' industries—chemicals, plastics, synthetic rubber, electronics, machine tools for Renault and Citroen cars, engineering and aircraft. The growth rate is faster than in the United States: in the years 1961–67, sales overseas of manufactured products have doubled. De Gaulle claims that he can double the standard of living in fourteen years. The population has increased by $4\frac{1}{2}$ million since he took office (it is now 50 million) and the demand for schools and houses is giving a new energy. The dams and barrages on the Rhône have given a vast increase of hydro–electric power; the South is enjoying a great boom; there are striking developments in transport like the Mont Blanc tunnel and much stimulus to regional development. However, the financial demands of the Algerian war, of modernization and of the atomic programme have been heavy. But oil from the Sahara is already proving a valuable asset: production that began in 1959 totalled 20 million tons in 1961 and 30 million tons in 1965 (50 million tons are hoped for by 1970). At present, about half of France's needs are supplied by Saharan oil. It is worth stressing that only by ending the Algerian war was it possible for the 'co-operative association' of 1965 to be established, which gives France the lion's share of all oil and natural gas in Algeria.

'*La Gloire*.' De Gaulle is preoccupied with the greatness and glory of France. He has been critical of the activity—and speech-making—of the United Nations; he disapproved of U.N. intervention in the Congo in 1960, and refused to contribute to the costs of that operation. He advocates a *Europe des patries* (Europe of states), is critical of the United States' role in Europe, and of NATO, which he sees as a disguised form of U.S. military domination. In 1960 he insisted on the withdrawal of American air squadrons from French territory; he refused to place his Mediterranean fleet under NATO control; in 1966 he requested NATO headquarters to be moved from Paris, and declared that France intended to withdraw from NATO. He is much less pro-American than post-war British Governments have been. He does not question the need for the Western Alliance, but it must be one in which France has the control of its own forces—land, sea and air, nuclear and 'conventional'. The French deterrent, or *force de frappe*, is necessary, in de Gaulle's view, both as a symbol of French independence and as an insurance against a nuclear attack upon Europe. 'France must have a sword, and it must be her own sword.' He resented bitterly that nuclear secrets shared by the United States and Britain should be withheld from France.

In February 1960 France exploded its first atomic bomb in the Sahara and in December 1960 a five-year programme was launched for the creation of a nuclear strike force of medium-range Mirage bombers and the provision of special army and navy equipment. The strike force is intended to be replaced, by 1970, by intermediate-range ballistic missiles, probably sea-borne (i.e. *Polaris*). The United States has criticized de Gaulle's determination that his nuclear forces shall be under exclusive French control.

From this, three conclusions follow: accord with Germany, separation from Britain, and the quest for a distinct foreign policy.

De Gaulle and Germany. De Gaulle's accord with Germany is partly economic, partly political. He saw in the European Economic Community, formed by the 1957 Treaty of Rome, a convenient Continental *bloc* in which French industry could profit by a wider market, French agriculture could be protected, and French power and influence could be extended, since the other five members would be irrevocably bound to France through the economic advantages of the Common Market. It would form also the nucleus of a Europe 'from the Atlantic to the Urals', equal in power to the United States or the U.S.S.R. This made it necessary for France to assure itself of the special friendship of West Germany. The Treaty of Franco-German Co-operation signed in Paris on 22 January 1963, at the conclusion of an official visit by the German Chancellor, Dr Adenauer, was an historic act of reconciliation. It was, in a sense, the result of a long process of mutual forgiveness and co-operation at which the Church, the universities, writers and youth organizations of both countries had been working for years. President de Gaulle rightly regards the Treaty as one of the great achievements of his life.

De Gaulle and Britain. The other five members of the 'Six' clearly wanted Britain to join them. Discussions to this purpose were held in 1962–63 (under the Macmillan government) and resumed in 1967 under the Wilson government. It was not possible for Britain to sign the Treaty of Rome as it stands, because of its existing commitments to the Commonwealth, its place in E.F.T.A. (European Free Trade Area), and because of its policy of subsidizing the British farmer—a policy which could not be altered overnight. In January 1963 de Gaulle imposed a veto on the discussions on Britain's entry on the grounds that Britain was not prepared to adapt itself to the conditions of membership and that its entry would transform the 'Six' into an Atlantic Community which would be guided not by France but by the U.S.A. Britain could hardly have been admitted without bringing in also its 'huge escort', the Commonwealth; and this would have altered totally the character of the Community. There can be little doubt that President de Gaulle was led to this decision by Britain's readiness, in the conference in 1962 at Nassau in the Bahamas, to accept the American Polaris missile as its system of defence—a decision that suggested to de Gaulle that Britain was not only an ally of the United States but a dependant. Nor has de Gaulle ever forgotten the contempt shown towards him during the Second World War by President Roosevelt and the American Administration; and the Americans were slow to give recognition to his Committee as the Provisional Government of France in 1942. For this reason, too, de Gaulle has opposed the setting-up of American bases in France and has hurried on the production of France's own nuclear weapons.

The man of pride and independence. France has hastened the development of the oil resources of the Sahara. In January 1964 it recognized the Mao régime in China, much to the consternation of the U.S.A. De Gaulle visited Mexico in March 1964, and later the same year (September/October) ten countries of Latin America (during which he covered 20,000 miles and ten countries in 26 days and gave 40 speeches). In June and July 1966 he visited the U.S.S.R., and in August and September South-east Asia and the French nuclear-testing site in the Pacific. In July 1967 he visited French Canada and gave support to 'free Quebec'. In September 1967 he was in Poland. He shows throughout a will of his own, especially a will to be independent of the influence of the United States, and of those governments, like Britain and Canada, he sees as American satellites.

By 1968, when he was 77 years old, his touch was becoming less sure. He lost much support in France by showing sympathy for the Arabs in the (May 1967) war with Israel; and his speech in Quebec in July 1967 identifying France with the cause of Free Quebec was an affront to the Government of Canada and embarrassed many Frenchmen. Many of them share his views of American policy, notably of the Vietnam war; and many believe he is right in arguing that Britain's entry into Europe will transform the character of the Common Market. But it is not true that he speaks for the majority of Frenchmen when he argues that the interests of France can be separated politically, economically or culturally from those of the Western European Community. It is doubtful if the French people any longer respond to his ultra-nationalist and anti-materialist notions of the glory of France.

De Gaulle's first term of office expired in December 1965. He was re-elected for a second seven-year term, in the first direct Presidential election by universal suffrage. But there was a heavy vote for his chief opponent, François Mitterand, and in the National Assembly elections of 1967 de Gaulle *plus* the Independent Republicans had a majority of only three over all other parties. Despite these checks, de Gaulle sees himself as the incarnation of France: a leader, above party, embodying the national identity. He calls his party the party of the Fifth Republic, the *Marseillaise* was his theme song in the elections of 1967, the tricolour his symbol. A leader, he believes, needs a strong dose of selfishness, pride, firmness and cunning. He is a truly great man, whose pride in himself and in his country twice saved it: in 1940 and again in 1958. The parallels with Churchill's career and his sentiments are very striking.

QUESTIONS TO CONSIDER

1. What are the principal regions of France? Give an account of any one of them.
2. What were the main problems facing France in the years from 1919 to 1939?
3. Why did the Fourth Republic collapse?
4. What main problems did de Gaulle have to face in 1958?
5. Assess the achievements of de Gaulle as President.
6. What is the significance of the present friendship between France and West Germany?

WORDS TO NOTE

Assimilation: Absorption, as of North Africa by France. The wish to absorb the French-speaking areas of North Africa into the way of life of metropolitan France.

Maquis: Corsican word for undergrowth and rough land. It was in the *maquis* of France and Italy that the war-time resistance movements hid. Hence the *maquis* has come to represent the 'underground' opposition to a government in power.

Monnet Plans: Jean Monnet was the author of the plans to modernize French industry after the Second World War. He was also one of the architects of the plan for the Coal and Steel Community.

Popular Front: Coalition parties of the Left and Centre.

Poujadist: Follower of Poujade: party of small shopkeepers who refused to pay what they thought were over-high taxes.

FOR FURTHER READING

Cobban, A.: *A History of Modern France*, Pelican—3 volumes, 1957, 1961, 1965.

Thomson, D.: *Democracy in France*, Oxford, 1958.

Brogan, D.: *The Development of Modern France*, Hamish Hamilton, 3rd ed., 1958.

Peacock, H. L.: *A History of Modern Europe*, Heinemann, 1961.

Beloff, Nora: *The General says No*, Penguin Books, 1963.

4. Germany

Of all the states of Europe, Germany is perhaps the hardest to understand. Of all the peoples of Europe, the people of Germany are closest to the British, especially to the Scots, in appearance, in respect for cleanliness and for orderly living, and in language. They are hard-working, highly educated and highly gifted. They have produced many scientists, philosophers, writers and musicians. Yet twice this century—for ten years out of 60—Britain and France have been at war with Germany, and France has had three wars with Germany since 1870. Germany went from victory in 1871 to defeat in 1918, from triumph in 1940 to disaster in 1945. For an older generation the Germans are the bogey-men of Europe. In two wars only a grand alliance of most of the rest of the world defeated them. How can today's Germany be understood?

The background: the rise of Prussia

There are—and have been—many Germanies. Today there are two, the Federal Republic established in 1949, 'West Germany', with a parliament at

106

Bonn, and the German Democratic Republic (Deutsche Demokratische Republik, or D.D.R.), 'East Germany', with its capital at Pankow, a suburb of Berlin, in the Soviet Zone. Together, West and East Germany occupy only three-quarters of the area of Hitler's Germany—Germany's eastern boundary was moved westwards in 1945 and fixed at the Oder-Neisse Line; east of that line is now under Polish control.

From 1945 until 1949 there were four Germanies, since on the defeat of the Nazis in 1945, the country was divided into four zones of military occupation (the British, the French, the American and the Russian).

Under Hitler, 1933–45, as with the Weimar Republic (1919–33) or William II (1888–1918), there was of course only one *Reich*. But until the creation of the German Empire in 1871, there had been at least 30 states inside what is now called Germany, and until the Holy Roman Empire was destroyed by Napoleon in 1806 there had been 360.

Germany seemed until 1815 a divinely ordained confusion of cities, small states and prince-bishoprics; the northern states were mainly Protestant, the southern mainly Catholic; in the Middle Ages what unity there was came from an elected Emperor, a title held by the rulers of Austria. Voltaire said that the Holy Roman Empire was neither Holy, Roman nor an Empire.

Germany has thus had a long, violent and disorderly history. It was the last European state to become united; it took great pride in the achievement of unity; it was largely the work of one of the states, Prussia, and of its rulers, the Hohenzollerns. The greatest of them all was Frederick II, the Great (1740–86), who conquered Silesia and was responsible for seizing part of Poland. The strength of the Prussian kings lay in their ruthlessness, their zealous civil service and still more in their formidable army, with its officers recruited from the landed class (the Junkers), and its N.C.O.s from the peasantry, of the great plains of Pomerania.

Prussia, the north-eastern edge of the Germany of today, has few natural defences. So it came to rely on a strong army, on a strong sense of discipline, and on pride in race and in power. Might, it seemed, makes right. By the time of Frederick the Great's death in 1786—three years before the outbreak of the French Revolution—Prussia was the chief state in Germany and a rival power to Austria.

Under the great Chancellor, Otto von Bismarck (1861–90), Prussia brought all Germany except Austria under its political control. Bismarck won three wars: Denmark was defeated in 1864; Austria, a large state with a powerful army, was defeated after a *blitzkrieg* of seven weeks in 1866; and France was defeated and Paris occupied in 1870–71. Prussia won Schleswig–Holstein from Denmark; Austria was excluded from the new Germany in 1866; and Alsace-Lorraine and a five thousand million franc indemnity was won from France in 1871. When the King of Prussia was crowned Emperor of Germany, as

Germany, 1933.

William I, in 1871, head of a federal empire of 25 states, the ceremony took place not in Berlin but in the Hall of Mirrors in the Palace of Versailles, outside Paris. The German Empire was built up by war; it was made, said Bismarck, of blood and iron.

Deutschland über alles

The first German Emperor, William I, died in 1888, and after the short reign of his son, was succeeded by his grandson, William II, who was also a grandson of Queen Victoria. Few rulers in history have gambled away a strong position so recklessly and completely as did William II.

In 1890 Bismarck was dismissed. It was then that the real danger of the German system of government appeared. The prestige of the army had been increased by Bismarck's wars. The Constitution of the Empire had placed supreme power in the hands of the sovereign, and, after 1890, a succession of weak appointments were made to the Chancellorship and the Foreign Office. Relations with Russia became cool and led to the first step in the isolation of Germany, when the Dual Alliance between France and Russia was signed in 1891. In 1900 a big increase in the German naval programme was announced, which was a clear challenge to British sea power. In these circumstances the British Government moved slowly towards the other European group: the *Entente Cordiale* with France was formed in 1904, and in 1907 a looser understanding was reached with Russia. A great race in armaments began. It led to the First World War.

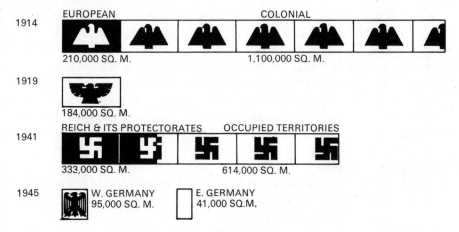

EACH SYMBOL REPRESENTS 200,000 SQ. M.

The results of changes in Germany's frontiers.

The outbreak of war led to the decline of the Emperor's power inside Germany, in favour of that of the Army High Command. When the western offensive failed, there began the cult of the victor of East Prussia, Marshal von Hindenburg. Soon after, Hindenburg was made Commander-in-Chief; together with General Ludendorff, his Chief of Staff, he dominated Germany.

For the last two years of the war Ludendorff, the brain of the High Command, was the effective ruler of Germany. In 1917 Germany came close to victory. In December 1917 Ludendorff defeated the Russians on the eastern front, and the new Bolshevik government asked for a separate armistice. Three months later, peace terms were imposed on Russia by the Treaty of Brest-Litovsk which brought Finland, the Baltic provinces, Russian Poland and the Ukraine under German control.

It was hoped in Germany that this victory would now make possible an overwhelming drive by the German armies in the west. This offensive was launched in March 1918, and came very near success. But it was slowed down, halted and finally driven back. On 8 August, Ludendorff realized that defeat was inevitable. Knowing that an approach from the High Command would meet with no favour among the Allies (and also wishing to saddle the civilian authorities with the peace negotiations, thus preserving the theory of the 'invincibility' of the German army), he insisted that executive power inside Germany should be transferred to a ministry responsible to parliament. The Kaiser fled to Holland. It was thus a civilian, a republican and a defeated Germany that surrendered in November 1918.

The real Germany

German history is not, however, merely the story of the organization of the state for war. The state itself, once united, was large—there were, in 1939, 70 million people in Germany proper, and it was the most populous state in Europe, except for Russia. It was rich in coal; by 1900 it was in places heavily industrialized. Germany, said Lord Keynes, was united not only by blood and iron but by coal and iron. The people were inventive, enterprising and industrious. They came late on the scene as an economic power, but they profited from the experience of others. They valued education, science and research, and in the late nineteenth century their universities and technical institutes were far ahead of Britain's.

Until 1914 the German chemical industry led the world and became almost an international monopoly. Germany used its ample supplies of lignite (brown coal) to generate electricity locally, and a great electrical industry developed. The country is rich in salts, and these too contributed to the development of chemicals; especially rich in potash, which is found in the Harz Mountains. The brewing industry became world famous—beer is the national drink of Germany. *Rathauskeller* (city hall cellars used as restaurants) and *Biergarten* are essential features of any German city's social and political life. And many a sinister political plot was brewed in Hitler's days in the Munich *Hofbrauhaus*. It developed a strong merchant marine. And it had—and has—an impressive transport system: 6,000 miles of rivers, 1,400 miles of canals, 36,000 miles of good, fast rail transport, and (though only with Hitler) good roads.

But after 1918 Germany as an economic power was handicapped. It lost the Lorraine iron ore deposits, which left the steel industry dependent on foreign ore. It had inadequate supplies of wool, copper, rubber, lead, phosphates and oil and lacked tin, nickel, asbestos and tungsten. Of important raw materials Germany had an exportable surplus of only two things: coal and chemicals. That it became a great industrial state was due not to mineral wealth but to skilful and frugal use of resources and the ingenuity of German chemists in producing synthetic products. Almost half the world's synthetic dyes were produced in Germany.

Germany's difficulties

Politically, then, Germany was united by Prussia, and by war; economically, it was industrial and progressive, with a vigorous and large population. Yet, as a world power Germany had four major limitations. First, it had few colonies. It acquired small colonies in Africa and in the Pacific but they were of small economic value, and Germany lost them in 1918. Unlike Britain there was no overseas empire in which to take pride, from which to draw raw materials and to which young men could go as governors and teachers and engineers.

Second, Germany had few defensible land frontiers. The Germany of 1918 consisted of two discontinuous parts separated by Poland. Czechoslovakia was a wedge pointing towards the Elbe Valley. The frontiers with France have been fought over for 1,000 years. The industrial regions are all close to frontiers: the Ruhr to France, Saxony to Czechoslovakia, Silesia to Poland. Germany was always prompt to feel encircled—and was in fact easy to encircle and to invade. A strong army was a necessity.

Third, as a sea power Germany was not as well placed as Britain—access to the open sea, which we call the North Sea and the Germans the German Ocean, could be blocked at the Straits of Dover or off the northern coast of Scotland. The longer shore borders the bottled-up Baltic. Stettin, the port of Berlin, has less than one-fourth the trade of Hamburg. To overcome the handicap, the Kiel Canal was built in 1895, cutting through the narrows at the German-controlled base of the Jutland Peninsula.

The beer cellars and beer gardens of Germany are famous. The one shown above is at the university city of Heidelberg.

111

And, fourth—and not least—its major river, the Rhine, runs to the sea through foreign territory. Germany does not control the outlet even of its major waterway.

The regions and their resources
Divided Germany: North and South

Politically, today, there are two Germanies. But any publication of the Bonn Government will describe Germany as a single country, implying that the line of division of 1949 is not permanent: West Germany wants to be reunited with East Germany and to hold free elections. East Germany wants Germany to be reunited but not with free elections, since there are 17 million people in the East but 51 million in the West, and in really free elections the Communist régime in the East would lose. For this reason, although the line of division is recent, it seems likely to last. Until 1945, where it existed at all, the line was a county boundary only. Now the control point at Helmstedt, or at the Branden- burg Gate in the middle of Berlin, is an international frontier; it is the 'Iron Curtain' where two worlds touch.

Local government in Germany can be strong—in Berlin and Hamburg, for instance, or in a state like Bavaria—almost as strong as the love of one's *pays* that is found in France. The real lines of division in Germany are, however, religious, economic, geographic and historical rather than political. The most permanent has been the division between those areas in the south and west, touching on the Rhine, that were for centuries influenced by Roman and Christian ideas, and those to the north and east untouched by them. That is, Frank *versus* Saxon. There is a Protestant, Nordic and military-minded (mainly north) Germany and·a Catholic, Alpine, easy-going (mainly south) Germany. The soils of the Northern Plain are not very fertile, whereas the Rhineland and South Germany are very productive. More important than the political division into East and West is this real geographical division into two regions, North and South.

The North German Plain. A winding line drawn from Aachen in the West through Dusseldorf, Hanover and Leipzig to Gorlitz on the Neisse leaves to its north a flat plain, with hardly any point above 700 feet. Much of it is marshy and wooded heath. It was only in the nineteenth century that much of it was reclaimed and settled, the first experiments having been made by Frederick the Great. The Plain begins, in fact, in Russia and runs across Germany into Holland—crossing all the man-made frontiers. Its marshy and sandy soil has held up the development of intensive agriculture. It was more suitable for large estates than for small peasant holdings and it has been traditionally the home of the great landlords, the Junkers. These were originally a military caste, ruling over a Slav peasantry.

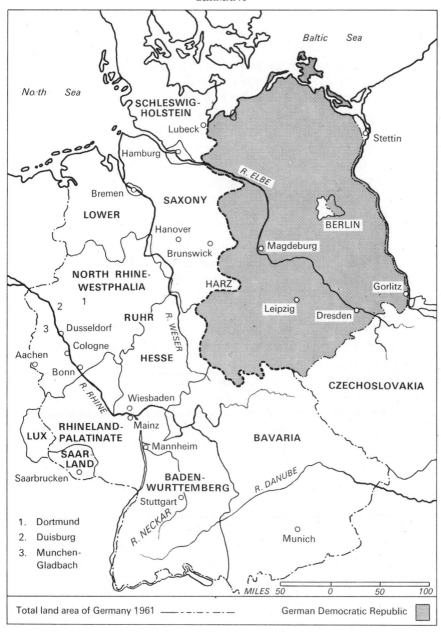

The main regions of Western Germany.

Map labels:

Baltic Sea

No.th Sea

SCHLESWIG-HOLSTEIN

Lubeck

Stettin

Hamburg

R. ELBE

Bremen

SAXONY

LOWER

BERLIN

Hanover

Magdeburg

Brunswick

NORTH RHINE-WESTPHALIA

HARZ

Gorlitz

1

2

RUHR

R. WESER

Leipzig

Dresden

3 Dusseldorf

Cologne

Aachen

HESSE

Bonn

CZECHOSLOVAKIA

R. RHINE

Wiesbaden

RHINELAND-PALATINATE

Mainz

LUX

BAVARIA

SAAR-LAND

Mannheim

Saarbrucken

BADEN-WURTTEMBERG

R. DANUBE

1. Dortmund

Stuttgart

2. Duisburg

R. NECKAR

3. Munchen-Gladbach

Munich

MILES 50   0   50   100

Total land area of Germany 1961 ——.——.——.— German Democratic Republic

Poor soil, a cold climate, and racial problems have long held back the development of the lands east of the Elbe. With modern methods of drainage and cultivation, most of it is now tillable. It produces wheat and rye, potatoes and pigs, milk and beef. Its western edge, Holstein, is much more productive than the eastern, East Prussia. Its chief ports are Lubeck, Stettin and Konigsberg (now Kaliningrad), the capital of East Prussia.

South Germany. South of the plains are the Central Uplands, where forested hills alternate with wide, fertile valleys or narrow deeply-incised gorges. It is the most beautiful part of the country, with ancient, picturesque cities.

The Uplands are 'block' mountains which take the form of steep-sided plateaux and, as they are composed of old, hard rocks, they are given over to coniferous forest, though on the flat, plateau surfaces there are extensive moorlands. Examples are the Thuringen Forest, Harz Mountains, Rhine Highlands, Black Forest and Bohemian Forest.

The valleys (of Weser, Rhine, Main and Neckar) are often narrow but sometimes they widen out into extensive rift valleys, with rich soils.

The Rhine Valley is the most important part of South Germany. It can be subdivided into three parts:

(*a*) from the German border to Bonn, largely industrial;

(*b*) the Gorge, from Bonn to Bingen, with its picturesque castles;

(*c*) the Rift Valley, from Bingen upstream to Basel in Switzerland.

The Rhine is important, first, as a route, for it provides an easy north-south corridor through the central hills. Together with the Rhône-Saône Valley, it was the main avenue through which civilization spread from the Mediterranean into Europe. Today the river itself is the most important inland waterway in Europe (Mannheim-Rotterdam). Second, the Rift Valley is an important agricultural region, vineyards being important on the slopes, wheat and tobacco on the plain, and cattle near the river. The Rhine Gorge and the Moselle are famous for their vineyards and wine. And third, industry based on coal brought by barge from the Ruhr is important also in the northern section of the Rift Valley. Here towns like Frankfurt, Mainz and Karlsruhe have engineering works and Ludwigshafen, a chemical industry. The upper Rhine has close relations with Alsace-Lorraine to the west of the Rhine. It is sheltered by the Vosges, the Jura and the Black Forest, and is one of the most beautiful parts of Germany.

South from the River Danube is the Bavarian plateau. It divides into two contrasting regions, (*a*) the Alpine Foreland, an undulating plain of gravel washed down from the Alps, which is mainly given over to forest and (*b*) the Alps proper—only a small area of which lies in Germany. South Germany is cut off, in the east, from Czechoslovakia by hilly forest country and on the west its boundary is the Rhine and the Black Forest. Munich and Augsburg, the only two big towns, have engineering industries and the former a brewing industry. Munich is the ancient and modern political capital of Bavaria, its greatest commercial centre—and for long it was the headquarters of Adolf Hitler.

Agriculture versus *Industry*

Alongside this rural Germany is industrial Germany, of which there are another four major industrial areas.

The Ruhr. Running into the Rhine at Duisburg is the main industrial river of Germany, the Ruhr, the equivalent of the Clyde or the coaly Tyne. This is the heart of German industry and the site of its grim and dirty towns. This was the area raided day and night by British and American bombers in the Second World War.

The Ruhr is one of the biggest coalfields in Europe and produces 140 million tons per annum (Britain 220 million tons). The seams are thick and easy to work and the coal is of excellent quality. It has easy access to the Rhine, to the sea, and to the Lorraine iron ore field farther up the Rhine.

It has given rise to one of the greatest industrial conurbations in the world, 45 miles long, stretching from Dortmund (population half-a-million) to Duisburg (a great river port on the Rhine) and including such centres as Essen and Gelsenkirchen, total population eight million. The Ruhr produces all kinds of heavy iron and steel goods (using imported iron ore). It is dependent on coal, but efforts are being made in the Ruhr, as on the Clyde, to diversify the economy.

The efforts are necessary, because between 1957 and 1962 the gross production of the Ruhr rose by only 30 per cent against 54 per cent for the Federal Republic as a whole. Coal and steel are declining industries (1938: 52 per cent of all Ruhr workers were either miners or steelworkers; 1961: 36 per cent). To offset this decline, manufacturing and chemicals have boomed. Bochum, the great (and grimy) coal town of the 1930s is now a major producer of Opel cars and of television sets; it is to have a new university and has one of the finest provincial theatres in Germany. The Ruhr could be a model for parts of Britain to follow.

South and west lie other industrial centres drawing power from the Ruhr.

(*a*) Wuppertal—on the Rhine Highlands—a textile town producing cotton, silk and rayon.

(*b*) Nearby is Solingen—the Sheffield of Germany.

(*c*) West of the Rhine are Krefeld and Munchen-Gladbach—cotton and rayon producing towns. Munchen-Gladbach is now familiar to many in Britain—its vast 'New Town' is the headquarters of the British Army of the Rhine. (B.A.O.R.)

(*d*) Aachen stands on a coalfield of its own and makes woollen goods.

(*e*) Cologne (population 800,000) and Dusseldorf are administrative centres

Part of the vast engineering works of Krupp, at Essen.

for Ruhr industry, but have engineering industries also. Cologne was the greatest Roman settlement and the greatest medieval archbishopric and city in Germany. Its centre is still the Dom (the Cathedral) and its bridges over the Rhine. A great commercial and cultural centre, it was heavily bombed in the Second World War, but has been splendidly restored, and has now a new opera house that is perhaps the finest in Europe.

This Ruhr-Rhine industrial complex is the power-house of West Germany.

Middle Germany. This area lies in East Germany. It contains many old cities with old-established industries and on the other hand many new modern industries.

Among the old industries are, first, on the slopes of the Erzgebirge, an old cotton textile industry located around Chemnitz (the Manchester of Germany). Second, agricultural industries are important, especially sugar refining and milling at Magdeburg. Magdeburg on the Elbe is now a Russian Command

116

Headquarters. Leipzig (population 700,000) (printing) and Dresden (engineering) are now cultural centres.

The new industries are based on deposits of lignite and salt. Most important is the chemical industry (lignite—synthetic rubber, plastics, etc.; salt—soap, fertilizers, explosives). Lignite is also used to produce large quantities of electricity, and an important electrical engineering industry has grown up.

Lower Saxony. If the British eighteenth-century kings came from Hanover, it was from the Saxon dukedoms—from Saxe Coburg, Gotha and from Anhalt —that many of their queens came. Hanover and Brunswick have engineering and vehicle industries, and railway stock; the former also has great rubber factories. Industry is widely scattered throughout the countryside.

The Saar. The Saar is a political problem child. Nothing so well indicates how pointless are political divisions than does this area. It is German in character and its people are German-speaking. But it is on the French-Belgian-German border, close to the iron of Lorraine and the coal of Alsace and to the Rhine waterway. With nearly one million inhabitants it produces about 16 million tons of coal per year; the French section to the south-west has produced about six million tons in recent years. The Saar developed, in the 1870–1914 period, in close relation to the Lorraine-Ruhr complex, and was thoroughly integrated in the German economy. According to the Treaty of Versailles in 1919, however, the coal-mines, iron and steel plants were passed to France for a period of 15 years. Since 1919 its international status has been changed six times.

(*a*) After the Versailles Treaty of 1919 France was awarded the coal-mines as war reparations. The territory was administered by the League of Nations for the next 15 years.

(*b*) In 1935 90 per cent of Saarlanders voted for reunion with Germany and this took place in March of that year.

(*c*) In July 1945 (after the Second World War) the Saar became part of the zone of occupation allotted to France.

(*d*) In 1946 France detached the Saar from the French Zone and put it under a special régime.

(*e*) In 1954 at the meeting of Foreign Ministers in Paris it was agreed that the Saar would be given a European Statute.

(*f*) October 1955. A referendum was held in the Saar. The people voted against the European Statute and for union with Germany. Reunion with Germany took place on 1 January 1957.

Thus twice in one generation (1935, 1955) the people have voted for union with Germany. Yet, economically, France (which is short of coal) needs the Saar, and Germany (which has a surplus of coal) does not. The Saar needs Lorraine (i.e. French) iron ore for its steel industry and needs French food supplies. In 1955, however, Germany held that the absorption of the Saar would serve as a model for the smooth reunification of Germany.

At last the problem appears to have been settled. Today the Saar is part of Germany. This is the result partly of mutual understanding and also of the development of the European Coal and Steel Community and of the growing common economic policy of the 'Six'. It appears that at least one milestone on the road to European unity has been reached.

Apart from these industrial areas there are a number of large cities, isolated, as it were, in the midst of relatively thinly-peopled rural land—like Munich, Stettin, Bremen, Hamburg and, biggest of all, Berlin.

Hamburg (population $1\frac{1}{2}$ million), the major seaport of Germany, is a splendid city on the Elbe, at the head of a broad estuary. It is 60 miles from the sea, on a river that is kept open to sea-going ships by dredging, and it overlooks its own inland sea, the Alster. For these reasons it is often called the Glasgow of Germany. Like Glasgow it is robust and enterprising, and it looks to the sea; a city of wharves and warehouses, shipyards and factories. Like Glasgow, also, it is the centre of a large industrial region. Mindful of its great past as a Free City of the Hanseatic League, it likes to call itself *Hansastadt* Hamburg. It was heavily bombed in the Second World War—in one single saturation raid more bombs were dropped on Hamburg by the R.A.F. and the U.S.A.A.F. than were dropped on London in the whole war and the sea itself, soaked in oil, caught fire.

Its smaller but similar neighbour, Bremen, on the River Weser, was the supply port after 1945 for the American Zone of Germany. It was in the nineteenth century the port used by German emigrants to the United States.

Berlin grew with the power of the Electors of Brandenburg who became (1701) Kings of Prussia and (1871) Emperors of Germany. It is surrounded by poor and sandy soil, producing rye and wheat. The city itself (Greater Berlin) now cut off from West Germany, covers 340 square miles. Its population in 1939 was $4\frac{1}{4}$ million (1960, $3\frac{1}{4}$ million). As capital of the Reich, it was a rail and administrative centre. It is also a great centre of the electrical industry, light engineering, printing and publishing. Heavily bombed, West Berlin has made a spectacular recovery. It is bright and gay. Much of East Berlin—the barrier is at the Brandenburg Gate—remains unrepaired, a bleak image of another world.

The Länder

There is, however, still another system of division, the administrative division into provinces or '*lands*' (German, *länder*). These were reorganized after the Second World War and there are now ten *länder*. The most important single state is North-Rhine–Westphalia, in which live 17 million people, one-third of the total population of West Germany.

Berlin is regarded by West Germany as a *land* of the Federal Republic but it cannot be so officially. It has representatives in the *Bundestag*, but they cannot vote. Each *land* has its own parliament and government. It raises its own taxes, has its own police force and has considerable economic control within its own territory. It is comparable to a state in the United States.

Land	Capital	Population (millions)
Schleswig Holstein	Kiel	2
Hamburg		2
Lower Saxony	Hanover	$6\frac{1}{2}$
Bremen		$\frac{3}{4}$
North Rhine-Westphalia	Dusseldorf	15
Hesse	Wiesbaden	$4\frac{1}{2}$
Rhineland-Palatinate	Mainz	$3\frac{1}{2}$
Baden-Wurttemberg	Stuttgart	7
Bavaria	Munich	9
Saarland	Saarbrucken	1

Germany between the Wars

When the Kaiser abdicated, a republic was proclaimed, headed by a socialist working man, Friedrich Ebert. This republic had enormous problems to contend with.

The physical situation of Germany was serious. The country had lost 2,300,000 men killed and another 4,200,000 were wounded during the war. Communication and transport (particularly the railways) were in a bad state. Jobs for the already demobilized soldiers became ever scarcer. Food was hard to get. Allied hatred expressed itself in a continuation of the blockade for many months after the war was concluded; necessary food imports were blocked, and people starved.

It is possible that Allied enmity might have taken more active forms if it had not been for the presence of a vigorous revolutionary movement all over Europe. The Allies' fear of revolution in Germany prevented them from imposing really harsh measures. Revolution was indeed a real danger and it was the Social Democratic Party which saved the country from Communism. President Friedrich Ebert directed the brutal Gustav Noske, his Socialist Minister of Defence, to suppress all revolutionary groups. The Spartacist revolt in Berlin was crushed, and the leaders of this Communist group, Karl Liebknecht and Rosa Luxemburg, while under arrest, were murdered by the authorities. Noske carried on this work with the aid of the so-called *Freikorps*, a paramilitary organization composed of mercenary soldiers and semi-criminal elements.

The Weimar Constitution (adopted July 1919) created the machinery of a democratic state. The Constitution was called after the town where the

119

Assembly met. It provided for a two-house legislature (the *Reichstag*), a President (Ebert) and a Chancellor, and granted universal suffrage. The upper house was removed from Prussian control through the institution of a system of proportional representation. An economic council functioned, in effect, as a third house. The states or *länder* now numbered sixteen, and controlled local affairs.

The British blockade was lifted in July 1919, after the population of Germany had been reduced to near-starvation. But Allied enmity did not end there. France feared the re-creation of a powerful Germany, and did everything possible to prevent it. French fear and hatred led to the imposition of very high indemnities upon the beaten Germans. British policy, however, was to prevent French domination of the continent, and this policy worked against the attempts to reduce Germany to a minor power. It should also be noted that the burdens imposed on Germany were appreciably lighter than those of 1945; the country was undivided, and, except in the Rhineland, was unoccupied.

Party politics were confused. Six political parties emerged. The Nationalists were the old Conservatives, representing the Junkers, the militarists, the friends of monarchy and private property. The German People's Party led by Stresemann were bourgeois liberals. The old Centre Party now called itself the Christian People's Party; led by Erzberger, it favoured bourgeois democracy. The left-wing middle-class reformers called themselves the German Social Democrats. They proposed the gradual introduction of socialism. Left-wing socialists who accused the Social Democrats of betraying socialism formed the Independent Socialists. The Communists boycotted the elections.

The Weimar Republic was attacked from the left and right. It failed to cleanse Germany of the reactionary forces—Junkers, militarists, monarchists— who hated the Republic and were determined to overthrow it. Nothing was done to purge the army or the bureaucracy of those sinister forces who paid lip-service to the Weimar Constitution and, behind the republican façade, prepared for the return to autocracy and militarism. The doom of the Republic was sealed by the failure to carry out fundamental reforms in 1918–21.

The first years of the Republic were filled with reactionary propaganda and intrigue. Monarchists and nationalists blamed the defeat of Germany upon the treachery of the republicans ('stab in the back' theory) and attributed Germany's woes to the Versailles Treaty which the republicans had signed. The reactionaries assassinated two great and liberal statesmen, Rathenau and Erzberger. In 1923 Ludendorff and Hitler attempted the famous Munich *Putsch*.

Inflation and the Ruhr

More serious than political threats were economic problems. There were three unfavourable aspects of the economic situation—(*a*) business was disrupted by the war and the blockade, (*b*) there was a great deal of unemployment and (*c*) the government had to pay reparations. The imposition of heavy reparations payments was one of the prime mistakes of the peace settlement. The enormous payments were bound to create social strains in Germany and in Europe.

Inflation appeared shortly after the end of the war. In 1914, one mark equalled one shilling in value. In 1919, a mark was worth only about twopence. By 1923, it became impossible for the government to meet reparations payments, and Premier Raymond Poincaré seized this opportunity to send French troops into the Ruhr.

The occupation of the Ruhr, which was in part caused by the inflation of German currency, itself contributed to an increase in the pace of that inflation. By June, 1923, one shilling exchanged for 50,000 marks.

Within two weeks, the mark had declined in exchange value to 500,000 to the shilling. This inflation was disastrous. People starved on the streets. The small business group was wiped out completely. People on fixed incomes, especially pensioners, were left destitute. The people suffered and the middle class was all but wiped out. But some groups profited. The inflation enabled the German Government to wipe out its internal debts by paying in the worthless marks. American capital did well in speculation, as did the top financial capital of Germany itself.

German recovery

In 1924, the Dawes Plan reduced the size of reparations payments and extended loans to Germany. In 1925 she succeeded in negotiating the famous Locarno Treaties with Briand, the conciliatory French Foreign Minister. Germany and France agreed to remain at peace; their frontier was guaranteed by themselves and also by Britain, Italy and Belgium; they agreed to settle all disputes peaceably. Germany was now permitted to enter the League of Nations. From 1925 to 1929, Gustav Stresemann exercised a strong influence in every cabinet. Under his guidance, Germany supported co-operation with the Allies. The German economic recovery was remarkable: industry revived, unemployment disappeared and production was increased. It seemed that Germany's internal problems had at last been solved. In four years (1926–30) Germany built one and a half million houses, and built skyscrapers and post offices and an athletic stadium—all with other people's money.

The illusion did not last long. The short period of prosperity ended with the collapse of the American stock market in 1929. American financiers halted their loans to Germany and called in those that they could. German banks, in turn, stopped their investments, and financial failure followed in both Germany and Austria. All countries raised their tariff walls against foreign goods. The resulting depression set the stage for the rise of Adolf Hitler.

Adolf Hitler was an abnormal man who rose to power in an abnormal situation and created an abnormal régime. To say this, however, is not to explain or dismiss the man and the phenomena. Hitler was a product of the First World War and the depression that followed it. He had been, before the war, a would-be painter (although some have labelled him a paper hanger) and had had an unsuccessful career in Austria, where he developed extreme anti-Semitic views. He welcomed the coming of the war; he thanked heaven for giving him the opportunity to be alive while Germany was at war. As a corporal, Hitler had a good record and won the Iron Cross. After the war, he apparently was in contact with the *Freikorps*, which was plundering and 'suppressing Communism'. In 1923, Hitler and Ludendorff attempted a *putsch* in Munich. It failed, and Hitler was sentenced to five years in prison. He served only five or six months, and in prison lived in some comfort.

During his prison term, Hitler wrote *Mein Kampf*, a work which detailed the political philosophy and programme of 'National Socialism' and became the Nazi Bible. Man, he asserted in this work, is a fighting animal, and the state is, therefore, a fighting unit. The fighting ability of such a unit depends upon its purity in a racial sense. Pacifism is the worst of sins, and brute force must and should triumph. These principles appealed to many elements. The idea of a 'great Nordic state' including all the Germans in Europe; the idea of eliminating all 'impure races' including the 'mongrel' French and the Jews; the pledge to repudiate the peace settlement—these were designed to appeal to racism and nationalism generally. The suppression of Communism interested big business. The promise to abolish unearned incomes and to embark upon a programme of pensions, social insurances and agrarian reforms appealed to workers and farmers. Hitler included in his approach to politics an appeal to emotion as well as to intellect, utilizing highly developed methods of mob oratory. He represented an appeal to force and discipline—Germany under him was described as a society for sergeant-majors.

The success of such a man and such a programme depended upon the desperate situation of Germany after 1932. With national bankruptcy and a renewal of depression, Communism began to grow. By 1931 over 6 million Germans were unemployed. In the presidential elections of 1932, Hindenburg secured 19 million votes, as against Hitler's 11 million and the Communist Thalmann's 5 million. The weak government of the nearly senile Hindenburg (now both deaf and half-blind and aged 85) was unable to suppress the Nazis. When Franz von Papen, with support from big business and the major newspapers, seized power in Prussia, the die was cast. Thyssen and Krupp, the businessmen, financed Hitler, and made it possible for him to equip a private army, the Storm Troopers (*S.A.*), clad in brown shirts, and an *élite* bodyguard (*S.S.*). Business elements, although they despised him, needed a fanatic and a gangster like Hitler to wipe out the Reds; they would, they thought, use a lowbrow to do their dirty work, and then get rid of him. They mistook their man. In January 1933 Hindenburg appointed Hitler Chancellor of the Reich (Prime Minister).

The Nazis then either arranged or at least profited from the burning of the *Reichstag* building (28 February 1933) as an excuse for terrorism during the elections of 5 March 1933. They charged the arson to the Communists, and with the support of Hindenburg they began a methodical suppression of that group. In an election policed by Storm Troopers, they managed to win a bare majority of seats in the Reichstag. It sufficed. All other parties were outlawed and a total dictatorship was established.

The Nazi seizure of power resulted in other casualties, too. The following year (30 June 1934) Hitler directed a great blood purge of the Nazi movement itself. Nazis who, like General von Schleicher, Ernst Roehm and Gregor Strasser wanted constructive social reforms, were shot, along with many others within and outside the movement. This was the 'Night of the Long Knives' when Hitler flew around Germany in a private plane, superintending the murders. And even before this purge, free trade unions had been destroyed, converted into organizations controlled by the government. The right to strike was abolished. Crushing attacks were made on labour leaders, on intellectuals critical of the régime, on Protestant and Catholic clergy. Although a concordat was signed with the Pope in 1933, friction with the Catholic Church continued until the end of the Nazi régime. Cardinal Faulhaber of Munich was as critical of the Nazis as Pastor Niemöller. The Vatican denounced German racialism and paganism.

Wholesale slaughter of Jews began, partly on grounds of race, partly on the grounds that they had come in from the Slav East and were Communists in disguise (Jewish-Bolshevists), partly because they controlled many newspapers and thus influenced opinion, partly because their wealth and savings could be seized. This was the greatest of all Hitler's many crimes against humanity, the most vicious deed by any people in this vicious half-century. Under the direction of Joseph Goebbels, the crippled Rhinelander whose wife had been brought up by Jewish fosterparents, a stream of racial propaganda poured out from press and radio. The state was ruled by secret police (the *Gestapo*).

In 1934 the separate German states were abolished. Hindenburg died in the same year, Hitler became President of the Third Reich, and took the title of Führer. *Ein volk, ein reich, ein führer.* (One people, one state, one leader.)

The Nazis instituted Four-Year Plans to make Germany self-sufficient. Production was increased, and a limited new prosperity did occur in farms and industries. But the regimentation was designed to produce guns, not butter. War seemed the logical end of the aggressive Nazi foreign policy. The German people were promised an eventual plenty—when they reached the Urals. The anti-Russian policy had a real influence in the West, for many in powerful

123

positions in Britain and France sympathized with such a policy and supported it. The hatred of Communism was an important part of the policy of appeasement, which did so much to strengthen Hitler.

Hitler received continuing internal support in large part because of his diplomatic successes in foreign policy. A combination of luck and shrewdness carried him forward. Nationalism was satisfied by defiance of the West. In the six years from 1933 to 1939 Hitler made six territorial gains without resort to war.

(*a*) When, in 1935, the people of the Saar area voted overwhelmingly to return to Germany, the vote appeared to be a demonstration of Hitler's popularity. Hitler realized the problem of the other major powers of the West, which were caught between their dislike for the Nazis and their dislike for the Communists. Feeling that he could defy them with impunity, Hitler announced that he intended to rearm Germany in defiance of the Versailles Treaty.

(*b*) By 1936, he felt strong enough to occupy the Rhineland with his troops. This move was a gamble, for if France had opposed it by force, the Germans would have had to retreat (as, indeed, they were under orders to do if they met opposition), and Hitler's régime would have fallen. The success of the occupation was a complete triumph for Hitler, over internal Nazi opposition as well as over other powers. He had already removed any threat from Poland by concluding a treaty with it (1934), after France had seemed to deny its Polish ally any help against the Nazis. Hitler drove a wedge between France and Britain by concluding a naval agreement with Britain in 1935, by which Germany was not to extend its navy beyond 35 per cent of that of Britain.

(*c*) On 11 March 1938, Germany forcibly incorporated into the Reich the independent state of Austria, with its seven million citizens, thus obtaining the great city of Vienna, a key-point in European communications, and rich resources of iron and timber.

(*d*) By the Munich Agreement made by Great Britain, France, Germany and Italy on 30 September 1938, large parts of Czechoslovakia inhabited by about $3\frac{1}{2}$ million people, mostly Sudeten Germans, but including at least 800,000 Czechs, were taken over by Germany. Hitler assured Neville Chamberlain, the British Prime Minister, that this ' was the last of his territorial claims in Europe'.

(*e*) In March 1939, Hitler broke his pledges and annexed the Czech provinces of Bohemia and Moravia, making them a German 'Protectorate'. He also occupied the state of Slovakia on the day after its independence had been proclaimed, and gave it purely nominal freedom. Czechoslovakia was thus completely disrupted, and its heavy industries, including the great Skoda armament factories at Pilsen, passed to Germany.

(*f*) On 22 March 1939, Germany demanded the return of the territory of Memel from Lithuania, who surrendered this, its only port, on the same day.

The annexation of the Czech territories in March 1939 marked the end of the policy of appeasement, which had made these successes possible.

On 1 September 1939, German troops invaded Poland. On 3 September 1939, Britain and France declared war on Nazi Germany.

After six years of war, Hitler shot himself outside his bunker in Berlin (30 April 1945). Dr Goebbels and his wife also committed suicide with their leader, having first poisoned their six children. On 7 May 1945, Germany surrendered unconditionally.

Post-war Germany

Allied occupation

In 1945 it was planned to occupy Germany until a peace treaty could be signed. The treaty would, it was hoped, settle the problems of Central Europe, and

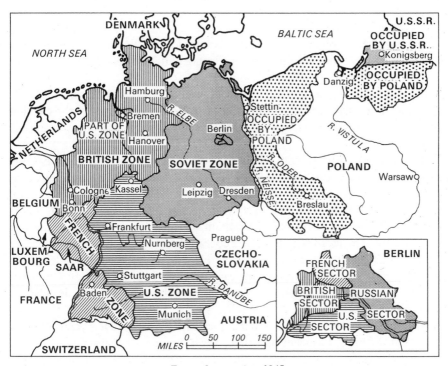

Zones of occupation, 1945.

create a peaceful Germany. Today there is still no peace treaty and no sign of one. The internal division of Germany today is the result of a series of one-sided decisions—and of the Cold War between West and East. Germany is thus paying the price of its own folly under Hitler, and of world tensions.

Largely under American pressure, she has been permitted to rearm and to become a Western military base against the U.S.S.R.

In accordance with the decisions of the Teheran and Yalta Conferences, Germany was divided into four zones of occupation under military government: the American Zone in the south (41,000 square miles and 17 million people); a British Zone in the north-west (37,000 square miles and 23 million people); a French Zone in the south-west (16,000 square miles and 6 million people); and a Russian Zone in the east, the mainly agricultural regions (41,000 square miles and 17 million people).

In 1949 a Federal Republic (*Bundesrepublik*) incorporating the three Western zones, was established with a parliament at Bonn. This development was followed by the creation of the German Democratic Republic (D.D.R.) in the Soviet Zone. From the four zones, two new states thus emerged, each claiming to be the real Germany and neither accepting the idea of permanent partition.

The Federal Republic

The Federal Republic now has a population of 58 million and covers an area of 94,700 square miles (compare Great Britain and Northern Ireland with $51\frac{1}{2}$ million in 1961, and 94,200 square miles).

In 1946 and 1947 the Germans were allowed to re-establish local and 'land' (provincial) governments, and the Basic Law of 1949 provided for the election of a Federal President as head of state every five years, and for a bicameral system.

The most important organ, the *Bundestag* (Chamber of Deputies) has 400 members elected every four years by direct suffrage, like the House of Commons. It is responsible for legislation and for supervision over the Federal executive. The *Bundesrat* was set up to represent the *länder*, or states, and is designed to ensure co-operation by them in legislation and administration; compare the American Senate. The Federal Government, under its powerful head, the Chancellor (from 1949 to 1963 Dr Adenauer), is responsible for the political initiative and represents the executive power of the state. A Constitutional Court decides disputes over the Constitution and the legality of legislation.

The most important political parties are the Christian Democratic Union (C.D.U.) with its Bavarian associate, the Christian Socialists (C.S.U.)—a Conservative and Christian party; the Social Democratic Party (*Sozial Demokratische Partei Deutschlands* or S.P.D.), a Labour Party seeking nationalization of the Ruhr industries but anti-Communist; the Free Democratic Party (F.D.P.), a Liberal and middle-class Party; and the German Party (*Deutsche Partei* or D.P.) which is Nationalist and Conservative. The Communist Party (K.P.D.) was declared unconstitutional in 1956. In the 1957 election the right-wing C.D.U./C.S.U. secured just over half the votes and the S.P.D. (Socialist

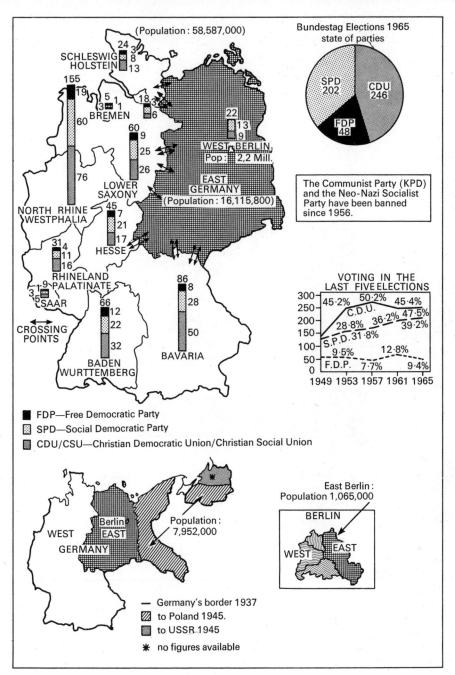

(Population: 58,587,000)

**Bundestag Elections 1965
state of parties**

SPD 202
CDU 246
FDP 48

SCHLESWIG HOLSTEIN
24 3
8
13

155
19
60
76
BREMEN
5 1
3 1
18 3
6

60
9
25
26
LOWER SAXONY

22
13
9
WEST BERLIN
Pop: 2,2 Mill.

EAST GERMANY
(Population: 16,115,800)

The Communist Party (KPD) and the Neo-Nazi Socialist Party have been banned since 1956.

NORTH RHINE WESTPHALIA
45 7
21
17
HESSE

31 4
11
16
RHINELAND PALATINATE

3 1 9
5
SAAR

CROSSING POINTS

66
12
22
32
BADEN WURTTEMBERG

86 8
28
50
BAVARIA

VOTING IN THE LAST FIVE ELECTIONS

300
250
200
150
100
50
0

45·2% 50·2% 45·4%
C.D.U.
28·8% 36·2% 47·5%
39·2%
S.P.D. 31·8%
9·5% 12·8%
F.D.P. 7·7% 9·4%

1949 1953 1957 1961 1965

■ FDP—Free Democratic Party
▨ SPD—Social Democratic Party
▨ CDU/CSU—Christian Democratic Union/Christian Social Union

Berlin
WEST EAST
GERMANY

Population: 7,952,000

East Berlin: Population 1,065,000

BERLIN
WEST EAST

— Germany's border 1937
▨ to Poland 1945.
▨ to USSR 1945
✳ no figures available

In 1965 the C.D.U. had 246 seats, the S.P.D. 202 and the F.D.P. 48. It was all but impossible for a S.P.D.–F.D.P. Coalition to govern with a majority of 4; Chancellor Erhard's position was undermined by the criticisms of Adenauer and by the opposition of the Bavarian brand of the C.D.U. In December 1966 a 'grand coalition' was formed, with Dr. Kurt-Georg Kiesinger as Chancellor; the S.P.D. were given 9 out of 19 Cabinet seats, including Foreign Affairs, held by Willy Brandt. The map shows the representation of each party in the various Lander. By the Potsdam Agreement in 1945 the territories east of the Oder–Neisse line (see bottom left-hand corner) were placed under Polish and Soviet administration pending the conclusion of a peace treaty.

A brass band, familiar sight in Germany.

leader Ollenhauer) was the main opposition party. In the 1961 elections there were 241 Christian Democrats, 190 Social Democrats and 66 Free Democrats in the Bundestag.

The Federal Republic has closely associated itself with the defence policy of the Western Powers and the movement for European unity. In 1949, it became a member of the O.E.E.C. and, in 1950–51, of the European Council at Strasbourg. In 1951, the treaty founding the European Coal and Steel Community (E.C.S.C.) was signed and in the following year the treaty founding the E.D.C. (European Defence Community). In 1954 the Paris Agreements provided for the inclusion of Germany in W.E.U. (Western European Union) and in NATO and are regarded as a preliminary treaty ending the state of war

128

with the Western Powers. Germany undertook to accept the principles of NATO, while the Western Powers agreed to support the reunification of Germany. Because of the division of the country the Federal Republic could not become a member of the United Nations Organization but joined the ten special organizations.

This development has been much debated, since any rearming of Germany (for Western defence against Russia) might lead to a return to 1914 or 1939. Equally, so long as Germany was occupied (and therefore defended) by the West, and had no army of its own to maintain, it was able to devote more money to non-military purposes, whereas Britain, France and the United States of America, although they had won the war, spent much of their money on troops with which to defend Germany. The solution has been to rearm Germany within the framework of NATO.

Diplomatic relations with the Soviet Union were resumed in 1955, but there is no diplomatic recognition of the German Democratic Republic (D.D.R.) which is not considered a foreign state nor as entitled to have its government represent Germans.

The Adenauer Government at the Messina Conference in 1955 and at Rome in 1957 agreed to the setting up of the European Economic Community.

The phenomenal economic recovery (the 'German miracle') began with the currency reform of 1948. This was designed to reduce inflation, to curb black-marketing and hoarding, and to give people renewed confidence in their money. It was followed by the ending of the dismantling of industries. These reforms were mainly the work of Professor Ludwig Erhard, then Vice-Chancellor and Minister for Economic Affairs. By 1956, therefore, the gross national product was 125 per cent higher than the 1949 figure and in 1958, for the first time since the war, West Germany replaced Britain as the world's second biggest exporter of manufactured goods (after the United States), and had also become Britain's most important market in Europe. In 1956 crude steel production, at 23 million tons, already exceeded that of Britain by 2 million tons. Despite the almost total devastation, Germany is now the most prosperous state in Europe. West Germany has also, since the war, absorbed 12 of the 16 million German-speaking refugees. One person in every five in West Germany is either a refugee or a child of refugee parents.

Berlin

Berlin is unique. And again there are two Berlins. West Berlin has 2.2 million and East Berlin 1.1 million inhabitants. The former is now the largest industrial city of West Germany but it is not incorporated in the Federal Republic, since it is surrounded by Soviet territory. Much the greater part of its trade is now conducted with the West. It is the centre through which refugees from the East, now numbering many millions, have passed.

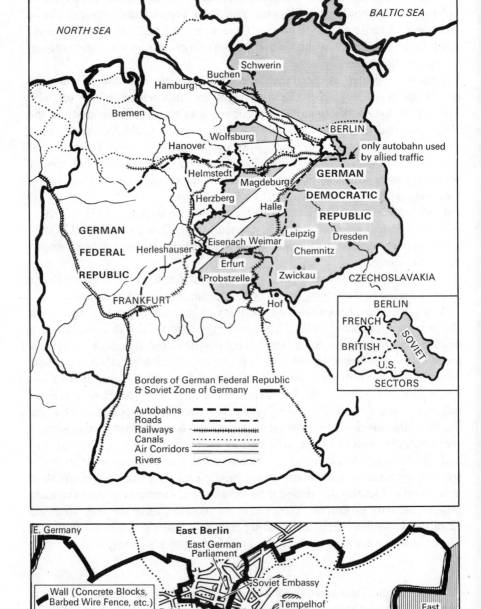

Lines of communication to Berlin from the West.

The vulnerability of its position was demonstrated by the blockade of 1948–49 when all road and rail traffic from the West was cut off. All supplies had to be flown in from the West. It was fed for a year from the West by an airlift, in which planes were arriving every 30 seconds. The D.D.R. has little influence on opinion in Berlin, and in the 1958 election the Communist Party (S.E.D.) failed to get one seat on the city council, while the S.P.D. polled 52 per cent and the C.D.U. 37 per cent of the votes. The former mayor of West Berlin, Willy Brandt, is a prominent figure and was in 1965 an unsuccessful candidate for the Chancellorship of Germany.

East Berlin is being built up as the capital of East Germany and it is here that the revolution of 1953, which was suppressed by the Russians, began. The question of Berlin had not caused trouble for several years but on 27 November 1958 the Soviet Government said that it intended to end the present situation; this led to the movement towards a 'Summit' meeting.

The German Democratic Republic (D.D.R.)

The D.D.R. was set up in 1949 with a population of approximately 17 million and 41,571 square miles of territory, as a unitary state with a strictly centralized administration. It was governed by a President of the State (Wilhelm Pieck), a Chief Minister (Otto Grotewohl) and a 'People's Chamber' (*Volkskammer*), while the leadership was concentrated in the hands of the German Socialist Unity Party (*Sozialistische Einheitspartei Deutschlands* or S.E.D.).

The former Soviet Zone bore the brunt of the programme of dismantling. Large estates have been broken up, 85 per cent of industry has been nationalized and the degree of state control over the individual is far greater than in the Nazi period. Since 1948 production has been progressively tied up with that of the Soviet *bloc*.

Since 1949 the Constitution of East Germany has been changed on a number of occasions. On President Pieck's death in 1960, the office of President was abolished, and a Council of State set up under the chairmanship of Walter Ulbricht, First Secretary of the Communist Party. Grotewohl remains Prime Minister, but, as with all the 'people's democracies', real power rests with the chairman. Elections to the People's Chamber are purely nominal: the voters are presented with a printed list of candidates, with no alternatives. In all essentials, East Germany is governed as a Russian satellite state.

East Germany is a totalitarian state, in which there is no freedom of opinion. The People's Police number 250,000, and are equipped with tanks, mortars and machine guns. The spontaneous revolt in Berlin in 1953 showed the helplessness of the population in the face of modern tanks and, during the Hungarian revolt in 1956, there was no sign of any anti-Soviet movement in the D.D.R. Economic and administrative wisdom has not been the strong point of the government; there are pronounced signs of progress (the average wage in

131

1959=95 marks=approximately £7 10s.), and education is far more heavily subsidized than in West Germany, but the government hopes of a higher standard of living than in the Federal Republic have not been realized.

The East German Government has not been recognized by the West. East and West Germany are, in fact, two distinct states, with different currency systems, different stamps, different police and laws. If you send a letter by airmail from Bonn to East Berlin, it does not go to the Tempelhof airport in West

| GERMAN FEDERAL REPUBLIC ::::::: | | GERMAN DEMOCRATIC REPUBLIC ▨▨▨ |
| Germany's border 1937 --- | to USSR 1945 ≣≣≣ | to Poland 1945. ||||||||| |

The two Germanies.

Berlin and from there the extra 1,000 yards over the sector boundary, but makes the astonishing detour via Frankfurt-on-Main to Prague in Czecho-slovakia and from there to the airport in East Berlin. If you want to telephone from West Berlin to friends in the Eastern sector, you can do this only over the line Frankfurt-on-Main to Leipzig in the Soviet Zone and from there to East Berlin. The Berlin subway is run by East Germany, since the station that supplies the power is in East Berlin, but there is great care taken to awaken any Western traveller who has fallen asleep lest he finds himself waking up in

Soviet-controlled territory. For 800 miles a rusty barbed-wire fence, dotted with 60-foot watch-towers, cuts off East Germany from West. Yet all Germans want a single reunited state. They still have the same national flag, of red, black and gold, the same language, and the memory of a common and stirring history.

The Eastern territories

These territories consist of East Germany beyond the Oder and Neisse rivers (i.e. Pomerania and Silesia) and East Prussia. The administration of the area east of the Oder-Neisse line was handed over to the Poles at the end of hostilities and they expelled the majority of Germans. The D.D.R. recognized the territory as a permanent part of Poland in 1950; to this the Western Powers have not agreed.

Adenauer and his successors

Konrad Adenauer (1876–1967)

West German politics were dominated after the creation of the Federal Republic in 1949 by the figure of Adenauer, whose position of authority in some ways resembled that of de Gaulle in France.

Dr Adenauer was born at Cologne on 5 January 1876, the son of a court clerk who was a devoted Catholic, as his son became. He was quite poor. He studied law at the universities of Freiburg and Bonn, and then climbed rapidly in local government, becoming chief burgomaster (Lord Mayor) of Cologne in 1917, a post in which he showed many of the characteristics he was to show as Chancellor.

He remained in the post continuously until 1933, when he was removed for refusing to hoist the Nazi flag on the town hall. After a commission of inquiry had failed to substantiate accusations of bribery and separatism, he was allowed to live quietly through the Nazi period, except for brief periods of arrest in 1934 and 1944. He wrote in his *Memoirs*:

> At the end of September 1944, I was re-arrested and sent to the Gestapo prison at Brauweiler, near Cologne, after a rather exciting escape from the concentration camp on the Cologne Fair Ground, where I had been taken during the aftermath of the rising against Hitler of 20 July 1944.
>
> The commissar in charge of the prison asked me on arrival please not to take my own life, as this would only cause trouble for him. I asked him what made him think that I might take my life. He replied that as I was now nearly 70 years old I had nothing more to expect from life, and that it therefore seemed quite likely that I would put an end to it.
>
> I told him not to worry. I would not cause him any trouble.

When American troops arrived in Cologne in March 1945 the once beautiful Rhineland city was in ruins. Of its 59,000 houses and public buildings only

300 were unscarred by war. The city had no water, gas or electricity. Of the city's 780,000 inhabitants, only 120,000 were left. Germany as a whole was destitute. By October 1945 Cologne had fallen under the occupation zone of the British, with whom Dr Adenauer soon quarrelled. The British Government accused him of 'incompetency' and of a 'lack of energy', which seems hard to accept; once again Dr Adenauer was dismissed as mayor of Cologne and banished from the city. He was dismissed, he says, because of the friendliness of the British Labour Government for the German Socialists, and 'because of the strong ties I was assumed to have with the Americans'.

He set about building up a successor to the old Centre Party, starting with the Roman Catholic Rhinelanders but gradually gaining the support of Protestants, and thus building up a party big enough to defeat the Social Democrats, whose main strength was cut off in the Soviet Zone. The result was the Christian Democratic Union, of which Dr Adenauer became chairman in 1946. It won the first Federal elections in 1949, and he was elected Chancellor (Premier) of West Germany by the Bundestag. When his son asked him later if he had voted for himself, Dr Adenauer replied, not untypically in the view of his friends, 'Since I was determined to accept the appointment I should have felt it sheer hypocrisy not to have voted for myself'.

He worked hard to establish Germany by stages as a sovereign country and in 1951, when it was permitted to set up a Foreign Ministry of its own again, he became Foreign Minister as well as Chancellor. In this dual capacity he can claim most of the credit for the achievement of sovereignty in 1955, only ten years after the surrender. He had won the trust of the Allies in record time. One of his biggest single achievements just before this was to get Parliament to approve large sums of money for restitution to Jews who suffered under the Nazi régime, and for the State of Israel.

Throughout his Chancellorship, Adenauer's dominant idea was the reunification of Germany, East and West. He pressed this repeatedly on the Western Powers, and insisted that the first requisite for reunification was the holding of free, all-German elections, to be followed by the formation of an all-German Government and the signing of a peace treaty.

Although he persuaded the German Parliament to make Bonn the Federal Capital, during his first two terms in office he paid frequent visits to West Berlin. This helped to discount the stories that he did not really believe in German reunification lest it bring huge gains in political strength to his Social Democratic opponents. His methods often annoyed his supporters as well as his opponents, and throughout his political life he had to face charges of caring more for the Rhineland and a 'little Europe' than for the national interests of Germany and—latterly—its reunification. In spite of this, he rarely had to yield to opposition, and in 1957 his party was the first to win an absolute majority in a democratic German Parliament.

What did Adenauer do for Germany?

In five main respects Dr Adenauer's Chancellorship was important.

First, he sought to re-establish Germany's honour and reputation. When he became Chancellor, Germany was in defeat and disillusionment. His first concern was to end the occupation, to stop the dismantling of industry (which Britain was urging), to obtain an amnesty for minor Nazi offenders, and to gain independent control of foreign affairs. In return, he offered the Allies a firm commitment to the West, and a military contribution. The result was the Petersberg Agreement of November 1949. He was helped by Russian rearmament of East Germany and by the Korean war and immensely helped by the Marshall Plan. When he left office, he had established an effective Government in West Germany and obtained for his country as full a measure of sovereignty as possible, given the present division of Germany. The Federal Republic is now securely integrated into the Western community as a free and equal partner. And his party rested on a balance of political forces: an alliance of agrarian Catholics, urban conservatives and middle-class liberals, 'the Adenauer balance'.

Second, he presided over the rebuilding of the West German economy. French Foreign Minister Robert Schuman's proposal in 1950 for a European coal and steel community was eagerly accepted by Dr Adenauer as the first step towards the permanent integration of Germany into the West European economy. He did everything possible to encourage the movement towards the economic and political unity of Europe.

Third, he won a measure of military security for the Federal Republic. With the growth of Russian threats to Berlin and the failure of Four-Power negotiations, the active build-up of the *Bundeswehr* (the German Army) became essential to Western European defence. In 1952 Germany was accepted as a member of a military union of five countries. When, in August 1954, the French National Assembly failed to ratify the European Defence Community, Dr Adenauer felt great bitterness towards France's Prime Minister, M. Mendès-France, and contemplated retirement from politics. In October 1954, however, he signed the Paris Agreement (largely Sir Anthony Eden's achievement), by which Germany acquired full sovereignty and a national army within the framework of Western European Union. In January 1958 Dr Adenauer told the *Bundestag* (the German Parliament) that he was prepared to equip the German Army with nuclear weapons. He called the Russian plan for a nuclear-free zone in Central Europe 'only a strategem to seize control of Europe'.

Fourth, he bound his country with France in a treaty of friendship. When General de Gaulle came to power in 1958, Dr Adenauer at first viewed him with distrust; but their first meeting at Colombey-les-deux-Eglises broke the ice. The failure of the Free Trade Area, impatience with Britain's attitude towards the Common Market, the death in 1959 of U.S. Secretary of State John Foster Dulles, and suspension of Anglo-American endeavours to seek a settlement with Russia all drew Dr Adenauer increasingly close to France—at the expense of relations with Britain. Mr Macmillan's Moscow visit in 1959 seemed to confirm Dr Adenauer's suspicions of Anglo-Saxon untrustworthiness. The Chancellor said: 'Germany and France are leaders on the Continent.' The return of the Saar to Germany in 1957, and its absorption into the German economy by 1959, removed the last obstacle to Franco-German reconciliation.

And fifth, while reunification still dominates political thought and action in the Federal Republic, the goal is no nearer realization. Dr Adenauer's central principle remained distrust of the Russians. In practice, therefore, West German foreign policy in the Adenauer era was firm, uncompromising and unimaginative. The Chancellor emphasized, time and again, that the West must not be fooled by any changes in Soviet tactics.

Dr Adenauer was 87 when he retired from the Chancellorship in 1963—an office to which he had been re-elected in 1953, 1957, 1961. Since 1961 there had been some criticism of his long 'reign' and of his rigidity and autocratic habits—in which he resembled de Gaulle; and in the 1961 elections Dr Adenauer's party, the Christian Democratic Union, lost its absolute majority.

The end of the economic boom, a string of Socialist successes in *länder* elections, and a series of political scandals resulting in an intricate government reshuffle at the end of 1962, forced Dr Adenauer to fix a firm date for his retirement (September 1963). He died in 1967.

Adenauer was strongly criticized for his arrogance towards his colleagues, for his pro-Western policy, and for his cunning—'the old fox'. But his achievement is striking. France and Germany are no longer foes. The European Common Market has brought economic unity to much of Western Europe; and by joining the North Atlantic Treaty Organization West Germany has sided militarily with countries it fought twice within a generation. To the German people, Dr Adenauer's long rule brought prosperity and a sense of moral resurgence from the dark hopeless days after the war; and not least he sowed the seeds of democracy in his native land. Winston Churchill described him as 'the greatest German statesman since Bismarck'.

Ludwig Erhard

Adenauer was succeeded as Chancellor in 1963 (re-elected in 1965) by Ludwig Erhard, the professor of economics who got the credit for the West German 'miracle'. Until June 1948 economic controls were tight, goods were rationed, 'black-market' rackets were rife and cigarettes served as a form of currency.

In July 1948 the controls disappeared. If Erhard got the credit for this, the facts behind the facts are perhaps harder to establish. There are Allied observers who maintain that the end of restrictions was planned by Anglo-American experts and that Erhard at first reacted with horror. Whatever the truth, the reform had immediate success. Overnight the shops filled up with hoarded goods. People began to work, buy and sell. After 1949, when he joined Adenauer's first Cabinet as Minister of Economics, Professor Erhard presided over the tremendous economic recovery which followed decontrol, and he preached that only free trade and a free market—and hard work—made it possible.

Erhard was a sharp contrast with Adenauer. Chubby in build and in manner genial, he was in fact shy and cautious; he abandoned Dr Adenauer's impressive symbol of authority, the elaborate police escort, with sirens screaming and lights flashing, that forced cars off the road as the Chancellor drove from his home at Rhoendorf, to the capital, Bonn. Dr Erhard drove unescorted in his official Mercedes 300 accompanied by one detective in the car. Often he used to stop at the city market to check prices or make purchases but his efforts to establish a popular image were marred by a number of peculiar contradictions.

He built a $500,000 official residence, thus distinguishing himself from his predecessor, who had no official residence but lived in his own home at Rhoendorf. He restored for his own use Hermann Goering's private train, reckoned to be the most luxurious in the world, with such lavish appointments as a marble bath-tub. And, while opposing increases in wages and prices, he raised telephone charges steeply.

The fact that the 66-year-old Dr Ludwig Erhard had been elected Chancellor in 1963 by 279 out of 484 votes in the *Bundestag* was mainly because the C.D.U. Deputies felt that only he could guarantee their return to the *Bundestag* in 1965. In the last year of Adenauer's 'reign', he was seen as the old man's successor, though not by Adenauer himself, who treated him with scorn. But to the public, Dr Erhard was the symbol of continuity and the guarantor of economic prosperity; both in politics and economics he was far more liberal than Adenauer. He was re-elected Chancellor in September, 1965.

West German Elections

	Seats		Votes		% age	
	1961	1965	1961	1965	1961	1965
C.D.U. — C.S.U. (Christian Democrats)	242	246	14,298,372	15,524,067	45	47
S.P.D. (Social Democrats)	190	202	11,427,355	12,813,185	36	39
F.D.P. (Free Democrats)	67	48	4,028,766	3,096,736	12	9
Others	—	—	1,796,409	1,178,748	6	4

He brought new emphases in foreign policy; he was less close to France than was Adenauer. He had always pleaded for an outward-looking Europe and backed the Free Trade Area project before agreement on the E.E.C. was reached, but E.E.C. made slower progress in 1964 and 1965 than before. In December 1963 Erhard was a guest of President Johnson on his ranch in Texas; and his activities during the first six months of 1964 included official visits to all the capitals of the member-countries of the European Common Market, as well as to Britain, Canada, the United States and Denmark. The Queen visited Germany in May 1965, the first royal visit in 50 years. At the same time, the replacement of Adenauer by Erhard improved German-American and German-British relations. The death of U.S. Secretary of State Dulles in 1959 and the retirement of President Eisenhower in 1960 had marked the passing of Adenauer's true friends in the West.

The improvement was not merely a question of personalities but also of policies. The views of the British and West German Governments moved closer together: for example, on the key issues of the projected NATO mixed-manned nuclear naval force, the so-called M.L.F. (multilateral force). After Dr Adenauer's departure, the Bonn Government became more enthusiastic about the M.L.F. The most conspicuous difference between the Adenauer and Erhard administrations, however, was Dr Erhard's cautious flirtation with the Soviet satellites. This was part of a long-term plan to isolate East Germany by gradually improving relations with other members of the Communist world. Trade missions, which are in fact only thinly disguised diplomatic representation, were exchanged with Poland, Hungary, Romania and Bulgaria. Both Dr Erhard and his Foreign Minister Gerhard Schroeder believed that the threat of closer West German relations with Communist China, and the approaches to the Soviet satellites, could be used to promote Russian action on Dr Erhard's other major foreign-policy objective: the reunification of Germany. In his 14-year rule, Dr Adenauer talked much about reunification but actually did little. His foreign-policy priorities had been Germany's relations with the United States, the unity of Western Europe, and the Franco-German partnership. To Dr Erhard the world looked very different.

But in domestic affairs, which was thought to be his strength, Erhard was oddly less successful; and certainly much less successful as Chancellor than he had been as Minister of Economics. Prices and wages went up much faster than industrial productivity; the shortage of labour increasingly put a brake on expansion. The rise in prices resulting from a rapidly growing consumption began to hamper the export drive. Productivity in industry is still rising, but at a much slower rate than before. In 1965 the G.N.P. (gross national product) rose by 8.4 per cent (it rose by 9.6 per cent in 1964), industrial production rose by 6 per cent (in 1964 9.2 per cent). Dr Erhard, generally considered as the principal promoter of the German 'economic miracle', was also the principal exponent of economic 'orthodoxy'. The professor ceased to be a miracle-worker. Where once there had been five available jobs for every available workman and unskilled foreign workers poured in, now it was 1 to 1 and mutterings were heard about the foreigners. Growth slowed down; there were balance of payments problems; confidence fell.

There were other problems troubling Erhard. The half-million-strong German Army resented the control over it exercised by civilian politicians; and some generals spoke out and were dismissed. But one point they complained of was certainly valid: the German Air Force equipped itself with 700 American Starfighters, and in five years 65 of them crashed. There was a natural hue-and-cry over this; and there was also criticism of the fact that Dr Erhard's Defence Minister, von Hassel, permitted and indeed encouraged N.C.O.s and officers to become trade union members. There were signs, too, of a resurgence of a Nazi spirit, in the success of the extremist National Democratic Party in *land* (State) elections. In 1966 they polled 7.9 per cent in Hesse and 7.4 per cent in Bavaria; in 1967 they polled 7 per cent in Lower Saxony; they hope to have representatives in the *Bundestag* (the national Parliament) in 1969. Their success seemed at least the final proof of a loss of confidence in Dr Erhard. He had never been a great orator. Adenauer had never thought him a good administrator. He resigned in October 1966 to allow a coalition government to be formed of the two major parties, because of the budget deficit and the fear of a slump, and because the margin between the parties was too small to allow effective government.

Kurt-Georg Kiesinger

Kurt-George Kiesinger (C.D.U.) became Chancellor and Willy Brandt, the mayor of West Berlin, who had been the unsuccessful S.D.P. candidate for the Chancellorship in 1965, became Vice-Chancellor and Foreign Minister. Kiesinger is a man of great charm, and a distinguished orator. He was a member of the Nazi Party in the Hitler period but has 'lived down' his past, and since the formation of the coalition his party (the C.D.U.) has won easily in the various *land* elections, a sign of popular support for his largely non-partisan policies. But the price of consensus is—in Germany as elsewhere—unrest among the young, especially in Berlin.

The strongest figure in his Government is Franz-Joseph Strauss, Minister of Finance and leader of the Bavarian wing of the C.D.U.

Willy Brandt

He was born in 1914, in Lubeck, as Herbert Karl Frahm. His writings in Socialist newspapers made him unpopular with the Nazis, and in 1933 he fled to Norway, using the pseudonym which has become the name by which he is known. He returned to Berlin in 1945 as a Norwegian citizen with the rank of major, and did not become a German citizen again until 1948. He entered politics and was elected mayor of Berlin in 1957.

Herr Brandt was identified with the effort of isolated Berlin to continue as a major part of a free and democratic West Germany. Ever since the blockade of 1948–49, Berliners have been very much aware of their vulnerability. This was heightened when in 1961 the Wall dividing East Berlin from West Berlin was built. All West Germans—whatever their party allegiance—are unanimous in the desire to see it removed. But by accepting the Vice-Chancellorship in 'the grand coalition', Brandt clearly does not see any early prospects of Socialist victory in West Germany.

In Kiesinger and Brandt, West Germany has two able and democratically-minded statesmen. They lead a people who are skilful, industrious and thorough and who are now, in their membership of NATO and E.C.S.C., proving to be good Europeans.

In the arrangements for the 'Six' (the Common Market), in the joint role in NATO, and in the close links between France and Germany, it looks as if Western Europeans are at last genuinely seeking to live in peace.

QUESTIONS TO CONSIDER

1. What are the main industrial areas of Germany?
2. What were the main ideas of Adolf Hitler?
3. Distinguish between the areas and resources of West and East Germany.
4. Outline the major developments in West Germany since 1945.
5. Give an account of the career of Dr Adenauer.
6. In what ways does the membership of the E.E.C. help Franco–German relations?

WORDS TO NOTE

Bicameral Parliamentary system with two houses; in this case the *Bundestag* and *Bundesrat*, the equivalent of the American House of Representatives and the Senate.

Biergarten: Beergarden—often the centre of political speech-making. Hitler's first attempt to seize power—at Munich in 1923—is known as the 'beer-hall putsch'.

Blitzkrieg: 'Lightning war'—applied to the tactics of Germany in 1939–45 and especially to the use of tanks in collaboration with air attack.

Deutschland über alles: 'Germany above all', 'Germany over all', 'Germany is better than all the rest'. From the old German national anthem.

Entente Cordiale: From the French, 'cordial understanding'. The phrase is usually applied to the understanding of 1904 between Britain and France.

Gestapo, S.A., S.S.: Special organizations in Nazi Germany. The Gestapo (short for *Geheime Staatspolizei*) was the Secret Police, organized in 1933 to terrorize the opposition to Hitler. Its head was Heinrich Himmler.

The S.A. (*Sturm-Abteilung* or Storm Troops) were the Nazi Party Army, designed at first to protect party meetings but becoming a private army of brown-shirted warriors (hence the Brownshirts). They gave military training to party members.

The S.S. (*Schutz-Staffel* or protective squadron) were a superior branch of the Nazi Party Army. They wore elegant black uniforms (Blackshirts) and were Hitler's own special bodyguard. In the Second World War crack units of the army were often drawn from the S.A. and the S.S.

Land: State or Province of Germany.

Putsch: Attempt to seize power by force.

Reich: German word for empire or kingdom. The *Reichstag* was the name of the German Imperial Parliament. Hitler called his Germany the Third Reich, implying that the Germany united by Bismarck was the Second Reich and that the First Reich was that of the Holy Roman Empire. The 'Reich' in general use nowadays in Germany means the boundaries of the old and undivided Germany.

Unitary State: A country which has parliament directly representing the people without any regional governments. This is the opposite of Federal states such as U.S.A. and U.S.S.R.

FOR FURTHER READING

Leonhardt, R. W.: *This Germany*, Penguin, 1966.

Adenauer, Konrad: *Memoirs*, Weidenfeld & Nicolson, 1965.

Bullock, A.: *Hitler, A Study in Tyranny*, Odhams, 1952.

Mau, H. and Krausnick, H.: *German History 1933–45*, Oswald Wolff, 1959.

Jarman, T. L.: *The Rise and Fall of Nazi Germany*, Cresset, 1955.

5. *Russia*

The land and the people

Of all the countries in the world, modern Russia is the hardest to know. Access to it is difficult—visas are hard to obtain. Almost all travellers from the West are carefully guided in their travels by Intourist and are not normally free to move where they will. The language and its script are real barriers to understanding. And so are the size and nature of the country itself.

Geographical extent

The U.S.S.R. is a vast country. It covers one-sixth of the earth's surface. In size it is Great Britain about 90 times over. It is more than thrice the size of the U.S.A.

The maximum distance of the Soviet Union from north to south is some 3,000 miles—as much as the extent of the United States from east to west; and the spread between east and west is well over 6,000 miles, roughly the distance between the Equator and the Pole. The total length of the Soviet Union's frontiers is more than 36,000 miles. When it is midnight at the easternmost end of the country at Cape Dezhnev, it is one o'clock in the afternoon at Kaliningrad, near the western edge. It is literally true that the sun never sets on the Soviet Union because it is always above the horizon in some part of the land. The Soviet Union is larger than the side of the moon that faces the earth.

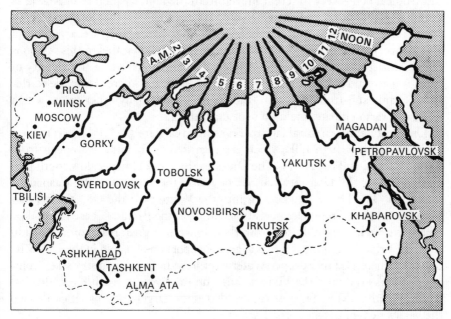

The Time Zones of U.S.S.R.

The Soviet Union occupies the eastern half of Europe and the entire upper third of Asia. Because of its size and location, it is both an Eastern and a Western power. Its Far East is farther east than China or Japan, while its western boundary is in the heart of Central Europe. The country has common frontiers with more than a dozen foreign states, as far apart as Czechoslovakia and China. At one point, Soviet soil is only five miles from an island of the United States in the Bering Strait.

The country is a vast plain which consists of four lateral belts:

(*a*) The northernmost is the Tundra, a dreary wilderness on the Arctic fringe. The land is permanently frozen a little below the surface of moss, lichens and coarse grass. In the summer it is swampy, and there are myriads of mosquitoes. Here live the Lapps and Samoyeds, occupied with fishing and the breeding of reindeer.

(*b*) A forested middle belt of fir and pine which covers most of Siberia; as it spreads south, the conifers are largely interspersed with silver birches.

(*c*) From the western Ukraine to beyond the Caspian stretches the treeless

143

plain, which is the Steppe. East of the Caspian it is a sandy desert, but in the west it becomes the fertile region of the 'Black earth', a golden cornland unbroken by hedges—there are none in the Soviet Union.

(*d*) Finally we reach the southernmost region of the Soviets. This is a green, sub-tropical belt—very different indeed from the familiar picture of Russia as a land of great snows and extreme cold. It is in this area that large collective farms raise sugar-cane and citrus fruits. Other fruits, too, are available in abundance. One of the major cities of the Soviet Union located in this region is called Alma Ata—'Father of the Apple'. The apples grown in the vicinity of Alma Ata are said to be the equal of those produced anywhere else in the world. In this same sub-tropical region, the farmers grow many other crops which require a warm climate, including cotton and tea.

The most definite natural landmarks on the plain are the Ural Mountains, a chain of not very high hills which are regarded as dividing European from Asiatic Russia, and the rivers. The Dniester, Bug and Dnieper flow south into the Black Sea; the Don into the Sea of Azov; the Volga into the Caspian, a closed sea. The Dvina flows north into the White Sea; the Ob, Yenisei and Lena issue in the Arctic Ocean and the Amur in the Pacific. These rivers flow quietly through a crumbly soil from their sources in great reservoirs of marsh (e.g., the Pripet Marshes); there is a larger proportion of marsh in the U.S.S.R. than anywhere else in Europe. Waterways have been the country's key communications ever since the Vikings sailed up the rivers to reach Kiev, the first Russian capital. Moscow later superseded Kiev, largely because it controlled the headwaters of the great river systems.

The country's rivers mostly run north and south. The two outstanding lateral lines of communication are (*a*) the great highway from the Polish border to Moscow, the road which Napoleon took in 1812, the road along which the German armies battered their way in 1941 and 1942, through Smolensk and Vyazma to the approaches of Moscow; and (*b*) the Trans-Siberian Railway, begun in 1891, which is the spinal cord connecting west and east.

This vast expanse of country imposes both advantages and disadvantages. It makes possible a large population and diversified economic development. Its size alone makes the country almost unconquerable. Napoleon in 1812 found it impossible to defeat the Russian winter, and retreated from Moscow through the snow; Hitler in 1942 got to Stalingrad and no further. Even when not able to defeat its enemies, Russia, like China, has always been able to trade space for time, to yield territory, to exhaust the enemy and to conserve its own strength. Although the country lacks some vital resources and has great deserts in the south-east, in mineral resources it is second only to the U.S.A., its forest resources represent one-fifth of the world total, and it has vast areas of corn and wheat.

With all its size, however, it is a land power, remote from the main oceans of the world. It has no adequate warm water ocean ports; many of its rivers flow into frozen seas; its climate is very severe in winter.

Moreover, there are no natural barriers inside Russia. The only mountains, the Urals, are in fact not mountains at all by European standards, but a range of rugged, broken hills like the Lake District in Cumberland. Only in the south are there high mountains, the Caucasus, the Altai and the Pamirs—'the roof of the world'. These have long been barriers against Russian expansion towards Turkey and India. Their effectiveness in an air age is more questionable. And with no barrier against invading Tatars or Mongols from the east, against Poles, Swedes or Balts from the north, or against Germans from the west and Turks from the south, Russia became, like Germany, a state depending on the ruler's power and his army; and the ruler, whether Tsar or Com-

Not all Russia is snow and ice, as this picture of Sochi, on the Black Sea, shows.

missar, became of necessity a strong man determined to brook no rival and tolerate no criticism.

The Russian people

There are today over 230 million people living in the Soviet Union. It is difficult to keep up with the statistics of population because 8,000 children (about 3 million per year) are born each day in Russia. It is thus quite unlike Britain not only in its size but in its mixture of peoples. It is equally unlike the United States where the various national groups have fused within a few generations into a single prevailing national type. In the Soviet Union the nationalities have in large measure kept their separate identities. And some of their languages are only now being recorded and written down.

The title of the state—The Union of Soviet Socialist Republics—indicates that no one national group shall dominate the rest. This union is a federation of 15 republics of which by far the largest is the Russian Soviet Federative Socialist Republic, covering most of European Russia and nearly all Asiatic Russia, and having a population of over 118 million. In itself it stretches from Finland to Vladivostok on the Pacific. Next in size comes the Ukraine Soviet Socialist Republic with over 40 million inhabitants. Among the smaller units are the three republics of Georgia (Stalin's homeland—Stalin always spoke Russian with a strong 'foreign' accent), Armenia, the land of oft-persecuted traders, and Azerbaijan on the Caspian Sea. This last, which is chiefly peopled by an Asiatic race, contains the famous Baku, Grozny and Maikop oil-wells.

On the other side of the Caspian Sea lies Turkestan, which includes five republics. These are all Asiatic peoples, mostly Mohammedans. The land is desert, but with large oases. In Uzbek lie Bukhara, Samarkand and Tashkent, the centres of an ancient civilization. Here many of the people lead settled lives as peasants, workers on cotton plantations or as shepherds, but numbers of them live like the nomadic Arabs—desert wanderers with herds of camels. Out east again, near the Chinese border, are the Mongols, while north of them, in the tundra region of Yakutsk, the inhabitants are mostly trappers and hunters, who look and live like Red Indians. In the west, Estonia, Latvia, Lithuania and Moldavia were added to Russia in 1940.

One of the most creditable features of the Soviet régime is its encouragement of local life and culture among the smaller nationalities of the Union, thus bringing to reality the idea of a 'United States of Russia', which was the demand of Russian liberals under the oppressive Tsarist régime. In some cases entirely new grammars have been compiled in order to help to bring civilization to the primitive peoples of eastern Soviet Russia. Along with this policy of enlightenment one can set the complete toleration as regards Jews in the Soviet Union, a toleration which is in sharp contrast to persecution under the Tsars.

There are so many nationalities that we can only guess at their number,

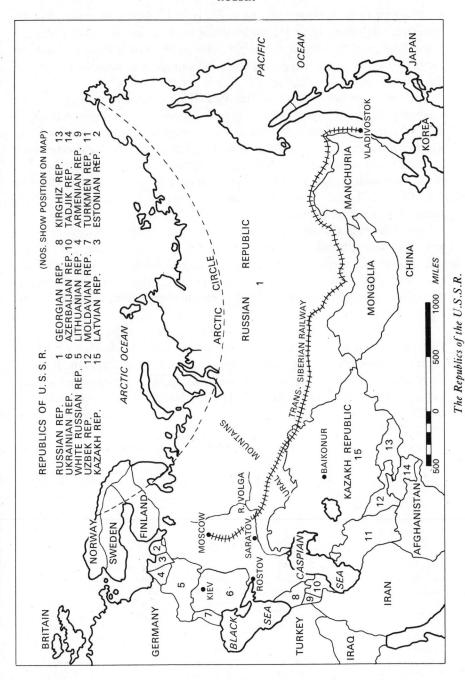

The Republics of the U.S.S.R.

REPUBLICS OF U.S.S.R.

(NOS. SHOW POSITION ON MAP)

RUSSIAN REP.	1	GEORGIAN REP.	8	KIRGHIZ REP.	13
UKRAINIAN REP.	6	AZERBAIJAN REP.	10	TADJIK REP.	14
WHITE RUSSIAN REP.	5	LITHUANIAN REP.	4	ARMENIAN REP.	9
UZBEK REP.	12	MOLDAVIAN REP.	7	TURKMEN REP.	11
KAZAKH REP.	15	LATVIAN REP.	3	ESTONIAN REP.	2

because new ones are discovered periodically and old ones drop out of sight. Estimates run from 110 to 150 nationalities in the entire country. There are 150 dialects, and 48 different languages. Most of the nationalities are found in the border areas, farthest removed from the European population centre and the powerful Russian influence.

There is a museum in Tbilisi (formerly Tiflis), capital of Georgia, where one may see exhibited the costumes and customs of some 40 nationalities living in the Caucasus Range. In one of these almost inaccessible valleys, there is a group which, until recently, retained a national costume much like the armour worn by the Crusaders of the twelfth and thirteenth centuries. It is quite possible that these people are the descendants of Crusaders who lost their way returning from the Holy Land, or were driven off their route by marauding natives and found shelter within the mountains.

One of the tactics which the old régime used to help maintain itself in power was to set one nationality against another. Opposing one another, they were less likely to cause trouble to their Tsarist masters. In this way, the Armenians and Georgians, representing the two main groups in the Caucasus, developed the bitter feud which resulted in generation-long fighting. The Caucasus Range became known as the 'Bloody Mountains'.

In this respect, the Communists broke with the ways of the past. Stalin, as a Georgian, was a member of an oppressed nationality. He knew by personal experience how the smaller ethnic groups resented the attempts to 'Russify' them, and he strongly supported the policy of encouraging national cultures, so long as they did not interfere with the basic policies of the Soviet state.

Constituent Republics of the U.S.S.R.

Republic	Area in sq. miles	Population (approximate)	Capital	Date of incorporation into the U.S.S.R.
Russian S.F.S.R.	6,569,000	130,000,000	Moscow	1918
Ukrainian S.S.R.	231,000	46,000,000	Kiev	1919
Byelorussian S.S.R.	80,000	10,000,000	Minsk	1919
Uzbek S.S.R.	153,400	9,000,000	Tashkent	1924
Kazakh S.S.R.	1,102,300	9,000,000	Alma Ata	1936
Georgian S.S.R.	27,700	5,000,000	Tbilisi	1922
Azerbaijan S.S.R.	33,460	5,000,000	Baku	1922
Lithuanian S.S.R.	25,500	3,000,000	Vilnius	1940
Moldavian S.S.R.	13,200	3,000,000	Kishinev	1940
Latvian S.S.R.	24,600	2,000,000	Riga	1940
Tadjikistan S.S.R.	54,600	2,000,000	Stalinabad	1929
Kirghiz S.S.R.	76,900	2,000,000	Frunze	1936
Armenian S.S.R.	11,640	2,000,000	Yerevan	1922
Turkmen S.S.R.	187,000	2,000,000	Ashkhabad	1924
Estonian S.S.R.	17,300	1,500,000	Tallinn	1940

A chorus of collective farm workers in Irkutsk region of Russia, celebrate the October Revolution in song.

Of the estimated population of 230 million in the Soviet Union, by far the largest number, however, are Russians. Together with the other Slavic strains —Ukrainians, Poles, Byelorussians—they account for about 170 million of the total.

The Russians are Slavs, which means that they speak the Slavic variety of the great Indo-European family of languages. The Slavs are supposed to be Eastern European in origin, but they have become mixed with other racial strains, not only Europeans from the north and west, but also Mongolians from the east.

Everybody has seen a portrait of the Soviets' famous leader, Lenin, a Russian by nationality. His features clearly show the typical Mongolian high cheekbones and suggestions of the slanted eyes. The Russians have received a large

149

intermixture of Mongolian blood in the course of the centuries during which they held sway over the heartland of Russia.

Originally there appears to have been little distinction between the various types of Slavs, but in the twelfth century a split developed. Today, there are the Great Russians—more mixed with the Eastern racial elements than the others—comprising about 65 per cent of the total Slavic population of the Soviet Union. Then there are the Ukrainians, also known as the Little Russians and sometimes as Ruthenians. They comprise more than 25 per cent of the Slavic group. Finally, there are the Byelorussians or White Russians.

Russia before the Revolution

The Russian nation has existed for well over a thousand years. It grew up around two important centres, first Kiev, then Moscow. Both looked to Constantinople for markets, and both drew from it their ideas and their religion; they followed the religion of the Eastern Roman Empire, and were Greek Orthodox, at a time when the Poles (also Slavs) and the Hungarians looked to Rome, and to Western Europe.

It also looked East. Russia reached the Pacific in 1647 and by 1800 dominated Northern Asia up to the Chinese frontier. By 1820 Russian fur companies had stations in Kamchatka, Alaska and California. It appeared to be an Asiatic state, cut off from Europe by Sweden, Poland and Turkey. The main movements in Western Europe—the Renaissance and the Reformation, the discoveries and the scientific inventions that made possible the beginnings of industry—passed it by.

Its spiritual centre, Constantinople, the second Rome, fell to the Turks in 1453, and although Moscow proudly called itself the Third Rome, it was the capital of a vast but a backward, remote and ill-governed state.

The reign of Peter the Great (1689–1725) was the first great turning point in Russian history. Territories thus far only Russian in name were unified. By 1721, Swedish power on the Baltic was overthrown and the 'windows on the West' annexed—Karelia, Estonia, Ingria and Livonia were won, and their proud symbol was St Petersburg (Leningrad), for the next 200 years the Russian capital. A standing army, a navy and an efficient civil service appeared; and the Tsar, who had come to Greenwich as a young man to see how ships were built, was tireless in importing foreign technicians and in seeking to enliven his backward state with Western ideas. By 1725, and by the energy of a single man, Russia was made a Great Power, and a European state.

The process continued under Catherine the Great (1762–96). Like almost all characters whom history calls 'The Great', she was a ruthless tyrant. Born a German princess, she married Peter III of Russia and had him murdered in order to rule in his place. In her reign the Crimea was taken from the Turks, and, in alliance with Austria and Prussia, Poland was completely destroyed and partitioned. Even when a small Polish kingdom reappeared after Waterloo in 1815, it was governed by the Russian Tsar.

On the collapse of Tsarist Russia in 1918, an independent Polish republic was set up, but it was again overrun in 1939. Some of its territory has been incorporated into Russia, and the Poland of today is a Russian satellite. Some of the strongest critics of Mr Khrushchev on his visits to the United States in 1959 and 1960 were the Polish Americans. The western fringe of Russian territory now consists of a variety of non-Russian nationalities—Finns, Estonians, Latvians, Lithuanians, Poles and Romanians—who are its outposts and bulwarks against the West.

The expansion eastwards was equally successful. Vladivostok was founded in 1860. Railways were built to give cohesion to this sprawling area and to give Russia control over Chinese Manchuria. But in 1904–05 the Russians were defeated by Japan—the first time in history that an Asiatic state defeated a European power. The control of China by Mao Tse-tung and the Chinese Communists in 1949 gave Russia a great new ally in the East.

The drive south was less successful. Despite many campaigns against the Ottoman Empire, and despite the support she gave to the Slav and Orthodox subjects of the Turkish Empire in the nineteenth century, Russia never succeeded in gaining Constantinople and the Straits. British policy in the nineteenth century was to support Turkey against Russia—as it still is today. The Crimean War (1854–56) was fought for this reason.

In fact, in 1907, by an agreement with Russia, Britain relaxed its opposition, and Turkey fell more and more under German control. In 1915, by a secret treaty, Britain and France offered to award Constantinople to Russia in the event of a victory over the Ottoman Empire (then an ally of Germany) in the First World War. By the time the Ottoman Empire was defeated in 1918, however, the Tsarist government, with whom the agreement had been made, had been itself overthrown by the Bolsheviks, and thus the agreement was not kept. On the collapse of the Tsarist system, the Bolsheviks made peace with Germany, demanded a peace treaty with the 'capitalist' powers, their ex-allies, and for their part announced a retreat from Imperialism. Since 1945 there has been no sign of retreat. In many ways the foreign policy of the Soviet Union in recent years has been hard to distinguish from that of the Tsars.

This is not to condemn or praise it. A state's foreign policy is shaped less by ideas than by geography. The Russians, Tsarist or Communist, need access to the sea by other than ice-bound routes—hence the persistent interest in the Baltic and the Black Sea. Lacking defensible natural frontiers in the west, they have always needed security in the Polish and German borderlands or in the Baltic provinces. Given the potential mineral wealth of Manchuria, they have for a century eyed it with interest. Whether their government is Tsarist or Communist, it is the government of the largest Slav state and as such automatically the power centre of all the Slav peoples, with interests in Czechoslovakia, Bulgaria and Yugoslavia today just as in the nineteenth century.

To seek to condemn this concern with security and survival by giving it a label like 'Imperialist' or 'Communist' does not change its character. It is a long and traditional strategic preoccupation of the people who happen to live in the middle of a great but landlocked plain. The Russians, like the Germans, are the great land power, as Britain—until recently—was the great sea power.

The State and its character

Whatever the motives or the direction of her policy, it has always been a result of direction from above. The Tsar was the heir of Rome, as the title indicated— Tsar was simply a form of the word 'Caesar'. He was responsible to no one— until 1904 there was no institution of a representative kind, no Parliament, no Reichstag. Industry came late, and until 1861 the majority of the people were serfs. Agriculture was backward; there was little industry; and government was corrupt. The only way to overthrow the system was by violence—and violence was a frequent occurrence. In the reign of Nicholas I (1825–55), who was known as Nicholas the Flogger, there were on the average 23 revolts against the Tsar in each year of the reign.

The single great reform was that of Nicholas's son, Alexander II (1855–81) who gave the serfs their freedom. He was not able to give them an adequate amount of land, however, and what he gave was poor in quality. Moreover title to it was vested not in the individual peasant but in the village community, the *mir*. So the majority of the Russian peasants remained discontented and open to revolutionary agitation. Many left the farms and moved to the cities, to form the labour force for the factories that sprang up in the 1880s and 1890s. By 1870 terrorism and violence returned. In 1879–80 there were three attempts on the life of the Tsar; in March 1881 he was assassinated by a bomb in St Petersburg. The result was a return to autocracy and the suppression of liberal influences under Alexander III (1881–94).

Alexander III's son, Nicholas II (1894–1917), was the last of the Tsars. He was a weak character who felt he must continue the programme; he was dominated by his wife, Alexandra, and by a sinister monk, Grigor Rasputin, who was his wife's spiritual adviser, and who preyed on her superstitious nature. The régime was largely maintained by the devotion of the masses to the Greek Orthodox religion.

By 1894 there were new as well as old problems. Industry was appearing. Many railway lines were built—especially the Trans-Siberian Railway (1891– 1905). The money to finance these projects was mainly French. As a result, Moscow and St Petersburg became industrial centres—and the living conditions of the two million workers, living in barracks, bred a proletariat and gave it a chance to prepare for revolution.

The war with Japan (1904–05) provided an opportunity. It stripped European Russia of troops and also demonstrated the incompetence and corruption of the government. In a riot in St Petersburg (January 1905) 1,500 people were killed or wounded. After the military disaster at Mukden and the destruction of the Russian fleet at Tsushima (1905), the crew of the battleship *Potemkin* mutinied, there were strikes in Odessa, and St Petersburg was for a time governed by a soviet, an elected council representing the workers, with Trotsky at its head.

The opposition, however, was disunited. The Social Democratic Party, which was Marxist, was itself divided into two wings—the *Bolsheviks* (or majority) and the *Mensheviks* (or minority)—who differed on the tactical question of how to seize power—and there were many other groups.

These groups had little effect on the Tsarist state. As usual after revolutions, a reign of terror followed. In two years (1906–07) over 4,000 officials or police had been killed, and 35,000 people were banished without trial; and in two months (September–October 1907) over 3,000 were executed. On the outbreak of the First World War none of Russia's fundamental problems had been solved. She was a primitive, autocratic and brutal society. The authority of the Tsar of all the Russias depended, in fact, on the army, on the secret police and on the Church.

The regions and their resources

As we have seen, the great Russian republic stretches from the western border to the Pacific, a distance of some 6,000 miles. White Russia or Byelorussia is flat and marshy. Crops have always been poor and life precarious. But the Soviet Government has been draining the land, and now there are many acres planted with rye and potatoes.

The Ukraine, on the other hand, is very fertile. It covers most of southern European Russia, and with the addition of the Polish Ukraine, won in 1939, and of Moldavia (formerly Bessarabia—won in 1940) it is twice the size of Great Britain. The climate is continental; burning sun in summer, icy winds and snow in winter. This is the great granary of the U.S.S.R.—the endless plain of waving corn. It is rich, too, in coal and iron. And it has access to the Black Sea ports of Odessa and Sebastopol, and the Russian 'Riviera'.

If the Russians are dominant, and the Ukraine perhaps the wealthiest of the Soviet Republics, there are many minor nationalities scattered among them. There are two other major regions. One is Trans-Caucasia, the remote highland republics in the Caucasus, between the Black Sea and the Caspian—Georgia, Armenia and Azerbaijan. The other is Russian Central Asia.

The Soviet Union has five constituent republics in Central Asia, on the borders of China, Afghanistan and Iran. At certain points India is almost within view, beyond a narrow Afghan 'panhandle', set up in years gone by as a

Part of a vast flock of sheep, said to be 60,000 in number, in the Zabaikal (Russian) steppes. The shepherd, Rabdan Albazhinov, is locally renowned for his work.

buffer between Russia and India's then rulers, Great Britain. This is a land of majestic mountains, forbidding deserts, and fantastic black sand. The names of the cities and regions here have a flavour of Oriental romance—Bukhara, Samarkand, Khorezm, Ashkhabad, Kara-Kalpak, Alma Ata, Khiva. Here we find the heart of the Islamic Soviets, with a population of some 20 million Moslems, the second largest religious group after the Greek Orthodox Church in the U.S.S.R.

The largest of these republics is Kazakhstan, with an area of over a million square miles. It is next in size to the Russian Soviet Republic and larger than all the other Central Asian Soviet Republics combined. It stretches for about 1,875 miles from east to west, and for almost 950 miles from north to south. This is a country of the great deserts, inhabited in 1939 by not more than 6 million people. Yet it is a treasure chest of valuable minerals, including the indispensable manganese, chromium, and many others in demand throughout the world.

Kazakhstan is regarded today as a potential home for many millions of migrants. Official government expeditions have reported that the barren 'hungry steppe' needs only water to become highly productive. Large hydro-electric projects are under construction, especially in the Kzyl Orda region, near the Syr Darya River. A dam here is expected to store water for the irrigation of 100,000 acres of rice lands and, later, for an additional 250,000 acres.

The other constituent republics in Central Asia bear the names of Turkmenistan, Uzbekistan, Kirghizia and Tadjikistan. In the first three of these republics, the people use languages which are variations of Turkish. The Tadjiks speak an Iranian dialect, which differs little from standard Persian.

The ruling race of the region were the Uzbeks, until the Russians came in during the third quarter of the last century. The Russians soon overthrew the native rulers, feeble and decadent successors of Tamerlane, great conqueror of the fourteenth century.

Today Uzbekistan provides 60 per cent of the total cotton production and 50 per cent of the total rice production of the Soviet Union.

Resources

Russia is rich in resources. Soviet mineralogists claim that their country contains 53 per cent of the world's iron ore, 50 per cent of its oil, 20 per cent of its coal. Even if these figures cannot be proved, it is clear that there is great wealth in Russia; but most of it is in potential resources, not yet in production.

Perhaps the richest area of mineral wealth is the Ural Range: with high-grade iron ore (Mount Magnitnaya and Mount Bakal); copper at Orsk and Sverdlovsk; and platinum, manganese, tungsten and molybdenum, all essential for steel alloys. There are also rich stores of precious stones, but inadequate quantities of coal.

The six major industrial areas of Russia are:

(*a*) Leningrad: machines, shipbuilding, trucks, railway equipment.

(*b*) Moscow: machines, planes, trucks.

(*c*) Ukraine, from Kiev to Rostov-on-Don: machines and tractors, shipbuilding, railway equipment; iron; coal; oil.

(*d*) The oil producing and refining centres: Baku and Batum.

(*e*) Urals, from Perm to Magnitogorsk: iron, vehicles, railway engines, machinery, minerals.

(*f*) Kuznetsk region from Novo-Sibirsk to Stalinsk in western Siberia: coal.

There is sufficient coal here to supply the whole world for 300 years. The Kuznetsk area has developed fast, linked to the iron of the Urals. Magnitogorsk and Stalinsk are new and thriving cities.

Industry in the Soviet Union is controlled and directed by the State. The State Planning Commission draws up plans every five or seven years and decides what shall be produced and where; it also fixes wages and prices. The planned economy, together with the rapid industrialization, has meant the absence of large-scale unemployment.

It is not possible in the Soviet Union to live by owning property on which others work.

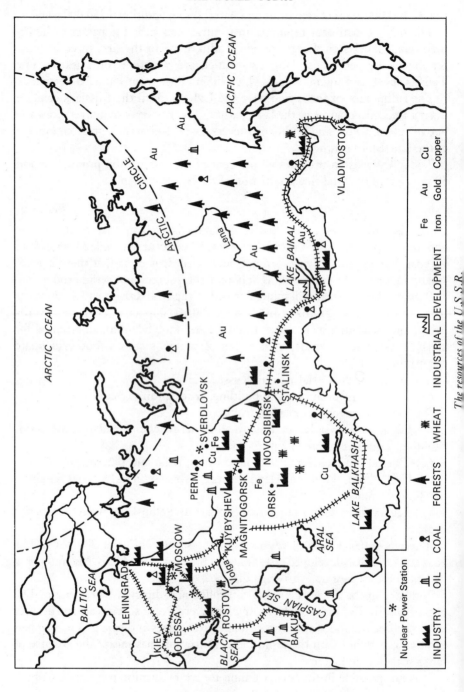

The resources of the U.S.S.R.

Today it is believed that some 35–40 million people in the Soviet Union are employed in industry. There are also some 3 million employed in the machine-tractor stations, to help the collective farms. Shops and factories are owned by the State; there is very little private enterprise. Industrial workers have to reach particular targets of production, but are encouraged to exceed these targets if they can. The best workers receive the highest pay, and are given prestige—by being featured in the wall newspaper, by being given theatre tickets or by decorations and honours. It is a great honour to be described as a Hero of Labour.

Despite the belief in equality, the Soviet Union encourages payment by results and rewards effort and skill. In August 1935 a young miner called Stakhanov, using a pneumatic pick, increased his output of coal from 7 to 102 tons in a single shift. Today 'Stakhanovite' is a term of high praise. The Soviet Union honours football stars as much as we do, and ballet dancers far more. Authors, ballet dancers and film stars, Communist Party officials and generals are among the people in Soviet Russia who earn really large incomes, and are able to live well—with some degree of privacy and with private cars and country villas, which few others can afford.

Under Lenin and Stalin

The Russian Revolution 1917

There were two Revolutions, not one. The first was the February/March Revolution (1917). During the early defeats in the First World War, Nicholas II did not alter his policies but continued to ignore the demands of the political parties and popular discontent increased. Strikes broke out and, with the help of the military garrison, a working men's council (soviet) was established at Petrograd. The failure of the army to stay loyal to the Tsar saw the collapse of the State. Nicholas II abdicated in favour of his brother, but the Grand Duke Michael did not attempt to carry on the Romanov dynasty because he knew it was hopeless. A provisional government was established with Prince Lvov as President. A programme of liberal reform was planned, and a constituent assembly was to be elected to draw up a constitution. The objective was a parliamentary system on British lines. There was to be a free Press and freedom of debate.

The second Revolution took place in October/November (1917). The attempt of the middle class to establish a democratic government was hampered by:

(*a*) the war and its problems—an empty treasury, no food, the collapse of the transport system;

(*b*) the numerous national groups within the country;

(*c*) the lack of any popular enthusiasm for an orderly democracy; and

(*d*) the proletariat which desired economic and social reform.

Soviets were formed in villages, towns and in the army. Discipline in the army became lax, and the soviets demanded peace with Germany. With the help of the Socialists, Alexander Kerensky tried to guide the Provisional Government, but the opposition of the Constitutional Democrats, Bolsheviks and Reactionaries was too great. The Bolsheviks increased in power and numbers.

The Bolsheviks had had no part in the first Revolution. Their leaders were in exile, and they had no following. Few in Russia could have predicted how powerful they would become. But with the freedom of debate after March 1917, Bolshevik ideas were overwhelmingly popular. Their leader, Lenin, was sent back to Russia by the Germans, in a sealed train, deliberately to inject an anti-war virus into the Russian people. All that the Germans wanted was a Russian surrender, so that they could turn all their energy to the western front. All that the West wanted was for Russia to stay in the war. Lenin in his train was like a Trojan horse—a leader armed with ideas rather than weapons. But in some situations, ideas are the most dangerous weapons. He wanted to seize power, and was prepared to be violent. He believed in discipline and leadership.

Yet he faced a danger—his opponents could describe him as a German puppet. Woodrow Wilson, the American President, always thought him a German agent, and misunderstood the Russian Revolution from the start. Lenin was no German. He quickly formulated a programme that expressed what the Russian masses wanted—immediate peace, all land to the peasants, all power to the people's representatives in the soviets. The slogan of 1917 was 'Peace, Land and Bread'.

In November, the Bolsheviks overthrew Kerensky's Provisional Government and gained control of the National Congress of Soviets. The political revolution of March was followed by the economic and social revolution of November.

Under the leadership of Lenin, whose real name was Vladimir Ulyanov, and Trotsky (Leon Bronstein), the Bolshevist programme was carried forward. The objectives were:

(a) to arrange a peace with the Central Powers;

(b) to make the proletariat supreme;

(c) to foster economic and social reforms;

(d) to consolidate Russia; and

(e) to spread Communism throughout the world.

Events in Russia were to herald a world revolution—'Workers of the world, unite' (Karl Marx).

The Theory of Revolution

Lenin derived his ideas from Karl Marx (1818–83), a German-Jewish philosopher who lived most of his life in London, and whose ideas were themselves a product of German thought (especially the writings of Hegel), of French Socialism (especially the ideas of the class struggle, in the writings of Proudhon and Louis Blanc) and of the British economists (the labour theory of value of Ricardo). Most of Marx's study, especially for his *Communist Manifesto* (1848) and his *Capital* (1870), was done in the British Museum. He lived a frugal life in Dean Street, Soho—a stern-looking, quarrelsome man, with a great black beard, a harsh voice and the manner of an Old Testament prophet. But, again, ideas are weapons that can influence millions of men, whatever their source.

Marx was a scientific socialist and a materialist. A materialist is a person who believes that the universe can be explained in terms of matter, and that minds, ideas and emotions derive from matter. Marx also believed that economic conditions are the basis of life. Other aspects of life, including politics, poetry, religion and thought could be explained on the same basis.

Hegel had taught that ideas were the most important part of reality, and that movement in thought depended on an endless process of contradiction, whereby one idea (a thesis) gave rise to its opposite (antithesis) and from their clash arose a final solution (synthesis) which became in turn a thesis, and the process began again. This pattern, following that of a good conversation, where one argument stimulates an opposing argument, was known as dialectic—from the Greek word for debate.

What Marx did was to see this process taking place in the material world rather than in the world of ideas—hence its name of dialectical materialism—and taking place in history. Each phase of human history, while determined by material forces, develops as a dialectical process, producing within itself its own opposite.

Thus capitalist society, in which the means of production are owned by private individuals or companies and are used for the making of profit, depends on a proletariat, a class of workers who have only their work or their skill to sell. This dialectic or conflict of the two classes is the 'class struggle'. The worker is paid only just enough; all the profit goes to the capitalist. As wealth increases, so does the worker's misery. He has nothing to lose but his chains. Eventually there is a crisis. The proletariat is the antithesis of the capitalist class and will, said Marx, rise to overthrow it. But the struggle between worker and capitalist, or between proletariat and bourgeois, will differ from all previous struggles, he said, in that, after a period of transition (the Dictatorship of the Proletariat) in the end a classless society will emerge. The State, the instrument of oppression, will then wither away.

This is not a matter of choice, or of human will, but a law of nature or of history.

The capitalist world in the West, especially the U.S.A., is seen, therefore, not only as the opposite of the Communist system, but as not yet having reached the final stage of the classless society. The Soviet Union is, it believes, approach-

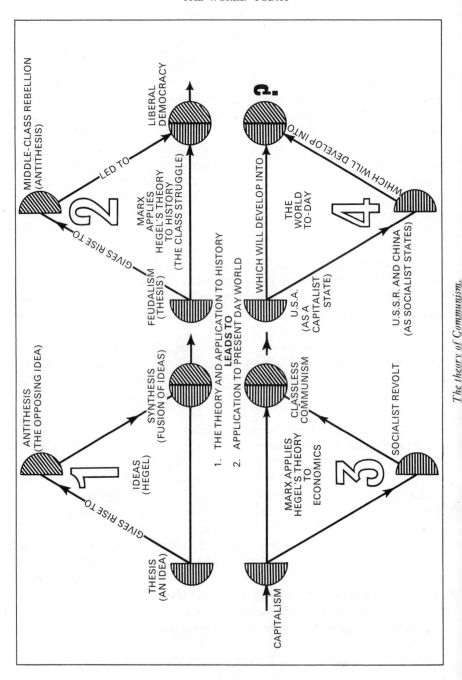

The theory of Communism.

ing this. The world revolution, when the workers will rise and overthrow their oppressors, is certain to come, said Marx.

More than eighty years after Marx's death, it is now obvious that much of his interpretation and prophecy has not been accurate. There has been no world revolution—although both the Russian and Chinese revolutions have been successful. Yet even here the prophecy has been inaccurate, because Marx predicted that the revolutions would be the result of industrialization and would come first in industrialized countries like Britain or the United States. They have come, in fact, in the most backward and agrarian, and only where they have been backed by military force. He did not foresee that the worker's conditions would steadily improve, so that in the affluent society of today it is becoming harder to distinguish between worker and capitalist.

Marx did not foresee the effect of liberal reform such as took place in Britain in 1908–15 or 1945–51, nor the effect of heavy taxation, which permits a redistribution of the national wealth and allows the payment of health and unemployment benefits. And, of course, many of the Marxist laws of history— that all history is the story of class struggle, that economic conditions determine the pattern of all else in society, that religion has been the opium of the masses— are not tenable as binding laws. They deny the whole story of Christianity, the belief in God and in His Church, the worth of the human personality and the belief that man's hope for his own and his society's progress depends on his use of his own mind.

Nevertheless the attitude of the Soviet Union to all problems is shaped by Marxism-Leninism. The plans for proletarian revolution are described in the official *Short History of the Communist Party of the Soviet Union* and in Stalin's *Problems of Leninism*.

Lenin himself was a prolific writer and added to the Marxist body of doctrine, particularly in his emphasis that Imperialism represented the last and decadent stage of capitalism. These writings have been published in millions of copies and are the Bible of the Soviet system.

The period of 'war communism' (1917–21)

Lenin's triumph was, however, a matter of tactics rather than of doctrine. The Russian Revolution was the result of the fusion of Marx's teachings with the revolutionary situation in Russia. There were no more than at most one-and-a-half million industrial workers in Russia in 1917, almost entirely confined to Moscow and St Petersburg; no more, that is, than one per cent of the population. The establishment of Communism, therefore, was the work of a very small percentage of the people.

Equally, although the Communist International was established in Moscow to foster world revolution, it was quickly apparent that world revolution was remote. The soviets in Hungary and Bavaria collapsed; the Red Army was driven out of Poland; the trade unions in the West failed to support the Bolsheviks, and in fact Western armies were landed to aid the White armies against the Red. Encirclement by the capitalist world allowed Lenin to appeal to Russian patriotism, as Stalin did again in 1941; this, and the civil war in Russia (1917–21), gave an excuse for dictatorship and the use of secret police, features of the Soviet system to this day. The country is governed by a tiny minority in the name of the people, but there is no popular participation in the government.

Nor was Lenin able to establish Communism inside Russia. After the loss of territory to Germany by the Treaty of Brest-Litovsk (1918), especially the loss of the Ukraine and of the major area of supply of Russian coal and iron, and after four years of civil war, there was economic chaos in Russia. There was famine in Russia in 1921, and between 5 and 10 million people died.

New Economic Policy (1921–28)

In 1922 Lenin was compelled to introduce a New Economic Policy, to encourage some private enterprise in commerce and minor industries; it lasted seven years. The State retained ownership of banks, railways and large industrial enterprises. But small shops appeared and the peasants sold their crops in the normal capitalist way.

Lenin was wounded in 1922 and ill at intervals thereafter; he worked overhard and had a series of strokes in 1923. He died in January 1924. His body was embalmed and has been permanently on display in the Lenin mausoleum in Moscow. St Petersburg was renamed Leningrad in his honour.

Stalin (1924–53)

On Lenin's death, there was a conflict for the leadership of the Party and the State between Stalin (whose real name was Joseph Djugashvili, 1879–1953) and Trotsky (1877–1940). Trotsky was the more colourful, a great orator, the creator and commander of the Red Army, and the diplomat of the Brest-Litovsk Treaty; he was Lenin's associate through the Revolution. Stalin, a Georgian from the Caucasus and the son of a shoemaker, was less dramatic, a poor speaker and much less conspicuous. But in 1924 he held the key position of Secretary-General of the Party. For a time he continued Lenin's policy and argued that Trotsky, who continued to advocate world revolution, was guilty of treason to Lenin's memory. By 1927 he had Trotsky exiled. In 1940 Trotsky was murdered by a man called 'Jackson' who, armed with an ice-pick, made entry into his barricaded house in Mexico City. Jackson (whose real name seems to have been Ramon Mercador) was released from prison in Mexico in 1960; he has since disappeared.

From his triumph in 1927, to his death in 1953, Stalin dominated Russia. He has been described as a man who was responsible for more deaths, outside wars, than any man in history.

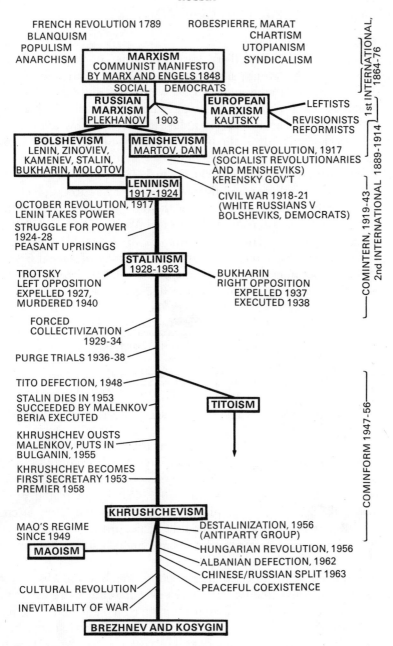

FRENCH REVOLUTION 1789
BLANQUISM
POPULISM
ANARCHISM

ROBESPIERRE, MARAT
CHARTISM
UTOPIANISM
SYNDICALISM

1st INTERNATIONAL, 1864-76

MARXISM
COMMUNIST MANIFESTO
BY MARX AND ENGELS 1848

SOCIAL   DEMOCRATS

RUSSIAN MARXISM
PLEKHANOV   1903

EUROPEAN MARXISM
KAUTSKY

LEFTISTS

REVISIONISTS
REFORMISTS

2nd INTERNATIONAL 1889-1914

BOLSHEVISM
LENIN, ZINOVIEV,
KAMENEV, STALIN,
BUKHARIN, MOLOTOV

MENSHEVISM
MARTOV, DAN

MARCH REVOLUTION, 1917
(SOCIALIST REVOLUTIONARIES
AND MENSHEVIKS)
KERENSKY GOV'T

LENINISM
1917-1924

CIVIL WAR 1918-21
(WHITE RUSSIANS V
BOLSHEVIKS, DEMOCRATS)

OCTOBER REVOLUTION, 1917
LENIN TAKES POWER
STRUGGLE FOR POWER
1924-28
PEASANT UPRISINGS

COMINTERN, 1919-43

STALINISM
1928-1953

TROTSKY
LEFT OPPOSITION
EXPELLED 1927,
MURDERED 1940

BUKHARIN
RIGHT OPPOSITION
EXPELLED 1937
EXECUTED 1938

FORCED
COLLECTIVIZATION
1929-34

PURGE TRIALS 1936-38

TITO DEFECTION, 1948
STALIN DIES IN 1953
SUCCEEDED BY MALENKOV
BERIA EXECUTED

TITOISM

KHRUSHCHEV OUSTS
MALENKOV, PUTS IN
BULGANIN, 1955

KHRUSHCHEV BECOMES
FIRST SECRETARY 1953
PREMIER 1958

COMINFORM 1947-56

KHRUSHCHEVISM

MAO'S REGIME
SINCE 1949

DESTALINIZATION, 1956
(ANTIPARTY GROUP)

MAOISM

HUNGARIAN REVOLUTION, 1956
ALBANIAN DEFECTION, 1962
CHINESE/RUSSIAN SPLIT 1963
PEACEFUL COEXISTENCE

CULTURAL REVOLUTION
INEVITABILITY OF WAR

BREZHNEV AND KOSYGIN

Development of Communism.

Stalin has, however, three achievements to his credit:

1. 'Socialism in a single country'

Stalin believed that before there was any chance of world revolution, Russia herself must be strong: she must show that socialism could succeed in Russia in order to set an example to the world; and since that world was capitalist and hostile, Russia must be strong enough to defend herself anyway. To be strong, Russia had to become industrialized; this was the only way to raise the living standards of the people; and it would also create a group of class-conscious workers, committed to the new system.

Stalin made Russia strong by introducing in 1928 the First Five-Year Plan to create basic heavy industry, and this was followed by a succession of plans. They set out goals to be aimed at, and for the most part they reached them. Between 1927 and the outbreak of the Second World War in 1939 Russia increased her annual production of coal from 32 to 140 million tons, of steel from 3 to 18 million tons, of oil from 11 to 30 million tons, of cement from 2 to 6 million tons and of motor vehicles from none to 170,000. Between 1939 and 1956 she had again more than doubled these figures.

Increase in production in Russia in millions of tons

	1913	1928	1940	1955	1963
Coal	30	33	140	314	532
Oil	10	12	31	71	204
Steel	3	4 ·	18	45	157
Cement	2	2	6	22	61

This was done by sacrificing the living standards of the people; few houses were built, and Russians still live in very overcrowded conditions; and few consumer goods like clothes or furniture were available. The emphasis was on capital goods, not consumer goods—on goods, that is, that could produce other goods, like factories, power plants, machine tools and heavy electrical equipment. Russia was transformed; and the achievement was all the greater since she had no reserves of capital at home, and obtained no large-scale financial help from abroad.

It was also done by a revolution in agriculture, which was mechanized and collectivized; individual holdings were taken over and run as large-scale units partly to release many millions of rural people for the new industries, partly because Stalin believed that the wealthier farmers (Kulaks) should be destroyed, partly because it was not intended that landless peasants should become individual owners of land—which would lead to a return to capitalism in a new form. There was great misery on the land, and thousands of people were killed, or exiled to Siberia. It is estimated that, in 1933, 5 million died of famine. But Russia was at last given the industrial base essential to a strong modern state. Without this she would never have been able to defeat Germany in the Second World War.

2. *The building of a strong State.*

Alongside the industrial and agricultural development of Russia went a fostering of education, especially technical education. In 1913, 67 per cent of the population were illiterate. By 1945 there were 770 colleges with over half a million students; education for all is free and compulsory; approximately 6 million children are in kindergartens. Throughout the Soviet Union, although local cultures are encouraged, education is based on uniform textbooks, based on Communist doctrine.

The outbreak of the Second World War interfered with the operation of the Third Five-Year Plan. It came just when there were some signs of improving living conditions. In 1935 rationing had been abolished, and food conditions improved. Some inequality in wages began to appear.

Along with state ownership and control of industry went political authority. The dictatorship of the proletariat over all other classes became in practice the dictatorship of one man, Stalin, over all—including the proletariat.

The first Constitution, which set up the Union of the Russian Soviet Republics with the other (then three) Soviet Republics in 1923, was based on the dictatorship of the proletariat. Lower soviets or councils chose higher soviets, and at the top was the All-Russia Soviet Congress. This met usually half-yearly or yearly, and was and is more a conference of delegates than a parliament in our sense. It elected a Central Executive Committee which sat permanently and made laws, and which chose the Government, the Council of People's Commissars (now Ministers).

In 1936 this Constitution was amended, after a great national debate. The 1936 Constitution has some remarkable features. It guarantees a right to work and to be paid for it—unique in modern constitutions. It guarantees a right to education. Equal rights to women are assured; equal rights to all races; also there is freedom for religious worship and also for anti-religious propaganda. There is freedom of opinion and of speech—at least according to the Constitution.

All soviets are now elected directly by the people; and the Soviet Congress has been replaced by a Supreme Council of the Union, a Russian 'Parliament', elected by all workers. It consists of two houses—the Council of the Union (one member for each 300,000 inhabitants) and the Council of Nationalities (25 members for each constituent republic plus some representatives of the territories). This meets yearly or half-yearly and is in form like an American party convention; it delegates executive power to a 'Presidium', the chairman of which is the official Head of State, and which in turn chooses the permanent

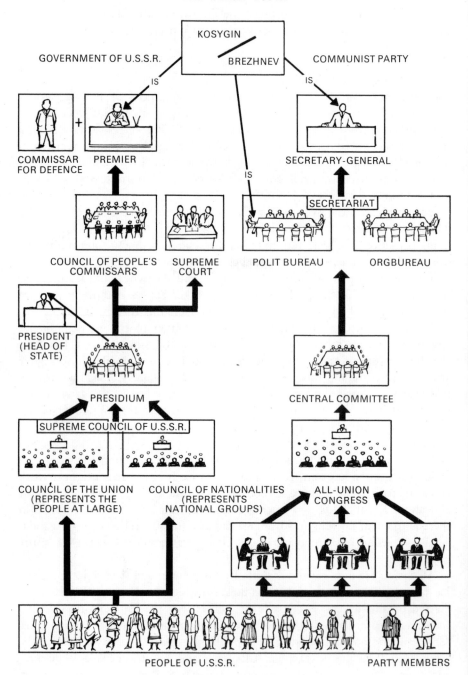

GOVERNMENT OF U.S.S.R.

KOSYGIN
BREZHNEV

COMMUNIST PARTY

IS

IS

IS

COMMISSAR
FOR DEFENCE

PREMIER

SECRETARY-GENERAL

COUNCIL OF PEOPLE'S
COMMISSARS

SUPREME
COURT

SECRETARIAT

POLIT BUREAU

ORGBUREAU

PRESIDENT
(HEAD OF
STATE)

PRESIDIUM

CENTRAL COMMITTEE

SUPREME COUNCIL OF U.S.S.R.

COUNCIL OF THE UNION
(REPRESENTS THE
PEOPLE AT LARGE)

COUNCIL OF NATIONALITIES
(REPRESENTS
NATIONAL GROUPS)

ALL-UNION
CONGRESS

PEOPLE OF U.S.S.R.

PARTY MEMBERS

How the U.S.S.R. is governed.

Council of People's Commissars (now Ministers). This acts as a sort of Cabinet and the President of this Council is in a sense a permanent Prime Minister. Reputations of the other members rise and fall over the years—as do, of course, the reputations of British Cabinet Ministers.

Unlike British politics, however, there is no democracy in the sense of free choice between opposing political parties. The Communist Party is the only authorized political organization, and only candidates approved by it are allowed to stand in elections. Membership of the Party is a great honour and is permitted only after searching examination—of one's past as well as of one's ability and zeal. The dominant body in the Soviet Union is the Political Bureau of the Party—a small group of dedicated revolutionaries, taking the real decisions on policy. Stalin was not only at times President of the Council of Commissars; he was also, almost all the time, Secretary-General of the only party in the State, and the dominant figure in the *Politbureau*. And behind the Party was the O.G.P.U., the secret police, controlling spies, penal labour camps in Siberia and prisons. Although a liberal federation in form, the Soviet Constitution of 1936 was a veiled tyranny in fact.

In 1936–37 there was a need, it seemed, for tyranny. There was much debate on the changes in the Constitution, in soviets and in factory groups throughout the Soviet Union. There was unrest at the hardships suffered as a result of the Five-Year Plans. The Plans themselves were not keeping to schedule. There was fear of Hitlerism in Germany, which preached a doctrine of hatred for 'Jewish-Bolshevism', and fears of spies and agents from the capitalist West.

And in 1936–37 came the Moscow Trials, a series of spectacular trials of prominent Communists. The result of these trials was the elimination of all who opposed Stalin.

From 1937 until his death in 1953—through the two years of truce with Hitler (1939–41), the four years of war (1941–45) and the eight years of Cold War (1945–53)—Stalin dominated Russia, and most of Eastern Europe. He came to be described as superhuman and to be revered; he was seen as all-knowing and all-powerful, and free from human frailty. His picture was everywhere. He was the symbol of the nation, he was 'the Great Teacher of the Toiling Masses'.

3. *The war for the Soviet fatherland.*

From the seizure of power by Hitler in Germany in 1933, there had been bitterness between Germany and Russia; Hitler made it plain that he would move East, if he could, to seize the Ukraine; he was the declared enemy of Communism. In March 1939 Stalin described Hitler's Germany as aggressive, and Britain and France as non-aggressive.

On 23 August 1939, however, Stalin concluded a non-aggression pact with Hitler, giving the latter a free hand in Poland. After a fortnight's war, Poland was partitioned between Germany and Russia. (This has sometimes been described as the Fourth Partition of Poland—the previous being 1772, 1793, 1795.) This decision of Stalin's was presumably made to give Russia time to prepare against Hitler, and to give it an extra defensive barrier in East Poland. With the same intent, the Baltic States were forced to make terms with the Soviet Union, to be incorporated as Soviet Republics in 1940. Finland resisted, expecting Western help. She was invaded in November 1939 and had to make terms in March 1940, ceding strategic areas of southern Finland—the approaches to Leningrad—to Russia.

Stalin wished to maintain neutrality in the war. He trusted neither side, and was gaining substantially as they exhausted each other. But Hitler struck at Russia, in 'Operation Barbarossa', 22 June 1941. And Mr Churchill promptly announced British help for the Soviet Union.

What followed was land war on a colossal scale, with millions engaged on both sides. There were 4 million Russians opposed to 3 million Germans, with the Germans much superior in tanks, planes—and experience. They planned to break Russian resistance in four months. At first the German tanks registered quick success; by October they reached the outskirts of Leningrad, penetrated within 60 miles of Moscow and overran the Ukraine. Russian losses were staggering. They lost millions of acres and hundreds of thousands of men as they retreated. In the grim winter of 1941–42, however, they pushed back, regaining one-fifth of the territory lost. In June 1942 the German drive on the oilfields of the Caucasus was launched and was held at Stalingrad on the Volga. At last, in October 1942, the German army at Stalingrad was defeated, and much of it was captured. Along with the Battle of Alamein, this was the turning point in the war. In the second winter counter-offensive, Russia regained 200,000 square miles of territory.

She suffered acutely in the war—half her coal and steel production was destroyed, and millions of her people were killed. As the Germans were driven back, the Red Army overran Poland, Romania, Hungary, Czechoslovakia and Bulgaria. Communist régimes arose in these countries, either spontaneously—as in Yugoslavia, whose resistance to Germany owed little to Stalin's help—or under pressure. During the war, Russian factories had been moved to the Urals, and the war brought a great stimulus to industrial development in the Urals and in the Kuznetsk basin. After the war the economies of the 'satellite' countries were closely linked to that of the Soviet Union; and in all of these countries there have been the usual purges in the leadership, often on direction from Moscow. By the time (April 1945) that Russian troops entered Berlin, much of Eastern Europe was under Russian occupation or control.

In 1946 the Fourth Five-Year Plan was begun, designed to restore the war-ravaged areas, to restore the pre-war level in industry and agriculture and to develop industry in non-European Russia. During it Russia was able to replace

Germany as a supplier of industrial goods to her satellites and to draw in agricultural supplies—and booty—from the territory she occupied. The Plan also provided for the maintenance of large military forces—estimated as high as 4 million men.

The army is now well trained, and is equipped with atomic and nuclear weapons and missiles.

On Stalin's death in 1953 he left his country very strong, commanding an empire—though no Communist would accept the term. In fighting the war he had appealed not to Communism but to nationalism. Other Communist leaders had done the same, like Tito in Yugoslavia; and when too much Russian control was pressed on Tito in 1948 he broke with Stalin. But elsewhere the Russian grip on the satellites was strong. Despite the Plans, however, Russian production was and is far behind that of the United States, both in total goods produced and in the production per man-hour of labour. Russia lacks skilled mechanics and craftsmen, but is training them quickly. Each year Russia devotes a higher percentage of total production to industrial and capital goods than does the United States, because of the latter's enormous consumer market in materials.

Russian foreign policy 1917–45

Throughout her recent history, Russia has had several permanent objectives in foreign policy: security against Japan in the Far East, including, if possible, control over ports in Manchuria and trade outlets into Asia; the Russianizing of, or at least access to, the Bosphorus, and from it to the Mediterranean; leadership of the Slav nations (pan-Slavism was a Tsarist policy as much as a Communist policy); security in the west, against the big powers of Europe, by the erection of buffer-states, friendly to Russia or under her control.

Her policy from 1917 to 1945 fell into five stages:

The period of complete isolation 1917–22. Russia withdrew from the First World War and made peace with Germany at Brest-Litovsk, March 1918. She was forced to abandon the Ukraine to Germany and lost most of her industrial resources. Russia, herself engaged in civil war, was invaded by foreign troops (British, French, American and Baltic) and was at war with Poland.

She denounced Imperialism and the secret treaties of the First World War. She set up the Communist International in Moscow to organize world revolution. But the revolutionary movements in Hungary and Germany collapsed.

Co-operation with Germany 1922–33. This began by Russia's signing the Treaty of Rapallo in 1922 with Germany; and exchange of goods and military supplies followed. It was a period of antagonism towards Britain, France and the United States. Stalin abandoned the idea of world Communism, at least temporarily, but gave aid to Communism in China. The First Labour Government in Britain (1924) recognized the Soviet régime, but relations were broken off later. The United States did not recognize U.S.S.R. until 1933.

Collective security 1933–39. Frightened by the rise of Hitler, U.S.S.R. joined the League of Nations. Treaties of non-aggression were signed with all her western neighbours and with France. Communists outside Russia joined with democratic movements in so-called 'popular front' governments, as in Spain and France, to fight Fascism; active Soviet help was given to the Spanish Loyalist cause in the Spanish Civil War. This policy was associated with the name of Maxim Litvinov, Russia's Foreign Minister.

Co-operation with Nazi Germany 1939–41. The non-aggression pact with Germany of August 1939 was due to the failure of Litvinov's hopes of an accord with the West and the belief that the West, as Munich showed, was not prepared to resist Hitler. Stalin therefore began a policy of insuring himself by seizing territory from Poland and from Romania (Bessarabia) and by annexing the Baltic states. Communist parties outside Russia found themselves in a confused and embarrassed position as 'unwilling allies' of the Nazis.

Co-operation with the Allies 1941–45. On 22 June 1941, Germany invaded Russia. On 12 July 1941, Great Britain and the U.S.S.R. became war-time allies. Communist parties throughout the world abandoned their hostile attitude towards the war and agitated for a total effort to defeat Germany. Russia participated in the war-time conferences which set up the United Nations Organization.

Russia since Stalin: Khrushchev and his successors

Since Stalin's death in 1953, the Russian Government has been much more liberal. Stalin was succeeded as Chairman of the Council of Ministers by Malenkov, but he resigned in February 1955 and was succeeded by Marshal Bulganin. In 1953 Nikita Khrushchev became Secretary of the Communist Party, an office Stalin held for 30 years, and Khrushchev was for the next 11 years Stalin's successor as the real ruler of Russia.

Khrushchev (b. 1894) is the son of a Ukrainian miner, who fought with the Red Army in the Civil War. He was responsible for the building of the famous Moscow underground, for which he got the Order of Lenin. In the Second World War he led the guerrilla war against the Germans in the Ukraine. He emerged as very different from Stalin—quick, shrewd and bubbling with energy and spirit, a jovial, roly-poly figure with great intelligence. In the years after 1953 he visited many foreign countries, including Britain and the United States (twice); Stalin only once left the Soviet Union to meet Roosevelt and Churchill at Teheran in 1943.

Khrushchev is a Marxist, like all Communists, and believes that there is an unbridgeable gulf between capitalist states and Russia. 'We shall forget about Marx,' he said, 'only when shrimps learn to whistle.' But his policy showed very striking differences from Stalin. In February 1956, at the 20th Communist Party Congress, he criticized Stalin because of what was called 'the cult of personality'. Stalin had deliberately built himself up into a hero, he said, and this was now condemned. Leadership, it was said, was now to be 'collective', not personal. Conferences were held with the Western Powers at Berlin and Geneva in 1954 and 1955; some Soviet bases in Finland and at Port Arthur were given up; Russian troops were withdrawn from Austria and at last a peace treaty with that country could be signed; discussions with Tito in Yugoslavia were begun after a six-year period of insults and accusation, and the doctrine was proclaimed of 'different roads to Socialism'—a view Stalin could never have accepted. But when Hungary revolted against Russian control in October 1956, Russia acted swiftly and ruthlessly, and the rebellion was crushed by Russian tanks.

Again, there has been little change in economics. Russia is still being directed by Five-Year Plans on similar lines to those of Stalin. The emphasis has been on heavy engineering; the world's largest hydro-electric power station has been built on the Volga near Kuybyshev; Soviet steel production has doubled since 1950; and the first steps have been taken to build up a third heavy industrial area in East Siberia, near Lake Baikal, to rival the Donbas and the Urals. There has been some decentralization of power: 105 planning councils were set up in 1957. But there is still neither political nor economic freedom in Russia.

Despite these facts, and his own showmanship, Khrushchev was a liberal. His policy can be summed up as de-Stalinization, decentralization and *détente*.

In two respects in particular he was genuinely more liberal than Stalin. (*a*) He reduced the power of the Secret Police and stopped the sudden arrests that marked the last years of Stalin. Leaders who failed or resigned were no longer ill-treated or executed; both Malenkov and Molotov survive, and the latter has recently been restored to major office. (*b*) The doctrine of inevitable war between capitalism and Communism seems to have been abandoned by Russia (although not, it seems, by the Chinese Communists). It has been replaced by that of 'peaceful co-existence': Russia and the West can live side by side, rivals but not enemies. This is partly due to the fact that both Russia and the West have nuclear weapons and can reply to nuclear attack in kind. It is also a recognition by Russia of its technical achievements, and that the more peaceful and successful it is, the greater the influence it will have over the African and Asian nations, the so-called uncommitted countries. It was for the leadership of these new nations that Khrushchev was bidding when he led his country's delegation to the United Nations in New York in 1960. He was a frequent and restless traveller, and in all his journeys, very much the extrovert. However different the strategy, the long-term hope of the Communist countries is to weaken the West and to win control over the neutral countries.

Since 1957 the challenge to the West has increased because of the development of Russian sputniks and technical skills. Russia was a leader in space research, the first country successfully to send animals and in 1961 a man (Yuri Gagarin) into space, and to bring them back alive, and the first to photograph from rockets the other side of the moon. There is now a state of 'competitive co-existence' with the West.

The fall of Khrushchev

In October 1964 Khrushchev was deprived of his posts and power, and replaced as First Secretary of the Party by Leonid Brezhnev and as Premier by Alexei Kosygin. It is not yet fully clear why Khrushchev was dismissed, but Moscow gave a list of 29 charges against him. The most important of these were:

Cuba. He committed errors in policy and invited the defeat of his policy by introducing missiles into Cuba in the autumn of 1962.

China. He reduced the Chinese-Soviet ideological conflict to the level of a personal feud between himself and Mao Tse-tung. He under-estimated the speed of scientific progress which permitted the Chinese to explode their nuclear bomb.

Personal behaviour. On his visit to Scandinavia in the summer of 1964 his behaviour defeated the purpose of his goodwill mission. Specifically, his remarks to a capitalist audience about his former political rivals in the Soviet leadership, Mr Molotov and Marshal Bulganin, were uncalled for.

Romania. His wrong policies led to an estrangement between the Soviet Union and Romania.

Planning. He committed errors in Soviet domestic economic policies. He disorganized the economy, first by ordering decentralization and later by going back to centralized planning.

Agriculture. He committed errors in his direction of Soviet agriculture, and this brought great discontent. Kosygin was especially critical of this.

Personality cult. He reintroduced a Stalin-type cult for his own benefit. Brezhnev and Kosygin argued that the epoch of 'self-congratulatory speeches' was over.

Statesmanship. His personal behaviour in office was unworthy of a Communist leader.

Leadership. He ended the 'collective leadership' that had begun after Stalin's death and instituted a new one-man rule of his own.

Industry. He over-emphasized light industry and consumer goods at the expense of heavy industry.

Whatever the reasons for Khrushchev's fall, the consequences seem clear and affect both policy and personality.

The New Men

Brezhnev and Kosygin are 'new men', reared in the Stalin era. At the time of the Revolution, Brezhnev was eleven and Kosygin thirteen. Their rise began in the late 1930s after Stalin's massacre of the Old Bolsheviks had opened up avenues of rapid ascent to young newcomers. Kosygin, who was born in St Petersburg in 1904, held a number of minor posts until 1938 when he became Mayor of Leningrad, his home town. In 1939 he became a member of the Council of People's Commissars (now Ministers) of the Soviet Union and head of the entire Soviet textile industry. In 1940 he was appointed deputy chairman of the Council of People's Commissars, a post he held for the rest of the Stalin era. During the war he also served as chairman of the Council of People's Commissars (equivalent to premier) of the all-important Russian Republic.

Brezhnev, the son of a Ukrainian steelworker and himself a metallurgical engineer, was made a party secretary of the important industrial region of Dnepropetrovsk in 1939. Since then he has moved steadily up the ladder: aide to Khrushchev, political commissar with the Red Army, commissar in Kazakhstan and then in the Kremlin. Thus the character and careers of both men developed within the same Stalinist pattern, but the skills and experience they acquired differed. In fact, each man represents the two major types of Soviet leaders: Brezhnev is the professional political organizer and Kosygin the economic administrator. Brezhnev has spent almost his whole working life within an organization of full-time political bureaucrats, the Communist Party apparatus. Kosygin, on the other hand, has spent his whole life in the management of the Soviet economy. He has never been a member of the community of professional political organizers to which Brezhnev belongs, and is more radical in politics.

Whatever may be the policy changes under Brezhnev and Kosygin, so far the most striking differences are differences of personality between them and Khrushchev. They have been cautious where Khrushchev was colourful, and deliberate in introducing changes where Khrushchev was apt to be the Great Improviser. It is probable that what Khrushchev's opponents found most intolerable about him was not his basic policies but his style of leadership.

The new emphasis

Within three weeks of Khrushchev's fall, a Communist Summit Meeting was held (November 1964). This meeting was attended by Chou En-lai, the Chinese Prime Minister—the first high-level meeting between Chinese and Soviet leaders since July 1963—and by all the Communist countries except Albania. Although the Soviet leaders cautioned against expectations of an early *rapprochement* with China, it seems clear that Mr Brezhnev and Mr Chou were seeking to arrange a truce in the war of words between their two states. They may even have made offers to resume Soviet economic aid to China—the aid which Khrushchev had stopped abruptly and totally in 1960 with devastating consequences for the Chinese economy. But there has been no evidence of a thaw here. The deep differences remain. The new leaders have continued the policy of peaceful co-existence with the capitalist West even more obviously than did Khrushchev, and much less dramatically. Mr Kosygin has emerged as an able diplomat: visits to China and North Vietnam, the mediation in 1966 at Tashkent to bring peace between India and Pakistan, the warm reception to de Gaulle in 1966, the visit to Britain in 1967. The major objectives thus far are clearly to prevent the nuclear re-armament of Germany (a view shared by de Gaulle) and the effort to stop the war in Vietnam.

They have emphasized the technical achievements of the U.S.S.R., its space programme and its industrial development. When de Gaulle visited Russia in 1966, he was taken on a visit to the great and fast-growing scientific city of Novosibirsk beyond the Urals and shown a Russian rocket-launching site. This, like the great May Day rallies, served also to demonstrate Russia's

May Day celebrations take place every year in Moscow. In this picture rocket weapons are paraded through Red Square.

military power and organization. In October 1965, the government under Kosygin approved the new Charter for Industrialists which has been described as a new Russian industrial revolution. The new system marks a complete departure from Stalin's 'command economy', and although factories must still operate within the general limit of the state plans, the greatest latitude is now given to each enterprise to exercise its own initiative in accordance with local conditions and requirements. A considerable personal incentive is given under this system to both managers and workers, which marks altogether a departure from the old concept of 'Soviet man', who was expected 'to work anyway for the good of Communism'. Now the personal profit motive has been strengthened and every factory, for instance in the clothing industry, must take account of the public's taste and requirements. In recent years there has been a wasteful accumulation of unwanted and unsaleable goods in shops.

Equally important are the changes recently made in the countryside. Under Khrushchev the cultivation of the collective farmer's private plot was discouraged through heavy taxation and in other ways; today, on the contrary, the farmer is helped to increase the production of his plot and to sell it profitably in the open market. Nevertheless, agriculture remains by far the weakest point in Soviet economy. Twice in the last few years—in 1963 and in 1965—Russia has had to import enormous quantities of wheat from abroad. At the 23rd Party Congress in 1966, Kosygin proposed revolutionary reforms to improve Soviet agricultural production. This Congress may prove the most important since the famous 20th ('de-Stalinization') Congress (1957).

Russia seems now to be ruled collectively. All the evidence indicates that decisions in the policy-making Praesidium of the party Central Committee, the twelve-man board of directors that rules Russia, are taken by majority vote of the collective leadership. That leadership includes (in addition to Brezhnev and Kosygin) such party stalwarts as ideologue Suslov, former security chief Alexander Shelepin, and deputy party secretary Nikolai Podgorny, who in 1966 replaced Mikoyan as President of the State.

One reason for the cautious leadership is the economic slow-down. This, attributed by Khrushchev to temporary factors, now appears likely to last at least for the rest of the decade. Forgotten are the slogans about surpassing the United States in economic development by 1970. The economic setback, aggravated by another bad agricultural year, imposes severe limitations on the flexibility of the leadership. With the volume of Soviet production only half that of the United States, Russia must devote a proportionately larger share of its resources to space and defence to match United States strides in the two fields. The Soviet growth rate will remain at about 4.3 per cent a year—the same level as the United States rate—until 1970. The Soviet rate must be much higher if Russia is to overtake the United States economy.

The big question is where the money will come from to finance these advances, particularly since bad weather and poor planning in past years have conspired to produce another poor grain crop. In a move reminiscent of the disastrous harvest of 1963, Russia buys wheat from abroad. Paying for these imports means using up foreign exchange that otherwise could permit the importing of machinery and chemicals to raise farm yields.

What, then, are the changes since Khrushchev? The only major foreign-policy move was the Kremlin decision to supply North Vietnam with much-needed military equipment. But Moscow, unlike Peking, apparently has been urging caution on North Vietnam. Russia's economic strains prevent adventurism; philosophical differences exacerbate tensions with China. Domestically, most of the changes are in degree, not substance. Agricultural policy has been revised. Khrushchev's recommendations to expand consumer-goods production have been followed, and his experiments with running industry on a 'profit' basis have been broadened. The Communist Party itself plays a less important role.

The big difference is in style. The new leaders appear rarely at diplomatic receptions, they rarely grant interviews, and their pictures rarely appear in the press. To their own countrymen and to the world, they appear as functionaries, not distinct personalities. They face grave problems—scarce resources, internal political pressures, the continuing feud with China. These pressures have in the past always led to the emergence of one man, the man who controls the party machine. If such forces continue, it seems safe to judge that in due course Brezhnev will become the supreme figure. He has received more publicity

Soviet cosmonauts. From the left: Gherman Titov, Boris Egorov, Yuri Gagarin, Andrian Nikolaev, Valentina Tereshkova (Nikolaeva), Pavel Popovitch, Valery Bykovsky, Vladimir Komarov, Konstantin Feoktistov.

Нас уже девять. Мы счастливы, что проложили первые трассы в космос. Верим, что 1965 год принесёт новые успехи в освоении Вселенной на благо нашей Родины, всех людей Земли.
С Новым годом!

recently than Kosygin. In January 1967 on his 60th birthday he became a Hero of the Soviet Union—the highest Soviet decoration. This could be the beginning of a process of manufacturing the next great Russian leader. After Stalin, Khrushchev. After Khrushchev, Brezhnev?

QUESTIONS TO CONSIDER

1. What are the chief features of either (*a*) the Russian S.F.S.R. or (*b*) Kazakhstan S.S.R.?
2. What are the main industrial areas of the U.S.S.R.?
3. Why did Revolution occur in Russia in 1917? Outline the main stages.
4. Distinguish between the views of Lenin, Trotsky and Stalin.
5. What did Stalin do for Russia? What criticism would you make of the régime?
6. What changes have occurred in Russia since 1953?
7. Account for the rapid growth in the production of oil, steel and coal since 1955.
8. Explain the serious rift in friendship between Russia and China since 1962.

WORDS TO NOTE

Politbureau: The top-level policy committee of the Russian Communist Party.
Proletariat: The main body of landless workers in Russia before the Revolution. (A term used by Marx and Communist politicians to describe the working people of any country.)
Soviet: Workers' council in factories or in the army.

FOR FURTHER READING

Crankshaw, Edward: *Russia and the Russians*, Macmillan, 1947.
Pares, B.: *Russia*, Penguin, 1941.
Baransky, N.: *Economic Geography of the U.S.S.R.*, Moscow, 1956. (English translation of a standard school textbook used in the U.S.S.R.)
Conquest, R.: *Common Sense about Russia*, Gollancz, 1960.
Crankshaw, Edward: *Khrushchev's Russia*, Penguin, 1966.
Cole, J. P.: *Geography of the U.S.S.R.*, Penguin, 1967.
Deutscher, I.: *Stalin*, Vintage Books, 1961.
Wolfe, B.: *Three who made a revolution*, Penguin, 1964.
Werth, A.: *Russia under Khrushchev*, Crest Books, N.Y., 1962.

6. *China*

China has a fourfold importance today.

It is, first, the scene of the longest continuous civilization in world history. 1,500 years B.C. there flourished in north China a rich society, based on the cultivation of wheat and rice and producing beautiful works of art. This civilization was perhaps at its height 2,000 years ago (the Han dynasty) and again at the time of the T'ang dynasty (seventh to tenth century A.D.). From time to time it was attacked from inner Asia by Tatar tribes, and the Great Wall was built to hold them out. Twice in its long history, however, China was ruled by foreign dynasties from Asia—by the Mongols (1280–1368) and by the Manchus (1644–1911). But each time the conquerors were absorbed, and the Manchus especially identified themselves with China. And throughout the 3,000-year story China changed very little in character; it was a great static agricultural society, governed by a class of scholars carefully chosen after public examination (the *mandarins*), and with a code of conduct shaped 500 years B.C. by the sage Confucius.

Its second importance is that on the collapse of the Manchus in 1911, China experienced the wave of nationalism that is the chief feature of this century. China, one of the oldest of civilizations, is also one of the youngest of nations. The revolutionary movement led by Dr Sun Yat-Sen in 1911 was an attempt by a group of foreign-trained Cantonese to replace the Manchu Empire by a republic; China was not ready for this, and 25 years of civil war followed. Sun Yat-Sen himself was educated in the United States, and the reform movement was largely a foreign product.

It was also, however, a revolt against foreigners: against the Western Powers who controlled the trade of China, and against their bases on the China coast. By 1898 Britain controlled some 40 ports on the coast, of which Shanghai and Hong Kong were the most important. European Powers had annexed parts of the country by 1898; and there was in 1900 a revolt against them, when the so-called Boxers, a group of Chinese who called themselves 'The Fists of Righteous Harmony', attacked the Western consulates. The Western Powers demanded compensation for this, and got it in the right to station troops in Peking (the Welch Regiment kept a battalion there until 1937) and in payment of an indemnity (the Boxer Indemnity). National bitterness against the West continued, and by 1937 it was a bitterness even more against Japan. Since 1894–95 when she defeated China, Japan had, like the West, been grabbing territory along the Chinese coast, especially Korea (annexed in 1910) and Manchuria (controlled in 1931). China hoped for a national revolution that would drive out the foreign barbarian, whether Western or Japanese.

The third feature of China today is that in October 1949, when at last a revolutionary government won control of the whole country, that régime was Communist. China is a Communist state as a result of a revolution in Asia. As in Russia in 1917, Communism in 1949 triumphed in a largely non-industrial society. This Asiatic form of Communism is now showing striking differences from that in Russia, but it was helped in its early stages by the Soviet Union.

Fourth, as in Russia, it is carrying through an economic revolution. As to Lenin, so it is to Mao Tse-tung—'Communism means state control, plus electrification'. China is being made a modern, industrialized, progressive nation. She is rich in coal (north-west) and iron (Manchuria), in antimony, tungsten, copper and tin (South China); she is reputed to be rich in oil, but little of it as yet has been developed. Her communications are still poor. In 1949 she had only 10,000 miles of railways (only four per cent of U.S.A.), and her rivers, her chief highways, suffer from periodic flooding.

One sign of progress is its increasing population. Today approximately one in five of all the people in the world are Chinese. The Chinese people belong to the Mongoloid race, of which Mongols, Tibetans and Manchus are related strains. The population was estimated in 1967 to be 700 million, it is increasing by 10 million a year and by A.D. 2000 it is likely to reach 1,000 million. The population is packed into one-seventh of the area—for much of China is hilly

Small children like to make a noise—in China as elsewhere. No doubt it's music to their ears.

and barren. Eighty per cent of the Chinese live on the land, producing mainly rice, wheat, millet and tea, sugar and milk. There are only six large cities— Shanghai, Nanking, Peking, Tientsin, Chungking and Canton—and industrialization has not as yet got far.

There is very strong family feeling; the family is large and a basic social grouping; great respect is shown to the head of the family and to the aged. But life is hard. A family might work a farm of less than three acres and earn £20–£25 a year. Implements are primitive; roads are poor; and there are periodic droughts.

The regions of China

China has 21 provinces, in addition to Tibet and Formosa, both of which it claims as Chinese. Inner Mongolia, Sinkiang and Kwangsi are also linked to it as 'autonomous provinces'. It is, after Russia, the second largest country in the world, covering over 4 million square miles.

180

China within and without the Great Wall

The essential China consists of the great plains lying to the east of the plateaux of inner Asia, which mark the limits of the fertilizing monsoon rains that support its vast population. For most of its extent from north to south of more than 1,200 miles it is backed by the immense tableland of Tibet with an average height of about 10,000 feet. On that side the ancient agricultural civilization needed no protection. But the lower-lying Mongolian Plateau to the north-west and the rich grasslands of Manchuria to the north-east were the homes of nomadic, pastoral tribes, who from time immemorial were a perpetual menace.

To protect the 'Peasant Empire' from the devastating invasions of these tribes, the wonderful scheme of frontier defence known as the Great Wall was built in the third century B.C. when China first became a centralized state. The Great Wall spans the gap between Tibet and the inner gulf of the Yellow Sea, known as the Po-Hai. It is over 1,500 miles in length. Its course marked one of the greatest social divides in the world. It separated 'the steppe and the sown'.

Outer China today

Whenever China has been strong it has exerted pressure on its neighbours across the Wall. This has been a feature of this century, especially since 1949. With the development of railways there has been an outward movement of Chinese peasants beyond the Great Wall, and that part of the Mongolian Plateau on the Chinese side of the Gobi Desert known as Inner Mongolia has been merged with China since the establishment of the Republic in 1911–12.

Still more dramatic has been the mass movement into Manchuria and the conversion of its former grasslands into a rich granary. Its seizure by Japan in 1931–32 and the creation of the puppet state of Manchukuo cannot alter the fact that it is now essentially Chinese in population and in culture. It is here that China, Japan and Russia have clashed. Manchuria is fertile and has mineral wealth; and across it runs the Chinese-Eastern Railway that joins up with the Trans-Siberian. It is the richest part of China today.

In the last few years strong pressure has been brought on Tibet, now part of China. Unlike Manchuria, however, Tibet and Outer Mongolia cannot be considered as part of the essential China, and, looking to the future, both the Tibetans and the Mongols have a definite claim to be regarded as distinct nationalities.

The most critical region of Outer China is the vast outlying 'province' of Sinkiang or Chinese Turkestan. Set in between Tibet to the south and Mongolia and Soviet Russia to the north, it is not only a prospective field for colonization but holds the key to China's communications with the West. Its scanty population is very mixed, and control over it has been an objective of Chinese foreign policy for more than 2,000 years.

Inner China

China proper within the Great Wall is approximately the size of Europe (excluding Russia). The Chinese provinces, 21 in number, are comparable, alike in size and population, to the individual countries of Europe. Only two are smaller than Scotland. Several are larger than Great Britain. Szechwan, the largest of the historic provinces, is approximately the size of Sweden but has nearly 10 times its population. The distances which separate Stockholm, London, Berlin, Moscow and Rome are roughly the same as those which separate the greatest regional centres of China: Peking in the far north, Nanking and Shanghai near the eastern seaboard, Hankow in the centre, Chengtu in the extreme west and Canton in the extreme south.

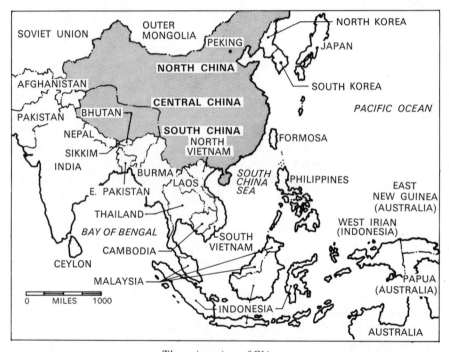

The main regions of China.

Inner China falls into three natural divisions:

North China lies south of the Great Wall. It is a vast plain some 600 miles from north to south through which flows the Hwang-Ho, the Yellow River.

It has a long and most bitter winter and is often swept by dust-laden winds from inner Asia. During this season agricultural operations are almost completely suspended. The summer is hot, and early autumn is beautiful, but the rainy season is short (about three and a half months) and precarious. There are years of drought and years of Yellow River floods, and, between them, famine conditions may be expected in one year out of five or six.

The severe climate has produced a race of sturdy peasant farmers, laboriously cultivating the 'dry' cereals (wheat and maize) and vegetables, which alone are adapted to the climatic conditions. Villages are innumerable but towns are few, and, in great contrast to Central China, the rivers are of little use for navigation. In the western highlands is 85 per cent of China's coal.

Central China has long been the main focus of Chinese civilization. Although there is much hilly country, the outstanding feature of its relief is the large number of rich basins linked by the Yangtse and its great tributaries, from the Red Basin in the extreme west to the plain of the Lower Yangtse, outstanding in agriculture, industry and commerce and studded with historic cities.

The climate is intermediate between that of the tropical south and the extreme continental conditions of the north. Its winters are cool but not cold, the temperatures closely corresponding to those of Britain in the same season. Its summers, on the other hand, are as hot and nearly as moist as those of South China, and it has a long and fairly reliable rainy season of seven or eight months. Its range of production is one of the greatest in the world, with rice, cotton, tea, wheat and many other cereals.

The Yangtse is its great artery from the Red Basin, almost under the snowy mountains of the Tibetan border, to Shanghai 1,600 miles away. When it issues from the Gorges into its great central basin it receives tributaries which are themselves comparable in size to the largest of European rivers: the Han, which links it with the north-west, and the Siang and the Kan whose valleys provide the two principal corridor routes to the south. The former is followed by the now completed trunk railway from Canton to Peking. This crosses the Yangtse at Hankow, the greatest junction in China and the head of ocean navigation, although it is in the centre of the country and 600 miles from the sea.

The Yangtse basin supports about 300 million people, nearly half the entire population, and the commerce of the country largely converges to a single outlet—Shanghai, the gateway of China.

South China is hilly and even mountainous. But in the coastal provinces the fertile valleys open out into busy, densely-peopled estuaries. The valleys of south-east and south China have a moist, virtually tropical climate all the year round, and here there is intensive tea and rice cultivation—two and sometimes three crops a year.

The valleys have tended to be little worlds to themselves and here in south-east China there is a multiplicity of dialects. In the highlands of the south-west, until recently almost completely remote, there are still many unassimilated aboriginal peoples, speaking tribal dialects.

The chief city of South China is Canton, one of the country's oldest ports, where thousands of people ('the river people') live permanently on their sampans or junks. Many Chinese cities are terribly overcrowded.

China between the Wars

The Manchu dynasty came to an end in the Revolution of 1911. This was led by Sun Yat-Sen who drew up the programme known as 'The Three Principles of the People'. They were (*a*) 'Nationalism'; (*b*) 'Political Democracy': i.e.

A Chinese worker carries home a fish he has caught in the river near Canton.

political institutions on Western lines; (c) 'The People's Livelihood'—or what might more usefully be called 'Social Justice' or 'Socialism'. He organized a People's National Party, the Kuomintang. Dr Sun was not a Marxist; his ideal was a free, educated, land-owning peasantry. But after 1918 he accepted help from the Soviet Union, and Russian advisers. In 1926 the advisers were recalled, and China struggled to find its own solutions to its problems.

The new republican government met opposition from the war-lords, who were part feudal landlords, part military chiefs, part brigands. To oppose them a new national army was organized by one of Dr Sun's followers, Generalissimo Chiang-Kai-Shek. Dr Sun died on a visit to Peking in 1925 but in 1926–28 this Kuomintang army won control of the Yangtse valley and eventually of Peking itself. Dr Sun's embalmed body was brought south to rest in a great mausoleum outside the new national capital, Nanking.

From his victory in 1928 to the outbreak of the Japanese war in 1937, in only nine years Chiang united under his control some three-quarters of the country and suppressed almost all the war-lords. Railways and roads were built, and some concessions were won from the Western Powers. The country was governed by the National Congress of the Party, and by the Central Executive Committee elected by it. A democratic system was to be introduced later.

Throughout this period, however, a bitter civil war continued between Chiang and the Chinese Communists. These were forces that urged far more sweeping reforms than Chiang was prepared to carry out, and a united front against Japan. They saw him as a tool of the West, especially after his marriage in 1927 to Mai-Ling Soong, one of three very attractive daughters of a Shanghai banker (her elder sister had married Dr Sun, her younger Dr Kung, also a banker). Madame Chiang, who was educated in the United States and who speaks flawless English, has long had great influence over her husband; in 1931 he became a convert to Methodism.

By 1934, after seven campaigns against the Chinese Communists in the south, Chiang was on the point of totally defeating the Communist Army in Fukien province. This army then carried out a famous march of some 3,000 miles through Szechwan to the north-west, where, in the mountains of Shensi and Kansu, they could reorganize and continue the fight. In 1936 Communist forces captured Chiang, and after some days of discussion he agreed to stop the civil war in order to present a united front to the Japanese, already occupying Manchuria and devastating the coastal provinces. In 1937, using an incident at the Marco Polo Bridge near Peking, Japan struck at Chiang, and a new war began.

The Japanese War (1937–45)

This was the ugliest war until then, in the ugly story of war in the twentieth century. It was marked by mass air bombing by the Japanese of defenceless civilians, especially the bombing of Canton. Pro-Japanese régimes were set up in the occupied part of China; Japan controlled many cities and railway lines and enforced a blockade of the coast.

Chinese resistance continued, however. The capital was moved inland to Chungking beyond the Gorges of the Yangtse, and a road, 700 miles long, was built from Burma to Chungking to convey British and American supplies. It was built without the help of machinery through mountainous and uninhabited country—a great achievement. A group of American volunteers, the 'Flying Tigers', led by Colonel Chennault, using old planes, flew in supplies over perilous mountains. The Chinese moved hospitals and schools and industry to the western hills—some 600 factories with about 12,000 workers—and continued a bitter guerrilla war. The war with Japan forced the speedy development of western China, and for a time brought a truce between Nationalists and Communists.

In 1941, when Japan attacked the Allies, China became an ally of Britain, Russia and the United States.

Two Chinas (1945–49)

In 1945 the civil war between Chiang and Mao was resumed. By 1948 Peking was in Mao's hands, and by October 1949 he controlled all China except Hong Kong, Hainan Island and Formosa. It was to Formosa that Chiang retreated, and from where ever since he has talked of 'liberating' the mainland. The People's Republic was set up in October 1949, with Mao as Chairman of the Central Committee of the Chinese Communist Party, and with Peking once again the capital. The Chief of the State Council (or Premier) is Chou En-lai, who has also been Foreign Minister since 1950.

The China of Mao Tse-tung

The first Communist movement had appeared in Canton and Shanghai in 1921, but by 1928 it had been destroyed in the towns. Communism, however, stayed alive in the Red Army in the southern provinces, and in some there were soviet governments. They wanted distribution of land to the peasants, schools and hospitals to be built, and a central agency for marketing—which provided rice and pork cheaper than elsewhere. Schemes were drawn up for flood control and irrigation. Gambling, opium smoking and religion were to be suppressed; many priests and missionaries were killed. The Commander of the Red Army was Chu Teh, but the political leader and strongest personality was Mao Tse-tung (b. 1893). Mao began to see in the Chinese peasantry the core of the future Communist state.

Mao led the Long March to the north-west in 1934. The Red Army had to fight against Chiang all the way on their march through the flat rice lands south of the Yangtse, north through Yunnan, past the borderlands of Tibet, until a year later they reached Shensi. Mao's first wife died on the march. By 1936 some 300,000 were in the new 'Utopia'; and, although they were by 1937 allies with Chiang against Japan, they now had a permanent base of their own, and they were nearer to Russia.

Why did Mao win?

By 1945 Chiang had lost whatever revolutionary appeal he had ever possessed. There were many accusations of corruption and the Soong and Kung families seemed to be prospering at the expense of the Chinese people. The Kuomintang had become a bankers' and landowners' party. Chiang's régime became corrupt and inefficient.

At the Yalta Conference in 1945 Russia was promised control over Manchuria when Japan was defeated. Because the atom bomb was dropped on Japan, Russia was at war with her only six days. Russian gains led to a loss of fighting spirit in the Nationalist armies. At one point, almost one million men left Chiang for Mao. This was less a preference for Communism than for peace, a weariness of 30 years of war, famine and inflation.

The Chinese Communists were not proletarians so much as peasants, concerned with land and livelihood. 'The land to him who tills it' had been the battle-cry since 1911. Chiang had done nothing to transfer land to the peasants. Communism was a protest against landlordism. Mao showed himself able to curb landlords and to improve social conditions.

Mao showed himself a disciplined and dedicated leader. He had had support from Russia in 1945, and when Russia withdrew from Manchuria in 1946, Mao was given much ex-Japanese war equipment by Russia.

On Japan's defeat in 1945 China was at last free from foreign armies and regained control of the 13 provinces the Japanese had occupied.

Why was the victory of Mao so important?

The Communist victory in 1949 is probably the most important event in the world's history since 1945.

The struggle between Chiang and Mao was important not merely for China. Chiang had had considerable American aid ($1\frac{1}{2}$ thousand million dollars during the Japanese War, and 2 thousand million dollars after it). The United States has continued to recognize Chiang's in Formosa as the legitimate government of China, and has prevented the Mao Government from sitting in the United Nations. The war in Korea (1950–53) in which Chinese Communist troops helped North Korea, and American, British Commonwealth and U.N. troops helped South Korea, has seriously hindered any improvement in Chinese-American relations. There was never much trade between the United States and China; today every effort is made to stop it altogether.

Britain has recognized—as it usually does—the government that is in control of the territory and can best protect British lives and property there, i.e. the government of Mao. Thus the Western Allies have been divided by the events of 1949 in China.

Russia has given considerable financial help to China, and Mao's victory in 1949 was in part a victory for Russia. Russian loans have surpassed a thousand million dollars; of the first 400 projects in the First Chinese Five-Year Plan, 160 were 'gifts' from Russia to China—machines, mechanics, even methods of book-keeping were all Russian. Russia has built two new railway lines to link up China and Russia; one across Sinkiang, one across Outer Mongolia; in 1955 it restored Port Arthur to China, without asking for any compensation for the installations built there; it has pressed for the admission of Communist China to the United Nations. The two powers have presented a common front to the capitalist world.

Nevertheless, there are three major differences between China and Russia. First, China is less interested in co-existence than Russia and readier to see the clash between the West and Communism as one that might lead to war; less industrialized than Russia, it feels it might even survive a nuclear war. Second, though still backward, China has three times Russia's population and in the long run will be the greater power. This could lead to a clash over the borderlands between them, especially in Manchuria and Outer Mongolia. It wants to regain Formosa; and is less tolerant towards India than is Russia. And, third, Mao as a Chinese Communist believes that he must lead the Chinese Revolution in the light of Chinese rather than Russian experience; other revolutions in Asia will, he thinks, take China rather than Russia as their model.

Mao's success has had great importance in South-east Asia. Whenever in its history China has been strong it has tended to expand into neighbouring territories. Between 1951 and 1958 it absorbed Tibet, and the religious leader of Tibet, the Dalai Lama, took refuge in India in 1959. It helped North Korea (1950–53); it helped Vietnam to expel the French in 1954; it helped Laos in 1960. In a sense these are China's 'satellites' today. It has claims against Burma. And scattered through the South China Seas are some 11 million overseas Chinese, who are often the leading merchants and traders in all the Asian ports. The Chinese communities are important in Malaya (3 million), Thailand (3 million), Indonesia (3 million), Indo-China (2 million) and Burma ($\frac{1}{2}$ million), If not Communist sympathizers, they take pride in the power of their mother-land. By Chinese law they remain Chinese nationals, with representation in the People's Congress. Fears about their loyalty are felt in all the countries of South-east Asia.

China is beginning to play an important diplomatic role. After Stalin's death in 1953, Mao became the senior world Communist. In 1955 Chou En-lai attended the Afro-Asian Conference at Bandung and made a considerable impression. In 1956 he visited Vietnam, Burma and India. In the rivalry, economic and diplomatic, between India and China, China is showing a spectacular lead. China's income per head was the same as India's in 1952; in 1970 it will be double that of India. Relations between the two are now tense, after the Chinese conquest of Tibet. Another important factor in China's prestige is the vast size of her army.

conto P.291

What has Mao done for China?

In 1949 China had been ravaged by eight years of Japanese war and 30 years of civil war. The system of river control had broken down and every year much fertile land was ruined by floods. There was famine and price inflation; only one-third of the country's railways and roads were usable.

Mao has rendered five great services to China:

(*a*) He has campaigned against corruption, disease and waste. He has campaigned for cleanliness—the 'swat that fly' movement, to get rid of the mosquito and the disease it carries, has been accompanied by attempts to eradicate rats and grain-eating sparrows.

(*b*) He has developed industry. The expansion in the power and in the

Communist China needs agricultural machinery to help to produce the food for many hungry mouths. This tractor was made in Red China.

industrial strength of China has been phenomenal. The First Five-Year Plan laid stress on industrial development; but since 1953 the need for producing more food has been increasingly important, as evidenced by the special programme for agriculture covering the years 1956–67. It was claimed that the major goals of the Five-Year Plan for 1958–62 were fulfilled three years ahead of schedule. By 1962 China produced nearly four times the amount of coal mined in 1945 (before the Communists took control). Shanghai alone now produces more textiles than all Britain. Industrial output has increased tenfold over that of 1949. Some cities, like Peking, Shanghai and Mukden, have doubled their population. Hydro-electric works and dams have been built on the Yellow and Yangtse rivers.

(c) He has carried through a great programme of collectivization on the land. The collective farms were often created by ruthless methods, and many landlords were killed in the great purge of 1950–51. In 1958 the 750,000 collective farms were further centralized into 26,000 communes. These became not only the agricultural but also the smallest administrative, economic, educational and military units. They usually provide communal meals and foodstuffs, and sometimes clothing, medical and housing facilities. Payment according to needs was, in 1959, superseded by payment according to results. 1958 was the year of the 'Great Leap Forward', and a popular slogan was: 'The East Wind prevails over the West.' In 1959 this was modified and some family plots restored. There has been a considerable increase in food production, but agriculture is run like a factory or an ant-heap by vast production brigades. Mao has been much less successful here than in industry. Drought and floods afflicted large areas of China in 1960 and 1961, so that there were very serious food shortages, which the withdrawal of Soviet aid at that time (the start of the Soviet-Chinese dispute) did not help to ease. Moreover, the population was estimated to have passed the 700-million mark in 1967 (and is expected to be more than 800 million by 1970, though this has caused little apparent alarm and the increase has been hailed as an addition to the labour force). The 1962 harvest was more satisfactory, and lately the Chinese leaders have been showing something of their former confidence.

(d) He has carried through a great educational programme. In 1949 less than 20 per cent of the people could read and write; today it is claimed the proportion is 75 per cent. Some 100 million students are being educated in schools and universities, four times the number in 1949. There is particular emphasis on the training of engineers and scientists. China now has an atomic reactor and a vast programme of scientific development.

(e) Mao has made the Chinese, not usually war-like, proud of their army and of their success, especially in Korea and Vietnam. They have a regular army of $2\frac{1}{2}$ million, and a semi-militarized adult population able to provide 200 million militia—the world's most formidable force. This has brought unity and pride. The army, as in all backward countries, has been used to help settle frontier areas, to build roads, to harvest the grain and to write and act plays—it is a political instrument. It was successful against India in 1962. The Minister of Defence, Lin Piao, is a major figure in the State. He appears to be seen by Mao as his successor.

But China has paid a heavy price for all this.

There is no individual freedom. The state is, like Russia, run on dictatorial lines by a single party (12 million members) and a benevolent despot at the top. After Stalin's death in 1953, there was a short period in which freedom of opinion was permitted; the period when the '100 Flowers could bloom and the 100 Schools contend'. There was, however, so much criticism that thought-control was reintroduced. There is no effective code of law and no real civil liberty.

There has been a disturbing revolution in thought. The Old China was marked by Confucian principles, by loyalty to the family, by respect for age and by veneration for ancestors and tradition. The New China has seen private property swept away, youth given special privileges and a great state machine set up. Many peasants have become cogs in machines, units in work gangs, fed in communal kitchens. The older folk-art is being replaced by popular arts on Soviet lines, by mass singing and folk dancing and a great emphasis on patriotism. The Red Guards play a privileged rôle. All the emphasis is on heavy industry. Basic foods and clothing are rationed. Refugees reaching Hong Kong tell of shortages and hunger and food queues.

The Home Front: The 'Cultural Revolution'

To these handicaps must be added 'The Cultural Revolution'. Since October 1965 Chairman Mao has been seeking to strengthen the party grip on the state, the army and the universities, and to purge these of dissident elements. His reasons are obvious enough: his régime was weakened by three years of very serious natural calamity—droughts and floods—which ruined harvests; the Great Leap Forward of 1958–60 failed to produce the results expected of it; and Russia abruptly withdrew all technical assistance. These difficult years shook the confidence that many people had in the system; the period of relaxation tended to wean them away from orthodoxy just as it gave the intellectuals more rein to express their opinions; and there developed among a small proportion of the party functionaries in China an attitude of bureaucracy. This minority has become status-conscious and unco-operative, and it has taken what is called the capitalist path.

Mao was frightened at this bourgeois development. He sees as China's greatest enemies revisionism as represented by the Soviet Union and imperialism as represented by the United States. His main instrument of the cultural revolution has been the Red Guards. His main lieutenants here are his

The art of writing, much revered in China, is put to propaganda use in these posters made in Peking.

deputy, Lin Piao, the Minister of Defence, and Madame Mao, the former Shanghai film actress, twenty years younger than himself, who is his third wife. His chief opponents are Liu Shao-Chi, the Head of State; much of the existing party machine; and some army units. The struggle has been one between on the one hand, moderation, the improvement of living standards, tolerance of difference of opinion and peaceful co-existence in foreign affairs (the views of Liu and the Party regulars) and on the other the sharp radicalism of Mao, who does not want China to lose its revolutionary zeal, and the Red Guards.

The clashes have become violent, as in Nanking and occasionally in Peking, and in the summer of 1967 there was an open anti-Mao rebellion in the military garrison of Wuhan, the main industrial city in Central China. There has also been increased tension between the Red Guards and foreign diplomats in China. The struggle has passed from one of emphasis and slogans and wall-newspaper diatribes to something close to civil war. It is clear that Mao is facing the gravest threat to his rule since he took power in 1949. The struggle weakens China's rôle in the world and hinders its material progress; it amounts to a revolution inside a revolution.

It is hard to obtain reliable figures on the Chinese worker's income, but an average city worker probably earns about 90 yuan (about £13) per month, in the main cities. In the communes workers earn considerably less, and in all categories of employment there are graduated scales of pay according to skill. Recent reports indicate there is still a labour surplus, with some under-employment and even unemployment in certain areas.

Rent consumes very little of the Chinese worker's pay packet—usually between half a yuan and five yuan (about two shillings to fourteen shillings) per month. Basic foodstuffs are cheap, and public transport costs very little. Clothing, however, is a major expenditure item. A wool-lined jacket for winter wear costs about 80 yuan (about £12) and an ordinary pair of working trousers can be over 20 yuan. One of the biggest items a family can aspire to is a bicycle. A new Chinese one costs about 140 yuan—rather more than a worker's monthly salary. A good second-hand British bicycle may fetch over double this amount. The only cars seen in China are those of officials. The roads are often almost deserted of motor traffic, even in Peking itself, and heavy loads of construction material are transported by hand-cart or pedicab. China is now producing her own cars and trucks, but the output so far is small. The shortage of motor transport and of petrol will continue to be a major handicap in construction and development.

China's leaders speak in terms of several decades when discussing her emergence as a strong industrial and technological power. Mao Tse-tung has mentioned from 20 to 30 years more, but Marshal Chen Yi, the Foreign Minister, who is probably more realistic, recently estimated the time required at 30 to 50 years. Whichever is right, most foreign observers in Peking believe the face of Chinese Communism is certain to alter substantially in the mean-time, just as that of Soviet Communism has over the past three decades.

What is Mao's foreign policy?

The predominating idea in the New China has been to end the humiliation of the last century and a half, and restore the 'Middle Kingdom' to what is regarded as its rightful position. To the Chinese Communist leaders, few of whom have much experience of the outside world, Formosa (Taiwan), Hong Kong, Tibet, Manchuria, Inner Mongolia and Sinkiang had to be regained: and many of the objectives of their foreign policy can be seen as purely national —in fact, they were shared by Chiang Kai-Shek.

Immediately after their victory in 1949, the Chinese Communists showed an enthusiasm for assisting 'national revolutionary wars' in Asia. After the

Korean war, however, and the evidence it gave that the West would resist an 'assisted' Communist revolution anywhere, there was a change. Instead of promoting world revolution, the emphasis was now laid (e.g. at the 1954 Geneva Conference and the Bandung Conference, 1955) on destroying the power of the West in Asia, and the idea of co-existence pervaded the 'Five Principles' of neighbourly relations agreed with India.

Later, in 1957–58, the Chinese attitude hardened. As American and Russian nuclear power increased, it became clear that each could destroy the other, and a mutual agreement to differ emerged between the Big Two. The prospect of a possible 'live and let live' agreement between the Russians and the Americans; the realization that Russian aid to China might dry up, that a test ban agreement might exclude China from the 'nuclear club', and that the loss of Formosa, Quemoy, etc., might be made permanent: all these reasons can be seen behind Chinese insistence on the necessity for solidarity in the Communist *bloc*. China insisted that Communist unity was necessary until the world victory of Communism was won in 10 or 20 years, that nuclear war was not to be feared, and that Communists should not stand idly by when the West suppressed revolutions by force (e.g. Lebanon, Jordan and Algeria).

Relations with the Soviet Union

Despite past misunderstandings with the Soviet Union, the new régime had no hesitation in adopting the policy of 'leaning to one side'—that is, towards the Communist *bloc*—in its foreign relations. This policy was strengthened by the event of the Korean war, during which China received Soviet military supplies on a large scale, as well as having many Soviet advisers attached to its armed forces. From 1949–57 China willingly accepted Soviet advice and models—as shown in the nature of the First Five-Year Plan (1953–57), with its emphasis on heavy industry and its reliance on Soviet aid. In their general strategical outlook in 1954–55, the Chinese reflected the growing awareness of the implications of nuclear warfare which was apparent in the Soviet at that time; this led, temporarily, to a greater moderation in China's foreign policy. Throughout the period of the First Five-Year Plan the Chinese Press and official pronouncements constantly praised the 'Soviet elder brothers'. The praise of the Soviet Union reached a climax in the celebrations in 1959 of the Tenth Anniversary of the Sino-Soviet Treaty of Alliance, which had given a guarantee of assistance in the event of attack. In fact the Chinese Communists had little reason to thank the Soviet Union for their victory in 1949, for Russian aid had been limited and, indeed, Stalin had discouraged their conquest of South China. Under the terms of the Alliance signed in 1950, the Soviet Union usually insisted upon a *quid pro quo*, for example in the form of food, however short that was at times in China.

For some seven years, relations between the allies were good. Though perturbed, the Chinese subscribed to Khrushchev's denigration of Stalin in 1956. They intervened in the Russian dispute with Poland to urge a greater degree of self-government for Poland, coupled with a recognition of Soviet leadership; and vigorously supported Russia's ruthless suppression of the 1956 revolt in Hungary, even taking the lead in drawing up the Moscow Declaration (November 1957) to recognize the Soviet Communist Party as 'head of the Socialist camp'.

Disappointment with the low position of Chinese interests in the scale of priorities of Moscow, coupled with anxiety over Soviet foreign policy, led in 1958 to the ascendancy of left-wing extremists in Chinese domestic policy, and to criticism of Yugoslavia for receiving Soviet as well as 'American Imperialist' aid. Soviet economic advisers in China were critical of much that was done under the influence of the Great Leap Forward movement of 1958. Resentment between them and the Chinese political, managerial and intellectual *élite* had been chronic and, given the relationship, perhaps inevitable. To the Russians, the Chinese political controls appeared crude, reminiscent of the worst days of Stalinism, a feeling exacerbated by Chinese attempts to impart political education to the foreign experts. From that date the 'Alliance between Brothers' (as Chou En-lai called it) has been an uneasy alliance. In 1959 Russia refused to give China the secrets of the atomic bomb—in order, the Chinese believe, to placate the United States—and this refusal rankled exceedingly with the Chinese leadership, especially in view of an earlier agreement that the Soviet would give China technical help in the field of nuclear armaments. From this time on all the other grievances between the countries were felt more acutely. In June 1960 the Soviet Government, angered at, among other things, the propaganda to which its experts in China had been subjected, suddenly withdrew them in large numbers with their work incomplete. They took with them essential blueprints, and in addition Soviet promises to provide vital equipment were not fulfilled. This was a major blow to China's development, especially as it came in the midst of a severe economic crisis. The Chinese increasingly challenged the Soviet leadership of the 'Socialist camp'. Although the quarrel was periodically patched up, patching up became less and less feasible, in spite of the fact that—especially at first—the dispute took the form of ideological arguments and veiled insults.

At the 21st Congress of the Soviet Communist Party (C.P.S.U.) in February 1959, economic difficulties and the weight of Soviet criticism forced the Chinese to a truce, when they recognized that the Soviet Union alone was on the way to the 'higher stage' of Communism. They were rewarded with an economic agreement. But Khrushchev's visit to the U.S.A., and the preparations for the abortive Summit Conference in 1960, again roused all China's fears and criticisms. Then Khrushchev, in February 1960, remained pointedly aloof from the Chinese disagreements with India and Indonesia. A cold war within a cold war seemed to be developing. And in December 1960, at the Moscow Conference of World Communist Leaders, Soviet monopoly of ideological authority—that is, its position as leading 'party'—was denied. This might almost be said to recognize China's right to compete with the Soviet Union for 'satellites', while not renouncing the overriding interest of Communist unity against non-Communist countries.

Khrushchev was obviously prepared for 'divergent unity' to last for a long time, with separate Soviet and Chinese spheres of influence. Yet he was not prepared for Chinese influence in the east of Europe. When he attacked the Stalinist leaders of Albania at the 22nd Congress in Moscow in October 1961, his position was publicly criticized by the Chinese, whose credits and aid to Albania had already made up for Russian credits and aid—which had been discontinued.

China itself was refused further Russian aid, and its extensive trade with the Soviet Union was halved in 1961. In addition, in spite of the acute shortage of food in China, the Russians insisted on large deliveries of agricultural produce in payment of existing debts, and technical assistance came to a halt. 'Comecon' —the Council for Mutual Economic Assistance, the Communist 'Common Market'—terminated Albania's membership at the end of 1961 and, equally significantly, made Mongolia a member in June 1962. Improved Soviet-Yugoslav relations, signified by the visit of Mr Brezhnev (then U.S.S.R. President) to Belgrade in September–October 1962, inspired Chinese attacks on Yugoslav 'renegades to Communism'. Nevertheless, President Tito of Yugoslavia was invited to Moscow.

The Chinese and Albanian Press and radio openly condemned Khrushchev's 'conciliatory' attitude toward the U.S.A. in the Cuban crisis of 1962, and his policies in general. The withdrawal of Soviet missiles from Cuba revealed not only that the Big Two had reached a balance of terror but that Khrushchev seemed afraid of a nuclear war, and thereby in Chinese eyes he 'lost face'. (It is interesting to note that when China detonated her first atomic bomb on 16 October 1964—and thus became the fifth nuclear Power after the United States, the Soviet Union, Great Britain and France—the Chinese Government immediately called for a world summit conference to discuss the complete prohibition and thorough destruction of nuclear weapons. The statement also solemnly declared that 'China will never at any time under any circumstances be the first to use nuclear weapons'.)

Reasons for the Chinese-Russian split

The differences between Russia and China can be summarized as:

First, a controversy over the rôle of the Communist state. Russia is, as a Communist state, 30 years senior to China; it gave some aid to Communist China—but not consistently and never enough—and it sees itself as the pacesetter. But Lenin, Stalin and Khrushchev insisted on industrialization as essential to Communist growth, whereas China, a vast agrarian state, relies on the peasantry. And Russia, geographically closer to the West and with more to lose, became more conciliatory under Khrushchev; having the nuclear bomb itself, it agreed with the American view that other Powers (like China) should not develop nuclear weapons, and in 1963 it signed the Test-Ban Treaty with Britain and the United States. By this time Russia believed in peaceful co-existence and the non-violent development of world Communism. China, on the other hand, claims that dependent territories and peoples can be liberated and world Socialism achieved only by warlike means. Within the next few years China and the Soviet Union came into open rivalry for the leadership of the under-developed world. China claimed that its revolutionary methods were more applicable to those regions, but the Soviet was able to give material aid in much larger quantities.

Second, a controversy between two Great Powers. Whatever the similarity or divergences of view of two Communist states, Russia and China remain two distinct and powerful countries, with a long history of tension and a debatable no-man's-land between them. In 1950–51 China attacked and overran Tibet and in 1962 threatened India's northern border; Russia stayed neutral. For her part, China criticizes Russia's readiness to aid some neutrals like Egypt, whose few Communists are in jail.

The stages in the quarrel

1924–27   Stalin exhorts small Chinese Communist Party to aim at an urban revolution. This misjudged the basis of Chinese society, and ran counter to Mao's strategy.

1939–49   Stalin supports Chiang rather than Mao to stop the Japanese. Mao seizes power despite this.

1956   Khrushchev attacks Stalin's dogmatism, but Mao denies Russia's right to speak for 'true' Marxism-Leninism.

1959   Russian nuclear aid to Mao stops.

1960   Russian aid to China stops, and all advisers withdrawn.

1963   Chinese proclaim that they are true heirs of Marxism-Leninism and call for a world conference of Communist States.

1964   Suslov, leading Soviet Russian thinker, attacks Chinese.

Third, a controversy between two men, Khrushchev and Mao. Khrushchev travelled widely outside Russia. Mao was never out of China until he visited Russia and Eastern Europe in 1949–50; he has never seen any non-Communist foreign country and speaks no foreign language. Mao believes that war is all but inevitable between Capitalism and Communism; Khrushchev apparently did not. The spread of communism is inevitable, Khrushchev said, but not war. Mao, the theorist and the intellectual mandarin, fought a civil war for 22 years before attaining power. To carry through a vast social revolution he needs dictatorial power. Khrushchev inherited the Communist state, a beneficiary of the second generation. History progresses, he said, by devious and unpredictable paths; 'only crows fly straight'. The Chinese say that Khrushchev had called off the fight against Imperialism. He forgot the hungry world, they say, and lined up with the 'haves' against the 'have-nots'.

These three major fields of controversy have been fought out thus far, however, not by war but by provocative statements by one leader or the other, each defending the purity of Marxist-Leninist doctrine against the other. To Communists, words are the weaponry of ideological war. This tension began in 1960, when Mr Khrushchev described Mao as another Stalin. In 1964 the Chinese Communists branded Mr Khrushchev as 'The greatest capitulationist, compromiser and appeaser of all time. He is leading the country back along the path to Capitalism.' But since both Powers are totalitarian, they control their own internal news, and their people do not know much of what is being said by the other Power—unless they listen to foreign broadcasts.

Relations with Japan

The split with Russia has improved China's relations with Japan. Large numbers of Japanese have been invited to Peking and entertained with great cordiality. The Japanese Government, in its turn, has shown itself not unmindful of the advantages of better relations with Mainland China. China exercises an exceptional fascination in Japan, as being in a sense the cultural motherland. However, the great obstacle to an improvement in Sino-Japanese relations is that at present this could come about only at the expense of Japan's relations with the United States, on which Japan depends for defence.

China's need for capital goods from non-Russian sources has improved its relations with some Western European countries, especially France. Political justification for closer links with capitalist powers has been given by a theory put out by Peking by which such powers are divided into two groups, of which one, consisting primarily if not solely of the United States, is bad and must be the object of unremitting struggle, while the other, a kind of intermediary zone in the world, which includes at least some of the countries of Western Europe, may be treated more favourably. This discrimination between the two groups was intended to exploit 'contradictions within the Western camp' and thus to split the forces of capitalism.

Relations with the United States

Hitherto, the United States had been the target for Chinese hatred. By recognizing Chiang Kai-Shek as the lawful ruler of China and preventing the acquisition of Formosa (Taiwan); by its part in the Korean War; by blocking the admission of the Peking Government to what it feels to be its rightful place in the United Nations; and by supporting anti-Communist governments in Asia, especially in Thailand and Vietnam, China's neighbours, the United States has been the major obstacle to the fulfilment of what the Chinese leaders regard as their legitimate aims.

Since 1962, however, Chinese criticism of Russia has been more strident than her criticism of the United States. If the Taiwan problem were solved, the Peking Government might find that there was less reason for continued friction with the United States than with the U.S.S.R. Many intellectual and professional groups in China would probably prefer their cultural and scientific links to be with America, where numbers of the older generation were trained. In addition, the United States is better placed than ever the Soviet was for providing the long-term credit that China needs. Improved relations with America would also open the way to more friendly ties with Japan. On the American side there is a strong residual sympathy with China, inherited from past generations, that would be ready to emerge at any sign of encouragement from China.

Conclusion

In spite of reverses, the economic development of China since 1949 has been impressive, though it is, as yet, too early to judge the effect in this field of the quarrel with the Soviet Union. The wisdom of the American determination to keep China out of the United Nations is very much open to question, especially in view of the Chinese leaders' lack of direct knowledge of the Western world. Of the six-man Standing Committee of the Politburo (the 'inner Politburo') only Premier Chou En-lai has been outside the Communist *bloc* since 1949, and even he has not seen an advanced Western industrial city since he was a student 40 years ago, only visiting Africa and the Middle East. It is doubtful whether China attaches much importance to membership of the United Nations, apart from the fact that admission would itself be a great victory. In the first years after the Communists came to power, the Peking Government appeared eager for acceptance by the United Nations, but since the Korean war this eagerness has evaporated. It is very doubtful whether Peking would consider a seat on the Security Council worth any compromise on Taiwan. But there is a serious danger that, by isolating China, its hostility towards and suspicion of the West will be increased.

THE WORLD TODAY

QUESTIONS TO CONSIDER

1. What are the main regions of China?
2. Outline the career either of Chiang Kai-Shek or of Mao.
3. Why did Mao win in 1949?
4. What has Mao done for China?
5. What are the main reasons for the Russian-Chinese split?
6. How far did the 'Red Guard' movement of 1966–67 change (a) Domestic policies; (b) Relations with other countries.

WORDS TO NOTE

Boxers: The Nationalists of 1900 (from their title of 'Fists of Righteous Harmony'), who were opposed to Western control of Chinese ports and trade.

Communes: A completely new development in Chinese society. Introduced by the government of Mao Tse-tung to make more efficient production on the land, by breaking down the family tradition and, instead, encouraging communal living.

Confucius: Chinese scholar-statesman who recommended moderation as the golden rule in life.

Mandarin: A governor of old China, chosen from scholars after rigorous examination, similar to our Civil Service.

Thought-control: The opposite of freedom of thought and opinion. The individual is directed to think along lines laid down by the government.

FOR FURTHER READING

Wint, Guy: *Spotlight on Asia*, Penguin, 1955.
Ping-Chia Kuo: *China, New Age and New Outlook*, Penguin, 1960.
McAuliffe, W. R.: *Modern Asia Explained* (Chapters 4 and 5), Blackie, 1952.
Snow, Edgar: *Red Star over China*, Gollancz, 1938.
Storry, R.: *A History of Modern Japan*, Pelican, 1960.
Wint, Guy: *Common Sense about China*, Gollancz, 1960.

7. The Middle East

The land and the people

The Middle East is a political, rather than a geographical, term which is used to describe an area the limits of which have been variously defined but which lies between European Turkey and West Pakistan and includes part of North Africa. It comprises Egypt, Iraq, Jordan, Libya, the Lebanon, Syria, Saudi Arabia, the Sudan and the Yemen (the countries of the Arab League), Iran, Israel, Cyprus, Aden and the remaining territories of the Arabian Peninsula. Turkey is both a European and a Middle Eastern country and provides a link between the two regions.

The Middle East is the centre of the Arab World, a world united by Islam and by the Arabic language, but not politically, although the United Arab Republic was formed in 1958. Arab nationalism is the most powerful force within the area. It is in general anti-Western and, of course, bitterly opposed to Israel.

The region is on the whole poor in natural resources except for its oil. Agricultural yields are low because of unfavourable climate, poor soil, pests, human disease and social factors, but there are a few areas (e.g. the Nile Valley) of exceptional richness. It is extremely backward industrially and the standard of living is very low.

Why is it important?

The importance of the Middle East is fourfold. First, its position as a bridge between three continents has given it great strategic significance (the Suez Canal performs a comparable function for the commercial sea routes linking the continents). Possession of the Middle East has long been recognized by military leaders as a key to world power. It has particular significance for Britain with her Commonwealth and her dependence upon foreign trade. The Cold War has increased its importance to the West because of its proximity to the Soviet Union. It is also of great strategic importance to Russia.

The area's second great asset is its oil, and (under normal conditions) it is the largest oil-exporting area in the world. Middle East oil is vital to Western Europe, and is becoming increasingly important to the United States. Iran, Iraq, Saudi Arabia and the small Sheikhdom of Kuwait are the principal oil-bearing territories there. Middle East oil is worked by Western-controlled enterprises—British, American, Dutch and French—though the oil-yielding countries receive a substantial share of the profits.

Third, the importance of the Middle East has grown because of the new

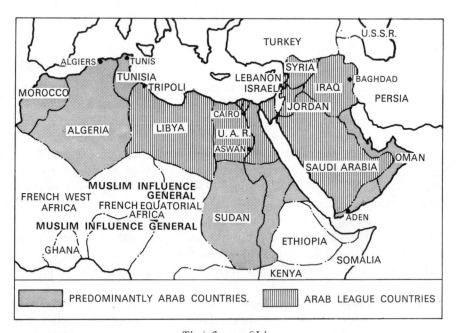

The influence of Islam.

rivalry of the United States and the Soviet Union within the region. It is a focal point of the Cold War and it is for this region, hitherto regarded as a British sphere of influence, that the United States formulated the Eisenhower Doctrine.

And fourth, the security of the Middle East is threatened basically by the Arab-Israel dispute, which remains the chief cause of instability in the region. The threat from Communism is growing, for the Arab-Israel dispute provides Russia with an opportunity to gain a foothold in the Middle East by selling arms to Egypt, Syria and other Arab countries.

How much is desert?

The Arab World is very dry. When Gertrude Bell, on one of her first journeys in Arabia, looked south from Palmyra and asked her guide Ahmed how far it was to Nejd, he replied: 'Forty-four waterless days.' Of the total area of two and a half million square miles of the Arab Middle East, less than a quarter receives an average annual rainfall of over five inches. Only on the coastal plains and highland valleys is there enough rain to allow cultivation without irrigation.

Soil, water and sand

The heart of the Ancient Near East was known as the Fertile Crescent, and it is still the geographical centre of the Arab World. It consists of the Twin Rivers, the Tigris and the Euphrates, in Iraq, the Orontes in northern Syria, and the Nile in Egypt. This was the Biblical Garden of Eden, the 'land flowing with milk and honey' of the Hebrews. But ancient Egypt and Mesopotamia were also dependent on a highly developed irrigation system. This tradition of irrigation has never disappeared in Egypt. Some scholars have even suggested that Egyptian civilization owed its origin to the need for community effort in the founding and maintaining of an irrigation system. Egypt's population has always been completely dependent on the long, thin ribbon of green created by the Nile waters, which have brought down from Ethiopia over thousands of years the silt in which they grow their crops and from which they build houses and make household utensils of all kinds. Over 95 per cent lives in 3 per cent of Egypt's territory. The traveller of today can stand on the desert near the Pyramids at Giza and see clear across the belt of green to the desert on the other side. He will find the width of the green steadily shrinking as he travels south towards Wadi Halfa and the Sudan. At Cairo it is ten miles wide, at Wadi Halfa, two.

What is true of Egypt and the Nile would have been true of Mesopotamia, but the irrigation system broke down and the population declined. Neglect overtook the Roman cisterns and aqueducts in Sinai with equally disastrous results. The Arab is not the son of the desert, but its father.

The settled areas

The Arab World is not quite all desert. In the centre is the Fertile Crescent of its river system, and it is here, in the Nile Valley, in Mesopotamia, or on the shores of the Mediterranean, that the mass of the people live. The majority are *fellahin* or peasants, producing cotton, wheat, rice, barley, dates and, on the Mediterranean, fruit. The flooded soil is rich; the normal yield per acre of Egyptian cotton averages four times that of the U.S.A. Four-fifths of the world's dates come from Iraq. Palestine is the land of citrus fruits.

These crops need water and regular attention. This means dams like the Aswan Dam in Egypt, to store water, or barrages, like that north of Cairo, to supply the feeder canals. They call for all-the-year-round irrigation, dykes to resist the flood waters, drains and pumps and wells. These things the West has brought to the Arab river oases. Nevertheless the industry of the *fellahin*—and there is no greater myth than that of Arab laziness—is untrained; his implements are primitive; labour is so cheap that there is no inducement to use machinery; modern soil techniques are little known and less practised; the biggest landowners are normally absentees.

Hard though the peasants labour, they make little by it; most of them hold less than an acre of land, and have to work as day labourers to eke out a living. Some estimates put the average annual income per peasant family in Egypt, the wealthiest of the Arab countries, as low as £20. The peasant is lucky if he can give his family one meal a day; he lives in a mud hovel, along with any animals he might have. He is often diseased, and suffers especially from eye diseases; the death and the birth rates are high.

Of industry, in the Western sense, there is little. Less than five per cent of Egypt's population is in industry, and the figures for other Arab countries are much lower. What industry there is is apt to be a one-man craft, or a family concern—in Egypt only three per cent of industrial firms employ more than ten workers. The reasons are obvious enough: the lack of industrial raw materials and of power; the poverty of the population which cannot provide a home market; and the predominant agricultural economy.

Villages and towns

In the settled areas, therefore, the traveller sees villages rather than towns. Or it is more likely that he will see a mosque on the canal bank, and next to it a few chairs in the open around the village coffee stall. There are few shops, since all the buying and selling are done at the weekly markets, but some of the villages will have a general store, usually owned by a Greek. Normally a traveller will see, not factory chimneys, but oxen at the plough or at the *saquieh*, the pump which draws water for the fields from the wells.

Of towns there are few in the Arab World. The cities we associate with the Middle East or Arab North Africa—Cairo and Alexandria, Beirut and Aleppo,

The Sphinx at Giza, symbol of Egypt.

Algiers and Casablanca—are less Arab than Mediterranean. Alexandria is
Jewish, Greek, Syrian, French, Maltese and British, much more than Egyptian;
the Lebanese in Beirut will be found speaking French, or, occasionally, good
American, quite as often as Arabic. The real Arab hardly belongs to such
environments.

There are, however, four cities that can justly claim to be native to the Arab
World. Damascus was a desert oasis on the Barada, which grew in importance
as a focus of the caravan routes. It is in many ways the natural centre of the
Arabs of the West, as Baghdad is of the East. Baghdad is the storied capital of
the Abbasid Caliphs and of Haroun al Rashid. For 400 years it was the centre
of the Moslem Empire. The third city, Jerusalem, is equally native to Arab,
Jew and Christian, having been fought over by Saracen and Crusader, and
more recently fought in by Arab and Jew. Jerusalem with its Mosque of Omar,
from which, in Moslem lore, Mohammed bodily ascended to Heaven, remains,
however, a city sacred to the Arab as well as to the Jew and the Christian.
Finally, there is Mecca, the Holy of Holies, not, like the other three cities, in
the Fertile Crescent, but in the desert.

Who are the Arabs?

What, then, makes the Arab? First, a certain sense of Semitic blood-kinship—
though a kinship that does not include Jews. Second, the memory of the period

205

of Arab dominance, when the Empire of Islam in the eighth century stretched from the Pyrenees to the Oxus and when Haroun al Rashid (763–809), and the Abbasids in Baghdad, outdid the Western Charlemagne in splendour. Third, because of the conversion of the Ottoman Turks to Islam, in effect the Moslem Empire lasted over a thousand years, though the role of the Arabs in it grew steadily smaller. Fourth, the memory not only of political, but of cultural dominance. Al-Azhar, the great Moslem University in Cairo, dates from the tenth century; the Greek classics reached the West via the Arabs; Arabs in the Middle Ages were famed as doctors and scientists, as mathematicians and as craftsmen. Damascus is still famous for its silver-ware, and Persia for its carpets and mosaics. But far surpassing these four unifying forces in effect are two others—religion and language.

Islam

Ninety-two per cent of the Middle Eastern peoples are Moslem. It is not quite true to say that all Arabs are Moslem, for the Copts in Egypt number about one million, and there is a similar number of Christian Arabs, Roman Catholics or Greek Orthodox, living mainly in the Lebanon or in the hills of Galilee. Yet both these groups speak Arabic, and until recently, one-quarter of the Jews in Palestine were Arabic-speaking. If there are, however, some non-Moslem Arabs, it has to be remembered that many more than Arabs worship Allah, and that to many millions in Pakistan, India, China, South-east Asia and North-west Africa, Mecca is the most important city in the world. The devotion of the world's 300 million Moslems to their religion is a very important fact. Islam is a great international force, like the Roman Catholic Church.

There is only one creed in Islam: 'There is no God but The God, and Mohammed is His Prophet.' There is no need for priest or liturgy; all who accept the creed and follow its simple precepts are Moslems, irrespective of colour, race or language. The creed was more fully outlined in the *Koran*, which the Prophet (570–632) dictated under inspiration, and in the various 'Sayings' attributed to him. These impose on the Moslem five practical duties:

(*a*) The public recitation of the creed.

(*b*) Prayer five times daily, at dawn, noon, mid-afternoon, sunset and nightfall.

Prayer must be preceded by ablution, and the postures for prayer are most rigorously prescribed. The Friday prayer in the mosque has special merit. This service is generally accompanied by a sermon, but did not the Prophet say 'Woe are ye when your sermons become long and your prayers brief'? The mosque, dominant though it is as architecture throughout the Arab World, is normally a simple building. Those in the cities may be splendid, like the magnificent mosque of the Omayyads in Damascus, but all that is necessary is the courtyard for the faithful to pray in, a mark to indicate the direction of

Mecca, and a supply of water for the ritual ablutions before prayers. There is usually a pulpit for the Friday sermon, and a minaret for the *muezzin* who calls to prayer. The muezzin is sometimes blind, lest he should see the faces of the women on the surrounding roofs. Of statuary there is none—no human or animal designs are allowed in Koranic law, and only simple geometric patterns will be found.

(*c*) Fasting from sunrise to sunset in the month of Ramadhan, the ninth month of the lunar year.

(*d*) The giving of help to beggars.

(*e*) The *Haj*, the Pilgrimage to Mecca. This is expected of all, but in practice only those older Moslems who can afford it undertake the long and arduous journey to Mecca, and the equally arduous duties prescribed on arrival there, which take up some ten days. The *Hajji*, however, is honoured on his return, if only by the title he can use thereafter.

Arabic

The unity of the Arab peoples is buttressed by the Arabic language. For four centuries all Moslems who wrote at all had to write in Arabic. Today Turkish and Persian, Hindustani, Malay and Kurdish are all Moslem languages. Arabic, however, is the common language of the Moslem world, whether it is the classical language of the Koran, or the various regional forms.

This religious and linguistic unity shows that the Arab World is akin to medieval Europe, when one Church and one language crossed all boundaries of nation, race and class.

The Middle East between the Wars

The Arab World before 1914 was not politically united. From 1841 Egypt was independent. Over Arabia and parts of Iraq the Sultan of Turkey had little authority. And elsewhere he was bitterly unpopular, as the First World War was to reveal. But until 1914 there was a sense of unity. The present boundary lines date from 1918 or even later. There is less sense of national differences than in the West.

By the close of the nineteenth century, however, real power in the Ottoman Empire was itself passing to the West. The Western interest in the cross-roads to Asia was, as we have seen, very old. For France it went back to the 'Capitulations'—whereby French and later other foreign nationals were exempt from Ottoman jurisdiction—and to Crusading times. It was revived by the Bonapartes and by the building of the Suez Canal.

Britain bought up some 40 per cent of the Suez Canal Company's stock, acquired Cyprus (1878), occupied Egypt (1882) and in 1898 declared a joint rule with Egypt over the Sudan. By the turn of the century Britain, like all other powers, was interested in the newly found oil of Persia and Mosul, and the naval building programme of the early years of the century gave a new value to the resources of the Arab East.

The Germans were interested in the Berlin-to-Baghdad Railway. Italians, Greeks and Jews, Maltese and Armenians, were there also, the universal middle-men living by trade in the cities—in Basra and Baghdad, Port Said, Suez and Damascus. By 1910 Americans were active as missionaries and teachers, and from 1920 they, too, were looking towards Mosul and the Persian Gulf for oil.

Arab renaissance

But from the West, the Arabs also learnt nationalism and liberalism. Societies came into being to agitate for Arab freedom from the Turkish yoke. The new literacy, the great Arabic language Press in Cairo, the coming of radio (which has had great unifying force in an illiterate area) gave an impetus to nationalism. Student rioters have chanted in every generation since 1918 'Better self-government than good government.'

The Western impact came to a climax in the events of the First World War. The years between 1914 and 1918 were, for the Arab World, an industrial revolution, a social upheaval and a political renaissance all in one.

The Arab revolt and its consequences

To assist us in our war effort against the Ottoman armies in the First World War we encouraged an Arab revolt, led by Hussein, the *Sherif* of Mecca, and sent the well-known T. E. Lawrence to help him. This led to three developments:

First, the Sherif of Mecca, in 1918, became King of the Hejaz. This increase in his status sharpened a long-standing feud that he had with his neighbour, Ibn Saud, King of Nejd. In addition, Ibn Saud, who had been in receipt of a subsidy from the Government of India that had now ceased, wished to make good this loss by getting hold of the valuable revenue from the Moslem pilgrim traffic to the Holy Cities of Mecca and Medina in the Hejaz. War followed and Ibn Saud conquered the Hejaz in 1924, and in due course united a large part of the Arabian peninsula into the present Kingdom of Saudi Arabia.

Second, two of the Sherif's sons, Feisal and Abdullah, were in 1920 and 1922 respectively placed on the thrones of Iraq and Transjordan, under British mandate.

Third, in revolting against the Turks, many Arabs hoped for a considerable Arab kingdom on the downfall of the Ottoman Empire. They were disappointed when Syria and Lebanon were turned into republics under French mandate instead of getting immediate and complete independence. These feelings of discontent were general among the Arabs of the Fertile Crescent.

Meanwhile, nationalism was gaining ground all over the Middle East. In Cyprus the cry for *enosis* (union with Greece) began. In the mandated territories nationalism caused chafing at the controls exercised by Britain and France. In Egypt it raised the issue of our special position and the presence of foreign troops on Egyptian soil, but in 1936 Mussolini's aggressive policies and conquest of Abyssinia caused Egyptians to scent danger, and a treaty was made which allowed British forces to remain.

Britain, therefore, had acquired by 1920 a much more definite set of interests and responsibilities in the Middle East than it had in the pre-war days of the Ottoman Empire. It had the political responsibilities of the mandates, the interest in oil and the interest in the increasing development of air routes across Egypt, Palestine, Transjordan, Iraq and the Persian Gulf, as well as the older sea route through the Suez Canal.

All these things, however, were bedevilled by another fact. During the war Britain had not only committed itself to Arab emancipation but (by the Balfour Declaration of 1917) to a 'Jewish national home' in Palestine, and had received a mandate for Palestine with the obligation to carry it out. The attempt to do so drew opposition from every Arab quarter.

The Arab states gain freedom

The defeat of the Ottoman Empire in 1918 brought about a revolution in Turkey, where a republic under Mustafa Kemal was declared. Turkey became confined to its present-day limits, and in 1925 Islam ceased to be the state religion. Turkey became a secular state. Palestine apart, the West fulfilled its promises to Hussein, though in qualified ways. The ex-Turkish territories became mandates of the League of Nations, to be governed and pushed towards independence by a Great Power acting on the League's behalf. Syria was mandated to France; Iraq, Palestine and Transjordan to Britain. Egypt remained unwillingly a Protectorate of Britain until 1922.

There followed, in each country, a generation of struggle against the mandates. In 1922 Transjordan was created, with Britain as mandatory power and Abdullah as Emir. In 1946 he became a king and in 1950 added Arab Palestine to his territory. In 1932 the Iraq mandate ended. And in Palestine itself Arab-Jewish conflict made the mandate unworkable by May 1948. France was forcibly expelled from Syria and Lebanon in 1945.

Egypt became an independent kingdom in 1922 after an outbreak of nationalism led by Saad Zaghlul. Some matters Britain reserved to itself— effective share in the Condominium over the Sudan, security over communications (i.e. control over the Canal), defence of Egypt, and the protection of foreign groups (i.e. the Capitulations). These were bitterly unpopular and various attempts were made to revise them. They were all unsuccessful until in 1936 Italy became a threat both to Britain and to Egypt. Then the military occupation of Egypt was declared at an end, and British garrisons were gradually to evacuate Cairo and Alexandria. They were, temporarily, to be given special facilities in a Zone on the Canal. Over the next 12 years the Capitulations were gradually to end. It was in accordance with this Treaty of 1936 that the British and Allied troops were based in Egypt in the Second World War.

The Arab World since 1939

The Second World War gave new impetus to the progress of Arab nationalism. The Free French authorities made a successful bid to oust the Vichy régime from Syria and the Lebanon by promising immediate independence to both these countries. The British Government, whose armies gained control of the area with the aid of Free French forces, carried out that promise.

After the German-inspired revolt led by Rashid Ali in Iraq had been suppressed in 1941, the people of Iraq also supported Britain.

Throughout the Middle East the war brought a rapid and considerable increase in communications. British and Dominion military engineers drew the Arab World closer together than ever before with hundreds of miles of new roads and railways. A central organization, the Middle East Supply Council, which aimed at making the Arab World economically self-supporting, emphasized the common factors in its domestic economy. Broadcasting, both by foreign powers and Arab states, spread the knowledge of a modernized form of literary Arabic. Socially and economically, then, the advantages of some sort of Arab *bloc* or federation were emphasized by war-time conditions.

In March 1945 a League of Arab States was formed in Cairo, in the names of the Kings of Egypt, Iraq, Saudi Arabia, Yemen, the Emir of Transjordan, and the Presidents of the Republics of Syria and the Lebanon, which countries are the League's constituent members. The idea of Arab unity is still very strong.

The Arab League's main preoccupation has been with supporting the Arab cause in the Palestine dispute.

The Palestine mandate and the Arab-Israel war

During the First World War, in the Balfour Declaration of 2 November 1917, Britain stated that it favoured the establishment in Palestine of a national home for the Jewish people. After the war, Palestine was mandated to Britain by the League of Nations; at the time the vast majority of its inhabitants were Arabs. The British Government promised that the rights of the latter would not be prejudiced by the fulfilment of its pledge to the Jews. Nevertheless the Arabs watched with growing alarm the proportion of Jews rising, while the Jews fiercely contested the limitations placed upon immigration, especially after the Nazi persecution in Germany.

At the end of the Second World War, Britain concluded that the mandate was unworkable, since it was impossible to reconcile the aspirations of the Jews and the Arabs. It therefore referred the question to the United Nations in April 1947. A U.N. commission subsequently recommended the division of Palestine into two independent states, one Jewish and the other Arab, linked together economically, while the city of Jerusalem would be placed under an international régime. The Arab countries announced their intention of resisting by force this 'partition scheme'. Britain declared that she would not enforce the U.N. decision and would relinquish the mandate on 14 May 1948.

The State of Israel was proclaimed at midnight on 14 May 1948, and was at once at war with its Arab neighbours. There were intermittent hostilities between May 1948 and March 1949. Early in 1949 the United Nations mediator succeeded in bringing about a series of armistice agreements between Israel and the Arab States directly concerned. As a result of the war, Israel secured more territory than she had been awarded under the partition scheme; the city of Jerusalem was partly in Israeli territory (the new city) and partly in the hands of Jordan.

The failure of the Arab League had important repercussions in the Arab countries. There was a series of *coups d'état* in Syria, and in Egypt it led to the murder of the Prime Minister and eventually contributed to the end of the monarchy (1953). Important territorial gains were made only by Abdullah of Jordan, whose British-trained Arab Legion put up the best showing on the

Jews in the Orthodox quarter of Jerusalem, Israel.

211

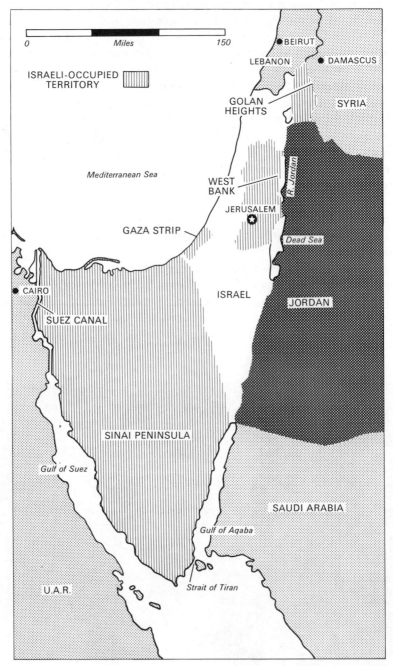

The Middle East after the 5-day war of June 1967.

League side; Abdullah's gains and the fear that he intended to recognize Israel aroused the jealousy of his colleagues in the Arab League, and led to his murder (1951).

The New State of Israel

Israel has developed under the most difficult circumstances. It has a land area of approximately 8,000 square miles with disproportionately long frontiers; yet at one point it is less than 40 miles wide. Roughly half the total area of the country is the still almost untrodden wilderness of the Negev which, however, the Israelis are making determined efforts to develop. In 1948, when the State was founded, there were about 600,000 Jews in Israel. Today there are over 2,500,000.

The economic position of Israel is precarious: today it has an adverse balance of trade of about £100 million. Gifts, loans and credits from the United States —and, from 1953 onwards, reparations payments from Western Germany— have alone enabled it to survive.

Since 1956 the port of Elath on the Gulf of Aqaba has been developed as Israel's link with the Gulf of Aqaba and the Red Sea and the symbol of the Israelis' determination to expand trade with the Horn of Africa and countries further south and east. By combining an intensive agriculture with an increasing variety of industries and industrial 'know-how' the Israelis hope to achieve a high standard of living and an important economic role in the Middle East.

Israel's task is made much more difficult by the continuing tension with the Arab States. The quarrel continues over:

(a) The use of the Jordan waters.

(b) The conditions of the Arab refugees from the former Palestine, now in Arab countries.

(c) Egyptian interference with Israel's shipping using the Suez Canal.

(d) The Arab bitterness over their two defeats: in 1956, in a 100-hour Israeli *blitzkrieg*, and in 1967, when the war was won and the Canal reached by the Israelis in 60 hours.

The Central Treaty Organization (CENTO)

The Arab-Israel dispute made it impossible for Britain to produce an agreed Middle East defence plan in the years after 1945. From 1950, the United States began to press for a 'northern tier' of defence linking Turkey (already receiving American military aid) and Pakistan (the most important Moslem state in the world and having a particular interest in the Middle East).

In February 1954 Pakistan accepted American military aid and in the following April signed an agreement on Mutual Co-operation and Defence with Turkey. This pact was inspired by the United States and was envisaged as the first step towards a wider alliance.

The Baghdad Pact itself was signed between Iraq and Turkey on 24 February

213

1955. Britain acceded to the pact on 5 April 1955; Pakistan on 23 September; and Persia on 3 November 1955. The United States joined the economic and military committees, though she has not so far become a full member of the Pact.

Egypt was greatly angered by the Pact and soon was organizing opposition to it. In October 1955 she signed military pacts with Syria and Saudi Arabia. An attempt by Britain to bring Jordan into the Baghdad Pact was unsuccessful.

In the summer of 1955 the Soviet Union made a new move into the Middle East. The Baghdad Pact was viewed with concern by the Russians and the hostility shown to it by Egypt and Saudi Arabia gave them their opportunity. A new Soviet drive was launched with the conclusion of an arms deal between Czechoslovakia and Egypt. The situation in the Middle East rapidly deteriorated.

When Israel attacked Egypt at the end of October 1956 and the British and French intervened, the United Nations passed resolutions, supported by U.S.A., which secured the withdrawal of the British and French and the evacuation by Israel of all but the Gaza Strip and the islands commanding the Gulf of Aqaba. But this did not solve the question of Middle East security, for which the United States had no option but to assume responsibility.

At the beginning of 1957, the U.S. Administration proclaimed the 'Eisenhower Doctrine' which would commit America to employ armed forces as the President deemed necessary 'to secure and protect the territorial integrity and political independence of any (Middle East) nation or group of nations requesting such aid against overt armed aggression from any nation controlled by international Communism'. The crisis in the Lebanon (1958) provided the first occasion for a show of U.S. strength in the Middle East. Since then Soviet influence has increased in the region.

Nasser: the Man and his Policy

Colonel Gamal Abdul Nasser (b. 1918) has become the symbol of Arab nationalism, and the Egyptian revolution the model for development in almost all other Arab States. He is a native Egyptian, the son of a post-office worker in Upper Egypt, and was educated at Cairo Military Academy. From 1942, as an Egyptian army officer, he planned to overthrow the government, because he wanted to bring about social reforms that the corrupt royal government would never consider. He formed the Free Officers' Movement which in July 1952 forced King Farouk to abdicate in favour of his infant son. From 1953–54 General Neguib was officially Head of State. In 1954 Nasser became Prime Minister and in 1956, when a new constitution was drawn up, he became President.

He is popular in Egypt and the Arab world, and Radio Cairo, the most powerful broadcasting station in the Middle East, spreads his propaganda.

The idea of leadership by a young soldier has been imitated in Turkey (General Gursel in 1960), in Iraq (Brigadier Kassem in 1958, Colonel Aref in 1963), in the Sudan (General Abboud in 1958) and in Pakistan (Brigadier Ayub Khan in 1958). Democratic government is still a novelty in the East.

Independent Egypt

The revolution of 1952 in Egypt was due to resentment at British occupation after the Second World War, to social discontent because of the wealth of the King and of a few pasha families, and to the consequences of war with Israel in 1948–49. In July 1952, after the revolt against King Farouk, a number of measures were enacted by the revolutionary régime, the Free Officers' Movement. They abolished civilian titles; they introduced proposals for land reform, limiting the area of land any one person could hold; they drew up plans to increase the production of cotton, rice and sugar and to build a high dam on the Nile; social welfare services were extended, and the Moslem Brotherhood was declared dissolved. Negotiations began with the United Kingdom on the question of the Suez Canal Zone, and in 1954 the Anglo-Egyptian Treaty of 1936 was ended, it being agreed that all British forces were to leave the zone by June 1956.

General Mohammed Neguib declared Egypt a republic in June 1953 and was President until November 1954, when he was accused of trying to concentrate all power in his own hands and relieved of all his posts. Colonel Gamal Abdul Nasser became Prime Minister, and in June 1956 President.

Suez, 1956

In 1955 and 1956 relations between Egypt and the Western Powers worsened. The country needed foreign capital to build the high dam at Aswan; when it found it difficult to sell its cotton to the West, it turned to Russia, which had offered to buy part of the crop; and, after unsuccessful attempts to buy arms from the West, the Egyptian Government concluded the Czech Arms Deal. In other words, Egypt moved—it seemed to the West—towards Russia. On 19 July 1956, the United States informed Egypt that it was not 'feasible in present circumstances' for American aid to be given for the construction of the Aswan High Dam; the United Kingdom and the World Bank echoed this view. Accordingly, Nasser announced that Egypt would immediately take over the Suez Canal and would use the revenue therefrom to build the Aswan High Dam. On 2 August the British Government said that it proposed to take 'precautionary measures of a military nature' to strengthen the British position in the eastern Mediterranean.

On 29 October Israel attacked Egypt in order to check the repeated Egyptian guerrilla raids, and on the following day the United Kingdom told Egypt and Israel that British and French forces would occupy the Suez Canal Zone unless

On a kibbutz in Israel, workers gather cotton left behind after the main harvest.

both sides were to 'stop all war-like action' and withdraw their forces to a distance of ten miles from the Canal. Egypt rejected this ultimatum, which would have meant loss of control over the Canal. Franco–British forces attacked Egypt and, on 5 November, seized Port Said. In response to appeals from the United Nations, the British and French ceased fire on 6 November, when they had occupied only the northern part of the Suez Canal Zone. By Christmas, a U.N. Emergency Force replaced the Franco–British armies, while the Israelis gave up their last foothold in Egypt, the Gaza Strip, in March 1957. The British intervention and then the withdrawal led to a 'loss of face' by Britain. Nasser remained in power, and could now appear at once as martyr and hero in Arab eyes.

United Arab Republic

On 1 February 1958, Egypt formed a union with Syria. Syria seceded from the Union in September 1961, since when Egypt alone has been officially known as the United Arab Republic (U.A.R.). Egypt has been a leader of the Arab League since its formation in 1945, and strongly opposed the signing in 1955 of the Baghdad Pact (Britain, Iran, Iraq, Turkey, Pakistan and the United States), which it considered weakened the League by attracting the support of

Iraq. (In March 1959 Iraq formally withdrew from the Pact, and in August 1959 the name of the organization was changed from Baghdad Pact to Central Treaty Organization.) The U.A.R. resents the existence of the neighbouring state of Israel which occupies a larger area of Palestine than was originally allotted to it by the United Nations. Egyptian troops were maintained from 1949 to 1967 in the Gaza Strip which the United Nations allotted in 1947 to a proposed new Arab state. The Tripartite Declaration of 1950—by France, the United Kingdom and the United States—was made partly in order to deter Egypt from attacking Israel.

Domestic policy. At home Nasser has been strikingly successful. Much of the land has been transferred to the people. In 1952, 27 per cent of the land was owned by 0.2 per cent (1 in 500). Now no family owns more than 100 feddans (Arab. *faddan:* a yoke of oxen—rather more than an English acre). Three-quarters of a million feddans have been redistributed to 120,000 families. There has been considerable success with rural school building and the rural health programme, and with land reclamation and irrigation. In 1960 all foreign trade, banks and some industries were taken over by the State, in what was described as the First Five-Year Plan. The charge that the Egyptian Government would be unable to operate the Canal has been disproved. Earnings from it in 1955 (14,000 vessels passed through) were £26 million; in 1965 (20,000 vessels) £70 million; and the Canal has been widened and deepened. Since the June 1967 war with Israel, however, it has been out of use.

But many problems remain: the population increases by about half a million per year, but there is no comparable increase in food resources; for this Egypt needs better irrigation—and for this the Aswan High Dam is being built with Russian assistance; the first stage was completed in May 1964 and ceremonially opened in the presence of Mr Khrushchev. When completed it will be two miles long and behind it will stretch a 300 mile-long lake; it cost hundreds of lives and £140 million. To obtain the machinery (and the arms) it needs, Egypt has had to commit its cotton crop to the U.S.S.R. It is still controlled autocratically, however benevolent the autocrat's intentions; and the old charges of corruption, inefficiency and bureaucracy can still be heard.

Egypt and the leadership of the Arabs. In foreign policy Nasser was also, until 1967, strikingly successful. So far the merger with Syria (1958–61, and again for a short time in 1963) and the hoped-for union with Iraq have not proved permanent, but they have at least been tried. So have attempts to shape a common Arab policy. At the invitation of President Nasser, representatives of the thirteen Arab League countries met in Cairo in January 1964. This conference greatly helped to ease the tension between Morocco and Algeria, Egypt and Saudi Arabia, and Egypt and Jordan. A second conference was held in Alexandria in September 1964 and a third at Casablanca in 1965. Nasser's propaganda is his most useful weapon. Cairo is the intellectual capital of the Middle East; Nasser's newspapers are read, and his radio broadcasts listened to, from Algeria to the Persian Gulf.

But he has met criticism, for his interference in their affairs, from Hussein of Jordan and Bourguiba of Tunisia. And his defeat in the war with Israel in June 1967—a defeat inflicted in 60 hours, during which time the Israelis destroyed the Egyptian Air Force, captured Jerusalem and the Gaza Strip and reached the Suez Canal—was the first major blow to his prestige. His country is now totally dependent on Russian military and economic aid.

Saudi Arabia. Nasser's efforts to dominate the Middle East have been seen particularly in three neighbouring areas: Saudi Arabia, Libya and Yemen. November 1964 saw the end of a long-drawn-out struggle for power in Saudi Arabia when King Saud was deposed and his younger brother, Crown Prince Feisal, was placed on the throne. Their father, Ibn Saud, who ruled Saudi Arabia from its founding as an independent state in 1932 until his death in 1953, had named Saud as his successor and Feisal as Crown Prince. In a further effort to avoid expected troubles, he had made his other sons pledge loyalty to Saud. For much of the time during his brother's reign, Feisal was Prime Minister; and an unsteady see-saw of power existed until, in March 1964, Feisal became regent and then king. Feisal has the backing of his other brothers, the country's religious leaders and tribal chieftains, while Saud's support came mainly from his sons. Seen at first as pro-Nasser, Feisal has gradually sponsored Islamic solidarity and built it on the Arab Kings, especially Persia and Jordan, and intervened in the Yemen to support the Imam. The United States and Britain have promised £100 million worth of military equipment to Saudi Arabia—to Nasser's loud displeasure. Saud now lives in Egypt as Nasser's guest, and there is now no pretence at friendship between Feisal and Nasser.

Since the discovery in 1938 of oil at Dammam, and its exploitation by the Arabian American Oil Co. (ARAMCO), the economy has boomed and the oil revenues of Saudi Arabia are among the highest in the world. Production soared from 26 million tons (1950) to 75 million tons (1962). ARAMCO was the first oil company in the Middle East to concede the principle of a 'fifty-fifty' division of profits between company and government. Apart from the oil-fields, the country is still undeveloped. A substantial amount is spent on subsidies for tribes in the interior and on the 325 Saudi Arabian princes of the realm.

Libya. In Libya, nationalism has been stimulated by the rise of Nasser and by the Algerian revolt against the French. Fewer than one million people live on the coastal belt which is cut into two areas by 550 miles of desert. In the West (Tripolitania) is the former Italian city of Tripoli, and in the east (Cyrenaica) the small provincial capital of Benghazi; around each is a fringe of settlement. The few thousand people who live in a series of oases known as the Fezzan—some 500 miles inland—enable Libya to claim that it has a population of just over a million.

Before the war, Mussolini tried to found prosperous Italian colonies in both Tripolitania and Cyrenaica. Roads and airfields were built, and the colonists heavily subsidized to establish fruit farms. The Fezzan was French, and the French forces evacuated the area only between 1955 and 1957.

The North African campaign of 1942–43 drove the Italians home, and after the march of the Eighth Army to the Tunisian frontier, a civil administration was established for the few remaining inhabitants. The present King, Idris, who had taken refuge in Egypt during the war, eventually returned as King, and a federation of the three provinces of Libya was proclaimed in 1951. The new kingdom relied on Britain and the United States for aid and technical assistance, which was given in return for the use of the desert for military training.

The United States built a huge air base near Tripoli (Wheelus Field), and Britain converted the much-fought-over R.A.F. station at El Adem into a staging post for aircraft flying from Britain to Egypt, Iraq or Aden. In addition, a small garrison of British troops was stationed in Tripoli and Benghazi. Defence treaties were signed with the U.S.A. and Britain, and considerable amounts of aid given. Despite this—but also causing it—Cairo Radio and the many Egyptian school-teachers brought in by the British administration have influenced the population and stimulated Libyan nationalism.

In recent years Britain and America have compromised by sending fewer and fewer troops to train in Libya. But the real power of the King has decreased, and his heir (his nephew, Crown Prince Hassan al-Rida al-Senussi) and the Government have grown increasingly nationalistic in their attitude. In March 1964 King Idris, then 74, talked of abdication but he later withdrew this threat. Further, important oil deposits have been found in Libya which make the Government there less dependent on the money Washington and London pay for their bases.

Nasser's main hopes in Libya are threefold:

First, to expand Egyptian influence westwards, especially as his efforts to spread eastwards have failed. The Egyptian-Syrian union has collapsed, and the Egyptian military venture in the Yemen was an expensive failure.

Second, to establish close bonds and possibly a union with Libya for material reasons. These include the use of Libya's Mediterranean coast for Egypt's surplus population and the exploitation of Libya's rapidly expanding oil resources.

And third, to end the treaties which give Britain and the United States air bases in Libya. This is part of Nasser's plan to deprive Britain of all Middle East bases—in Libya, Cyprus, Aden and Bahrein—before Egypt threatens or carries out military action against Israel.

Yemen. On the death of the Imam, Ahmed bin Yehya, in September 1962, a situation of great confusion arose. Within a week of ascending the throne, the Imam's heir, Mohammed el Badr, was overthrown and reported killed in a revolution; but in fact he took refuge in the almost inaccessible and rugged hills of the north. For three years civil war raged in the Yemen, with the new Imam, supported by Saudi Arabia, controlling the north and interior, and the revolutionary government, led by Abdullah Sallal, controlling the south and the two capitals of Taiz and Sana. This government is recognized and supported by Egypt, which supplied over 60,000 troops to the Yemen. A truce was signed in 1965, but not all the troops have yet been withdrawn.

President Nasser has three main objectives in the Yemen:

First, to seat the revolutionary régime firmly in power, and so establish a form of government in the Arabian peninsula which can, in time, be imposed on Saudi Arabia, Jordan and the Persian Gulf sultanates.

Second, to complete the military defeat of the Yemeni royalists and restore badly damaged Egyptian prestige.

And third, to form a base for military operations which would be used against the South Arabian Federation and the former British base at Aden. British troops left Aden in November 1967, independence having been granted and a government created from elements of the N.L.F.

The central theme of President Nasser's foreign policy at present is thus the expulsion of Britain from its remaining military bases in the area (Cyprus, El Adem in Libya, and Bahrein in the Persian Gulf). Nor does he want the United Nations to take over any bases which Britain might relinquish. He has also been supplying the Greek Cypriots with arms. Beyond this, his long-term objective remains the destruction of the state of Israel. This objective, he proclaims, can only be attained if Britain first loses its Middle East bases. His defeat by Israel in June 1967 confirms him in this view.

The British interest in the Middle East

Since 1839, when it acquired Aden, Britain has been involved in the affairs of the Middle East. In 1876 it acquired a major share in the Suez Canal (opened in 1869), and in 1882 occupied Egypt; from 1878 until 1960 it controlled Cyprus; in both world wars much of the Middle East was under Allied control, and for much of the inter-war years Palestine, Jordan, Iraq and the Sudan were either British mandates or were largely under British guidance. At the present time the British direct interest is largely confined to the Persian Gulf and two small areas in Cyprus (Dhekelia and Akrotiri).

In the Persian Gulf, British involvement goes back three centuries, when trade with Persia was being developed by the East India Company. British interests gradually changed from purely commercial affairs to 'moral' issues such as suppression of piracy and slavery, and to Great Power 'status' issues such as protection of the line of communications to India opened up by the Suez Canal, and, after 1908, the exclusion of European and other rivals from the oil-rich Persian Gulf.

Piracy was virtually ended in the 1850s with the signing of a 'Perpetual Maritime Truce' with the worst offenders: hence the name 'Trucial Coast' states which has stuck to this day. Later came a series of so-called 'Exclusive' agreements under which Arab rulers undertook not to cede, mortgage or give up any part of their territories to any one except Britain, nor to enter into a relationship with any other state without British consent. In return, Britain undertook to protect the Arab rulers from outside attack, sometimes implicitly (the seven Trucial States), sometimes explicitly (Qatar).

Central to these defence arrangements was Aden. Its stark, forbidding crags —the main centre is an extinct volcanic crater, windless and sweltering— shelter a busy harbour and an important oil and coal bunkering station. From 1839 to 1937 it was administered from India; in 1936 it became a Crown Colony; since 1963 it has been part of the South Arabian Federation, a merger of Aden with the thirteen neighbouring eastern and western protectorates. This Federation became independent in 1967. The 13 sheikdoms and emirates are feudal and backward: they extend over two thousand times as much land as Aden, and their world is that of the oasis, the camel, the tribe—and the rifle. Many of Aden's population (220,000 in all) are, however, Yemenis from the north (the Yemen describes Aden as the Southern Yemen), and Aden, a boom town, is vulnerable to Yemeni infiltration; the borders of the Federation are frequently under attack. The chief guerrilla force was FLOSY: Front for the Liberation of Occupied Southern Yemen. And behind FLOSY were Nasser and Egyptian aid. A rival of FLOSY is NLF, the National Liberation Front, with which Britain negotiated in 1967. There are no official figures for the cost of the Aden base, but the defence establishment there is believed to have pumped into the economy of the area something like £11 million a year. This will lapse gradually after independence. Behind defence lies the politics of oil. The total value of oil produced in the territories around the Persian Gulf is conservatively estimated at £1,200 million a year, of which the British-protected sheikdoms, including Kuwait, contribute about one-third.

In all the territories except Saudi Arabia and Bahrein, British oil companies have major interests; and the sterling income from Kuwait's oil, especially, is regarded by the British Treasury as vital to the British balance of payments. Two-thirds of the world's proved oil reserves lie under or around the waters of the Persian Gulf. For the last decade the area has been the world's biggest and cheapest exporter of oil, and Britain's biggest supplier in particular—it imports £150 million worth of Middle East oil each year. For the next decade, according to current estimates, the Gulf oil-fields, old and new, will need to double present production to keep pace with the world's oil consumption.

In 1961 Kuwait replaced its old British protectorate treaty with a simple treaty of mutual defence and a declaration of full independence. But elsewhere the old nineteenth-century treaties continue, and entangle Britain in an unhappy web of responsibility without power, obliging it to support a battery of more or less archaic régimes without having the authority or the power to insist on any changes in their internal affairs.

One vestige of Empire does linger here still, the Trucial Oman Scouts, which includes some 40 British officers and 100 British N.C.O.s. With their uniform the Arab head-dress, their grey shirts enclosed by red belts and worn hanging outside sand-coloured trousers, and their footwear the popular sand boots, they are a picturesque Imperial survival. They have five mobile squadrons operating from headquarters at Sharja, and from points inland and along the coast. The orders of the Scouts are that, unless in dire straits, they will not fire back even if some nervous finger fires on them in the Trucial States. Much of their work is police-like; and because only Abu Dhabi and Dubai have police forces of their own, a police wing of the Trucial Oman Scouts has been formed. There is also a small British force helping to train the South Arabian Federation Army. At present it is mainly a collection of tribal levies.

Country	Dominant language	Dominant religion	Area (square miles)	Population	Government	Trade	Military strength
Egypt (The United Arab Republic)	Arabic	Islam	383,000 (only 13,600 cultivated)	26,000,000	Independent Republic joined to Syria, 1958–61, United Arab Republic.	Mainly in cotton, with Eastern Europe.	German-trained and Russian-equipped forces, of which 50,000 had experience in the Yemen. Not yet recovered from defeat by Israel in 1967.
Iraq	Arabic	Islam	150,000	8,000,000	Republic since 1958.	Mainly in oil and with Western Europe; oil exports constitute 60% of national income.	Five army divisions. Handicapped by civil war with Kurds in northern Iraq.
Syria	Arabic	Islam	70,000	5,000,000	Independent Republic joined to Egypt to form the United Arab Republic, 1958. Withdrew 1961.	Receives transit revenue from oil pipelines across it.	Estimated at two divisions.
Lebanon	Arabic	Islam and Christianity (Maronite)	3,400	1,750,000	Independent Republic.	Oil pipelines terminate at Saida and Tripoli. Beirut important and cosmopolitan trading city and international airport.	Tiny.
Hashemite Kingdom of the Jordan	Arabic	Islam	40,000	1,500,000	Kingdom (1946) (King Hussein since 1952) Close ties with Britain.	Negligible. State financed by Britain, U.S. and United Nations.	Arab Legion British-trained and equipped and well disciplined.

Country	Dominant language	Dominant religion	Area (square miles)	Population	Government	Trade	Military strength
Saudi Arabia and Arabian Peninsula Countries	Arabic	Islam	900,000	9,000,000	Independent Kingdoms of Saudi Arabia and Yemen; Persian Gulf sheikhs in association with Britain; South Arabian Federation; Britain has close relations with Kuwait.	Saudi Arabian Government derives 80% of income from oil revenues. Oil exports worth $1,200 million each year.	Estimated to be 60,000.
Libya	Arabic	Islam	700,000 (mainly desert)	1,500,000	Kingdom (King Idris) since 1952.	Small, mainly almonds and fruit. Egypt main trading partner.	Less than 5,000. Cyrenaican Defence Force British trained. Much British and U.S. military aid, but this now ceasing. El Adem (British) and Wheelus Field (U.S.) important air bases.
Tunisia	Maghrebi variant of Arabic	Islam	48,000	4,000,000	Independent Republic since 1956. (President Habib Bourguiba).	Wheat and barley, olives and wine. Most of its trade is with France.	Small, to protect Algerian frontier. The state is non-aligned.
Sudan	Arabic in north	Islam	900,000	10,000,000	Independent Republic since 1956.	Cotton exports important.	Sudan Defence Force originally British trained; well-disciplined.
Algeria	Maghrebi Arabic and Berber	Islam	900,000 (mainly desert)	10,000,000 (mainly in the three Northern Depts.)	Independent Republic since July 1962.	Agriculture along coast. Sahara rich in oil and natural gas.	Strong and well-trained after long war with France.

224

Morocco	Maghrebi Arabic and Berber	Islam	200,000	11,500,000	Independent since 1956. (Hassan II).	Agriculture, but also manganese, cobalt and phosphates.	Defence forces mainly.
Israel	Hebrew	Jewish	8,000	2,500,000	Republic (1948).	Citrus fruits, phosphates, potash.	Large army: all able-bodied citizens have some military training.
Iran	Persian	Islam	650,000	26,000,000	Monarchy (Mohammed Reza Shah, since 1941).	Major source of world's oil.	Mainly on border duties. Much American equipment.
Turkey	Turkish	Lay in theory, but Islam is strong	300,000	31,000,000	Republic since 1923.	Agriculture, especially currants.	Large army; member of CENTO; good record in Korean War.
Yemen	Arabic	Islam	75,000	4,500,000 (approx.)		Self-sufficient in food. Coffee chief export.	Tribes provide army of 20,000.

QUESTIONS TO CONSIDER

1. What do you understand by the Middle East?
   What countries are in this area?
   What are the main features of the life of the people there?
2. Why is this area important to us in the West? Will its importance tend to decline?
3. Outline the main events in the Middle East since 1945.
4. Why is Colonel Nasser important? Give a brief outline of his career.

WORDS TO NOTE

The Capitulations: System in Ottoman Empire of giving special privileges to foreigners, especially right to be tried in their own courts.

Condominium: A country or region governed jointly by two or more powers.

Coup d'état: The seizure of power by force.

Emir: An independent chieftain.

Enosis: The union of Cyprus with Greece (from the Greek word for unity).

Fellahin: The field workers of Egypt.

Haj: The pilgrimage to Mecca.

Hajji: One who has made the pilgrimage.

Koran: The Moslem Bible.

Mandate: Area governed by a Great Power on behalf of League of Nations.

Minaret: The tower of a mosque.

Muezzin: The man who calls the faithful to prayer five times a day.

Ramadhan: Term used to describe the ninth month of the lunar year in the Moslem calendar.

Saqieh: The pump that draws water from wells or rivers.

Sheikh: Chief of a tribe.

Sherif: The Guardian of the Holy Cities of Mecca and Medina.

FOR FURTHER READING

McAuliffe, W. R.: *Modern Asia Explained (Chapter 1),* Blackie, 1952.

Connell-Smith, Gordon: *Pattern of the Post-War World,* Penguin, 1957.

Wint, G. and Calvocoressi, P.: *Middle East Crisis,* Penguin, 1957.

Childers, E.: *Common Sense about the Arab World,* Gollancz, 1960.

Pounds, Norman J. G. and Kingsbury, Robert C.: *An Atlas of Middle Eastern Affairs,* Methuen, 1965.

8. *International Relations 1919–45*

The peace settlement, 1919

In January 1919, 72 delegates from 32 victorious nations met in Paris to make peace after the four and a quarter years of the First World War. Of these delegates, those representing the British Commonwealth (especially the British Prime Minister, Lloyd George), France (especially Clemenceau), Italy (Orlando), Japan (Saionji) and the United States (President Wilson) were the chief figures. The defeated nations—Germany, Austria, Hungary, Turkey and Bulgaria—the neutral nations and Russia (now Communist) were not represented at the Conference.

The Conference faced appalling difficulties. Much of Northern France was in ruins. Millions of lives had been lost: in battle the British Commonwealth had lost over a million men, France 1,300,000, Germany 2,300,000 and Russia over 4,000,000. Of the Allied armies, 13,000,000 men had been wounded. Perhaps a further 10,000,000 people had died of famine or disease. Everywhere in Europe there was exhaustion and despair, and in places there was revolution.

Before the end of the war, President Wilson had proclaimed the American peace goals. In January 1918 he had embodied them in his Fourteen Points, which included the following: the removal, so far as possible, of all economic barriers; the adjustment of colonial claims; the principle of the freedom of the seas; the reduction of armaments; the abolition of secret diplomacy; and the creation of a system to guarantee security to all nations. The specific points in Wilson's programme included the return of Alsace-Lorraine to France, the readjustment of the frontier of Italy, the evacuation and restoration of all territories occupied by the German army, and self-determination for the people living under Austrian and Turkish rule.

But the Allies were not as noble as was Wilson. Although Germany had lost the war, Allied losses had been tremendous. The French were anxious to reduce Germany's industrial and military strength in order to ensure their own future security. They wanted the reduction of Germany to impotence. The British were mainly anxious to deprive Germany of her naval and commercial power and of her colonies.

The final peace treaty with Germany was signed on 28 June, 1919. The terms of the treaty were severe. Germany was deprived of Alsace-Lorraine in the west and territories in the east. Allied armies occupied the Rhineland and were supposed to stay there for 15 years. Germany was compelled to surrender war materials, its fleet, its submarines and its merchant marine. It was permitted to keep an army of 100,000 men but was forbidden to possess tanks, airplanes and heavy artillery. Germany's investments and property abroad were also taken. Furthermore, the country was stripped of its colonies. They became League of Nations mandates to be administered by France, Britain and Japan. Having been declared guilty of causing the war, Germany was told to pay the cost of it (reparations) to the Allies. The sum was in the end fixed at £8,000 million, a sum the country, according to some opinions, could not possibly pay. It was also forbidden to join the League of Nations.

The German people bitterly resented this treaty, signed at Versailles. They objected to the loss of colonies, to enforced disarmament, to the war guilt clause and to the occupation of the Rhineland. Furthermore, the continued blockade after the end of the war produced hardship in Germany.

The Treaty of St Germain settled the fate of Austria, which was reduced to a small state and was forbidden to join Germany. The Treaty of Trianon reduced Hungary considerably in size. The Treaty of Neuilly reduced the size of Bulgaria. The Turks repudiated the Treaty of Sèvres, however, and in 1923 were able to obtain better terms in the Treaty of Lausanne.

With the destruction of the Austro-Hungarian Empire, a number of new or newly enlarged states came into existence. An independent Poland was established. Czechoslovakia became an independent nation. A number of

Europe after 1919.

small states came into existence in the Baltic: Estonia, Latvia, Lithuania, Finland. Serbia became an enlarged territory and was henceforth called Yugoslavia. Romania's territory was also increased. The Turkish and Austrian monarchies had already, like the German and Russian, collapsed. It was assumed that with their destruction something much better would automatically take their place. But with the disintegration of these empires, southeastern Europe became a chessboard on which great powers, using the small nations along the Danube as pawns, played power politics to gain access to the economic and military resources of the region. In the end, fourteen new and largely powerless states appeared.

The League of Nations

One result of the Versailles Peace Conference was revolutionary—the setting up of the League of Nations. At Geneva a permanent organization was established, with an internationally-recruited secretariat, to which were linked the kindred organizations, especially the International Court of Justice and the International Labour Office. The League was to consist of an Assembly, or Lower House, meeting annually, and a Council, meeting three or four times a year, with both permanent and non-permanent members. At the first Assembly of the League (1920), though Russia and the ex-enemy states were absent, 42 countries were represented. At first it had some success; in 1924 there were present at the Assembly in Geneva seven prime ministers and 16 foreign secretaries. Its membership rose to 57 in 1932 and to 60 in 1934. Indeed the U.S.A. was the only major power which never, at some stage, joined the League.

Why did the League of Nations fail? First, the Conference was the worst possible setting in which to found such an institution. The Covenant of the League, describing its purpose, was made part of the Treaty. Many of the statesmen in Paris were concerned with problems of power politics instead of concentrating whole-heartedly on building an organization that would ensure world peace.

Second, despite its title, it was never a universal organization. The United States of America never joined the League, although President Wilson had been its main architect. The defeated central powers were also not allowed to join at first and Russia, under Bolshevik control when the League was formed and unpopular with the Allies, was also not invited. Germany entered the League in 1926 but withdrew in 1933, the year before Russia finally gained admission. Japan left the League in 1933 after criticisms of her aggression in China.

Third, the League eventually failed because it lacked the power to make its decisions effective; there was no powerful means at its disposal by which erring states could be brought to heel. Economic sanctions—depriving a country of certain vital raw materials—were tried against some aggressors like Italy but they were never really effective.

And, fourth, the chief reason for the League's failure was the existence of national sovereignty. The majority of states were unwilling to give the League real authority over their own affairs.

How successful was the Versailles Settlement as a whole?

The League of Nations nevertheless represented a constructive effort to replace the old system of military alliances and secret diplomacy by friendly, intelligent and co-operative action. Furthermore, certain nationality groups which had been persecuted for centuries, such as the Poles, Czechs and Jews, were given freedom and a chance for self-government and national development.

But the disadvantages of the peace far outweighed the advantages. The distribution of nationality groups was still dangerous. Large German minorities remained in many of the areas allotted to other countries. The German-populated state of Austria, shorn almost to nothing, was forbidden to become part of the new Germany, though both countries requested the union. The new republics of Czechoslovakia and Poland contained a number of distinct national groups that resented the domination of their new rulers.

The distribution of the mandates, made with the strategy of Imperialism still in mind, did nothing to lessen international tension. The failure to give Italy a fair share of the colonial spoils of war led it to abandon its policy of co-operation with the Allies and pushed it towards Fascism.

The gravest error of all was the treatment accorded to Germany. Many of the German people were horrified when they learned the terms of the Versailles Treaty. Many of them would have preferred continuing the war, but the terms of the armistice had given them no choice in the matter. It was hard to persuade anyone to affix his signature to the document on behalf of Germany.

Proud and powerful before the war, it was ridiculous to suppose that, however temporarily weakened, Germany would be content to remain an inferior state. It was inconsistent to saddle it with a huge debt, and to strip it at the same time of nearly all means of paying that debt. It was stupid to suppose that, surrounded by hostile nations, it would submit for long to be without adequate means of defence. Finally, it was absurd not to realize that the burden of war guilt would create a national inferiority complex that would create problems for the future.

The peacemakers had in fact set the stage for the next war. The First World War and the Peace Settlement changed completely the economic and military position of Europe. Until 1914 Europe had been the home of six great states: Britain, France, Germany, Austria-Hungary, Russia and Italy. As a result of the war, Austria-Hungary disappeared altogether from this category, and so for a time did Germany and Russia. For a decade after the war, there were only two great powers in Europe: Britain and France. And the Ottoman Empire, Germany's ally, was also overthrown. Austria-Hungary, Germany, Russia and the Ottoman Empire ceased to be empires and became republics.

The end of the European Age

Two non-European nations, however, became important: the United States and Japan. Japanese industries developed considerably during the war. Japan strengthened her position in Asia and received some of the spoils of victory. And as a result of the war, the economic balance of power in the world shifted to the United States. Instead of London, New York became the financial capital of the world. Under the leadership of President Wilson, America's diplomatic position became stronger than ever before in her history. For the first time since the founding of the republic, the United States asserted her influence in world, and particularly in European, affairs. The military position of the United States became more significant also. The expanding American navy soon became the equal of Britain's, thus ending Britain's supremacy on the seas.

The road to the Second World War, 1919–1939

For the first 15 years after 1919, Europe was in a state of uneasy peace and France was the major power in Europe. It sought to drain Germany of its resources by the demand for reparations; the Ruhr was occupied in 1923; by alliances with Belgium and Poland and the members of the Little Entente—Romania, Czechoslovakia and Yugoslavia—Germany was encircled. The French Army was believed to be the strongest in Europe. In spite of these French alliances, the principle of collective security as laid down by the League of Nations was generally accepted by 1924. It was hoped that peace could be maintained by collective security, disarmament and arbitration through the Permanent International Court of Justice. By the Locarno Pact of 1925 the powers of Western Europe pledged themselves to settle disputes by peaceful means; Germany joined the League of Nations in 1925; and in 1928 in signing the Kellogg-Briand Peace Pact the Powers declared that war was outlawed as an instrument of national policy. But these years of uneasy peace were shattered by the Depression in the United States.

After a decade of a giddy prosperity—the Jazz Age—in the autumn of 1929 a financial crash occurred in the United States that was bound to have world-wide effect. The stocks of leading corporations fell sharply in value, and confidence disappeared. The panic was followed by the collapse of banks, railway companies and other corporations. At first it was assumed by many that this slump was only a temporary matter, but by 1931 there were nearly 15 million unemployed in the United States.

By 1930 the depression was world-wide. Unemployment and panic affected many nations. In 1931 the banks of Vienna failed, and there was a second severe economic crisis in Germany. President Hoover had tried to stop the general financial collapse in Central Europe by proposing that payments of all debts to the United States should be suspended for a year. But the situation in Germany became worse, and the banks were closed. The economic and financial crisis affected Great Britain, which had to abandon the gold standard. Many other nations in Europe and South America and some of the Dominions also abandoned the gold standard. The depression became acute in France after 1932.

The economic situation in Central and Eastern Europe did not improve. Plans to remove trade barriers were not successful. In 1932 the reparations problem was settled, and Germany practically ceased making payments. In the same year, almost all nations stopped paying their debts to the United States and made only token payments. Finland alone continued to meet its obligations. The American people were displeased by the failure of European nations, including Britain, to meet their financial obligations. In 1934 the Congress forbade American loans to foreign governments which did not pay their debts.

It was in this situation of unemployment, poverty, repeated crises and despair that Hitler came to power in 1933. Nazi Germany left the League in the same year. There followed a race between the plans of the aggressors (Germany, Italy and Japan) and the efforts of the peaceful states to build up an effective system of collective security through the League of Nations. This effort was handicapped by Western suspicions of the U.S.S.R.—the United States of America did not recognize the U.S.S.R. until 1933. Britain and France continued to try to make arrangements of their own with Germany and Italy, Britain especially with Germany (the Anglo-German Naval Agreement, 1935, the Munich settlement, 1938), France especially with Italy. This became known as the policy of appeasement, and was far from popular.

In particular, Britain and France made little effort to stop the aggressors.

The Second World War

The causes of the war

Hitler was responsible because of his policy and his annexations.

Although not as harsh as Germans said it was—the Treaty of Versailles was much kinder than their own treaty (Brest-Litovsk) with Russia in March 1918 —and although the reparations demands were scaled down in 1924 and 1929, yet the Versailles settlement was unacceptable to Germans since it was a dictated treaty. Opinion in the West also saw it as harsh, and this 'softened up' early opposition to Hitler.

Moreover, national self-determination as attempted in 1919 was unsuccessful. A large and stable society, like the Austro-Hungarian in Central Europe, disappeared. None of the small states that emerged could stand on its own feet economically. All contained minorities that did not fit in with the majority, and Hitler exploited the grievances of the German minorities, as in Czechoslovakia and Poland.

The League of Nations failed to settle the major diplomatic problems.

The economic depression in Germany, the United States, Britain and France undermined the democracies. The poverty (spiritual as well as economic) produced Fascism in Italy, Nazism in Germany and the Falangist movement, led by Franco, in Spain. It weakened the middle class in all countries and weakened faith in democratic government.

Britain and France failed to show a consistent policy of opposition to Hitler and Mussolini. Had Britain not signed the Naval Agreement of 1935; had France moved against German troops in the Rhineland in 1936 (they had orders to withdraw if France did act); had Britain and France been firm towards

Mussolini in 1936; had Britain, France and Russia made a concerted effort to oppose Germany in 1936–38; had the West not been too ready to appease—Hitler might never have risked war.

The West did not make its policy clear until March 1939. Even then Hitler thought they would once again give way. In these senses, then, he was not solely responsible for the Second World War.

The course of the war

In September 1939 Hitler passed from diplomacy to armed conflict. On the 1st, land and sea forces attacked the Polish Corridor while the Luftwaffe bombed Warsaw. On the 3rd, after an ultimatum demanding the cessation of hostilities had not been answered, Britain and France declared war. The war was to run through six main phases.

First phase: the assault on Poland, 1939. The first phase of the war opened with the attack on Poland on 1 September 1939, and came to an end on 9 April 1940, with the invasion of Norway and Denmark. Poland was completely overrun by the Germans and Russians in 28 days. On the seventeenth day Soviet forces entered eastern Poland and, after meeting the advancing German troops near Warsaw, withdrew to an agreed line. With the occupation of Poland as complete as that of Czechoslovakia, the Nazis argued that there was no cause for continued hostilities with Britain and France. A joint German-Soviet invitation for a negotiated peace was issued in December but was rejected by Britain and France unless the evacuation of Poland was agreed to as a preliminary.

The static phase of the war (i.e. the 'Phony War') on the western front came to an end on 9 April, 1940. Almost at the same time Britain extended her naval blockade to Norwegian territorial waters and Germany invaded both Denmark and Norway. The success of this move demonstrated the possibilities of fifth-column activities in assisting a Nazi invasion. The Danish reaction was one of protest and official non-co-operation, but not of armed resistance.

In Norway, where the government decided unanimously for resistance, it was found that the army and all key services had been honeycombed with Nazi sympathizers and, as soon as the occupation was effective, the leader of the Nazi party, Vidkun Quisling, was made head of a government, acting in collaboration with Germany. His name has become synonymous with that of traitor.

Second phase: the campaign in the West, 1940. The occupation of Denmark and Norway was a means of bringing an increased strategic threat to bear on Britain and France. On 10 May the Nazis invaded Belgium, Luxembourg, the Netherlands and, in a few days, France.

A war of rapid movement followed, in which the Allies were outnumbered by the Germans, particularly in armour and aircraft: 350,000 British troops were rescued from the Dunkirk beaches. On 22 June France signed a separate

Armistice. Under the armistice terms three-fifths of France, including Paris, the north and the entire west coasts were occupied, while a government officially co-operative with Germany installed itself at Vichy.

Twelve days before the French capitulation Italy had declared war in support of Germany, and occupied Nice and Corsica. It began to plan an invasion of the Balkans.

All Europe expected an immediate large-scale invasion of Britain. No one knows today precisely why this was not attempted. Probably, on the advice of Ribbentrop, Hitler believed Britain would ask for terms and might even be of some value in a campaign against Russia. Possibly there was some doubt whether German air superiority without adequate naval power could neutralize the Royal Navy's command of the Channel, and time was wasted in fruitless negotiations to get the active assistance of the French against their late allies.

Third phase: the Battle of Britain. The Battle of Britain, which was fought in the air by R.A.F. Hurricanes and Spitfires, blunted the German air attacks and gave Britain a breathing space for reorganization. Hitler then decided to use Goering's Luftwaffe in an attempt to bomb her into submission. Heavy destruction took place, in London and other towns, but the attack failed to lead to British surrender. The air attacks did little damage to the British war effort, although 60,000 civilians were killed, and every month that passed made the prospects of a sea-borne invasion more doubtful. At some date in the first half of 1941, the project must have been written off. For 12 months Britain stood alone—and survived.

Meanwhile, a joint Italo-German attack had been launched against Egypt, but this failed to gain control of the Suez Canal.

Fourth phase: the German assault on Russia, 1941–42. A fourth and revolutionary phase of the war opened on 22 June 1941, when the full weight of the Nazi armies was thrown against the Soviet Union. Here again it is difficult to be certain of the reasons which led Hitler to make the mistake that every German strategist had denounced since 1914, that of starting a major war on two fronts.

In *Mein Kampf* Hitler made clear his belief that the Europe of the future was to be a German-dominated continent as far as the Urals and the Caucasus, with Italy and Britain as allies of Germany in the West, and an understanding with Japan in the Far East. The flight of Rudolf Hess, Hitler's deputy, in 1941 to Scotland to obtain British support for this campaign failed, but Hitler may still have thought that Britain would be convinced of Nazi 'sincerity' once the attack took place. In this he was promptly disillusioned by Churchill's speech on the day the attack opened.

The invasion came perilously near its objective. But the Soviet Government did not capitulate, and the advance was finally halted before Moscow, and stopped at Stalingrad at the end of 1942.

Meanwhile Japan, no doubt counting upon the success of Hitler's Russian adventure, had declared war on the British Empire and the United States, and Germany and Italy had committed the folly of declaring war also against the United States.

By the end of 1942, Japan controlled Indo-China, Malaya, the Dutch East Indies, Siam, Burma and was on the doorstep of India. Germany controlled France, Belgium, Holland, Luxembourg, Norway, Denmark, Czechoslovakia, the Baltic States, Yugoslavia, Poland, Greece, Austria and most of European Russia.

Fifth phase: the defensive retreat of Germany, 1943–44. The defeat before Stalingrad, coinciding with the start of the great British advance at El Alamein, represented the turning point in the war, and in Hitler's career. Notwithstanding catastrophic losses, the Red Army began its counter-offensive which pressed the invading armies slowly back to their point of departure.

In North Africa the German-Italian armies were defeated in Libya and forced subsequently from Tunisia, Sicily and southern Italy, until the Axis alliance was finally broken by the defection of Italy in September 1943.

On 6 June 1944, Anglo-American forces landed in France, and, after breaking the hard crust of Nazi resistance in Normandy, reached the Rhine on 20 September. Meanwhile German losses in the field led to an increased demand for imported labour from the occupied countries, and this stimulated the resistance movements.

This fifth chapter of the war led to widespread unrest inside Germany itself. This was reflected in the rapid changes within the army command, in the reports of increasing numbers of German citizens sentenced to death by the so-called People's Courts, and in the fact that an S.S. army of more than a million picked troops was immobilized in the interior, in spite of the demands of the front.

On 20 July 1944, an attempt was made on Hitler's life by a South German aristocrat, Count Stauffenberg, and this was the signal for a revolt by a large number of officers with the support of certain civilian personalities. The rising failed and the immediate effect of it was an intensification of the Gestapo terror. Himmler became Commander-in-Chief of all German armed forces.

Sixth phase: the defeat of Germany. By the end of 1944 all France and Belgium had been liberated. The attempts with air-borne troops at Arnhem to seize a Rhine crossing did not succeed, however, and German troops made a stand in the Ardennes Mountains in December 1944. But on 23 March 1945, the Anglo-American forces, after concentrated bombardment from the air, crossed the Rhine for the final all-out offensive. Some days later, the Russians, who had been halted at the Oder, began their last advance on Berlin.

On 9 April a fresh offensive was launched in Italy. This final campaign revealed extraordinary disorganization inside Germany. In some places the

Nazis, and sometimes even the Hitler Youth, fought with the expected fanaticism and ferocity. In others, such as the Ruhr, the opposing troops proved very weak. Plans for a stand in the difficult country of Bohemia and Upper Austria, where supplies for a long guerrilla war have been found, seem to have been disorganized by Hitler's romantic resolve to fight and die in Berlin.

On 24 April Himmler offered unconditional surrender to the Western Allies, but this was refused by the British and Americans, unless it were made also to the Russians. On 1 May Admiral Doenitz, the organizer of the U-boat war, announced Hitler's death, in Berlin, and his own appointment as Head of the State to continue the war. On 7 May a general unconditional surrender of the German forces on land, sea and air to the allied nations was signed by Doenitz's representatives at Rheims and ratified at midnight in Berlin. The Nazi system went down in total ruin after almost six years of war.

On 6 August 1945, an atomic bomb was dropped on Hiroshima and on 9 August on Nagasaki in Japan. She surrendered on 14 August.

QUESTIONS TO CONSIDER

1. What were the terms of the 1919 settlement? How successful was it?
2. Why did the League of Nations fail to solve the diplomatic problems of the inter-war years?
3. What were the causes of the Second World War?
4. Give a brief outline of the events of the Second World War.

WORDS TO NOTE

Appeasement: The attempt to placate Hitler by giving way to some of his demands between 1936 and 1939, hoping that he would then rest content.

Collective Security: The system by which the security of each country is guaranteed by all others. This is the idea that is expressed in the Covenant of the League of Nations and the Charter of the U.N.

War guilt clause: Article 231 of the Treaty of Versailles 1919 accused Germany of being guilty of causing the First World War. This article was bitterly resented in Germany. After the Second World War, the governments of the defeated powers of Germany and Japan were accused of crimes against peace, of war crimes and of crimes against humanity. The German leaders were tried for these offences at Nuremberg in 1946; most of them were found guilty and some of them were executed.

FOR FURTHER READING

Wales, P.: *World Affairs since* 1919, Methuen, 1958.
Priestley, H. E. and Betts, J. J.: *The Momentous Years* 1919–1958, Dent, 1959.
Elliott, F. and Summerskill, M.: *A Dictionary of Politics*, Penguin, 1959.
Robert, S. H.: *The House that Hitler Built*, Methuen, 1937.

Savage, Katherine: *The Story of the Second World War*, Oxford, 1957.

Peacock, H. L.: *A History of Modern Europe*, Heinemann, 1961.

Churchill, Winston: *The Second World War* (Abridged), Cassell, 1957.

Fergusson, Bernard: *The Watery Maze* (The Story of Combined Operations), Collins, 1961.

Thomas, R. H.: *The Post-War World*, Philip, 1966.

The World and the School, quarterly (since 1964) Atlantic Information Centre for Teachers.

9. *The Post-War World*

Russian foreign policy since 1945

The Second World War left Russia in military occupation of much of Eastern and Central Europe. Russia gained, as a result of the Second World War, the eastern provinces of Poland; the former Baltic States of Estonia, Latvia and Lithuania; Bessarabia and Northern Bukovina from Romania; Ruthenia from Czechoslovakia; Karelia and Petsamo from Finland; Konigsberg from Germany. Between 1945 and 1948, Poland, Romania, Bulgaria, Czechoslovakia, Albania, Hungary, Eastern Germany and Yugoslavia (for a time) were brought under its control. These are called by the Communists 'People's Democracies', and by the West 'Russia's Satellites'. They are closely linked with Russia and each other, economically, militarily and politically. Yugoslavia was in the Russian sphere of influence from 1945 until 1948.

On 5 October 1947 it was announced that a Communist Information Bureau (Cominform) had been set up in Belgrade to co-ordinate the activities of the Communist parties of Bulgaria, Czechoslovakia, France, Hungary, Italy, Romania, Poland, Russia and Yugoslavia. Its headquarters were subsequently moved to Bucharest. It published a journal, 'For a Lasting Peace, for a People's

U.S.S.R. IN 1939

AREAS ANNEXED BY
U.S.S.R. SINCE 1929

SOVIET OCCUPIED ZONES
IN GERMANY & AUSTRIA

COMMUNIST CONTROLLED
COUNTRIES

COMMUNIST BUT NOT
UNDER SOVIET CONTROL

FINLAND (NOT UNDER
COMMUNIST CONTROL
BUT IN RUSSIAN SPHERE)

BOUNDARIES OF 1939

SCALE OF MILES
0   100   200

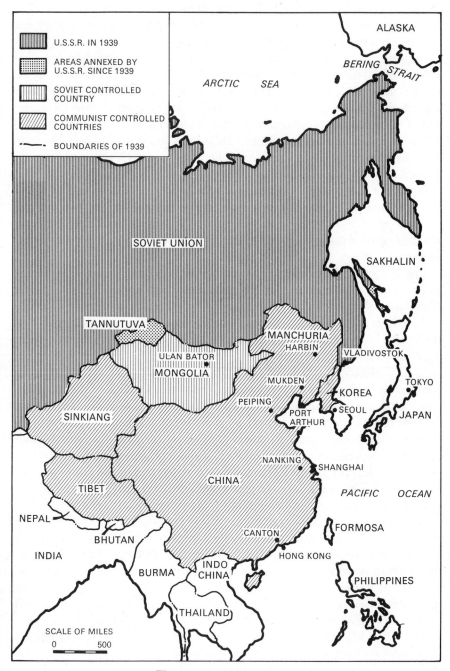

The expansion of Soviet Russia.

Democracy' from November 1947, in which the party line was expressed. The Cominform was dissolved in April 1956, but in 1955 a Communist unified military command was set up, the Warsaw Pact.

In June 1948, Tito was denounced and Yugoslavia expelled from the Cominform. Tito was accused of many 'crimes' of which the most serious was being a national deviationist. This meant he was altogether too independent from Stalin's point of view. The basic factor in the quarrel—and the reason why Tito was able to make a successful stand against Stalin—was that the Yugoslav leader and his Communist colleagues had built up their own state machine without Russian direction. The army and civil administration remained loyal to Tito.

In the Far East Russia obtained South Sakhalin and the Kuriles from Japan in accordance with the Yalta agreement. It regained the former Tsarist rights in Manchuria, Port Arthur and Dairen, and its position in Outer Mongolia was confirmed. Russia occupied North Korea and established a puppet government there.

The victory of the Chinese Communists in 1949 gave Russia what seemed to be an important new ally, and it eventually gave up most of its rights in Manchuria, Port Arthur and Dairen to the People's Government of China.

Russian expansion, the breakdown of Four-Power Control in Germany, the Berlin Blockade, the Greek Civil War; these led to the Cold War and the forming of an alliance against Russia under American leadership. Americans were especially affected by the news of the death of Jan Masaryk (1948), Foreign Minister of Czechoslovakia, who was well known in the U.S.A.; he was found dead below his bedroom window and believed to have been murdered. After the outbreak of the war in Korea (24 June 1950), the defence efforts of the Western Powers were greatly increased. It was made clear that Russia could expand no further, in Europe, at any rate, without precipitating a world war.

Since the death of Stalin (5 March 1953) there has been much talk of peaceful co-existence. This was associated at first with the Malenkov régime, then with the name of Khrushchev. The most important single event in support of it was the signing of a truce in Korea (27 July 1953) after the long stalemate over the prisoners-of-war question. When finally a conference was held between the Western Powers and Russia at Berlin in January 1954 specifically to discuss the German problem (a test of Russia's intentions, in the view of the West), however, it was soon evident that the Soviet Union was not prepared to give up Eastern Germany. In October 1954 the Western Powers signed the Paris agreements which brought Western Germany into NATO.

The fall of Malenkov in February 1955, and the emergence of Khrushchev, led to further changes both in domestic policy and in foreign policy. An Austrian peace treaty was signed in May 1955; the Russian leaders visited Tito in Belgrade later in the same month: the Geneva Conference 'at the summit'

The world today, as seen from a satellite circling 22,300 miles above the earth's surface.

passed off amicably in July and raised new hopes; and Dr Adenauer visited Moscow in September 1955. He entered into diplomatic relations with the Soviet Union and secured the release of German prisoners-of-war still detained in Russia ten years after the war.

When the Foreign Ministers (of U.K., U.S.A., U.S.S.R. and France) met at Geneva in October 1955 to discuss the specific questions of German reunification and 'European security', however, it was soon clear that the Russian standpoint had not basically changed. No agreement was reached.

Similarly in 1956 the Hungarian revolt was crushed and a puppet régime headed by Janos Kadar installed there. Tito's relations with Russia remained cool and national Communism was criticized by the Soviet Union. Nor was it possible for Communist governments to exist in most of the satellites without Russian support.

The use of Soviet tanks against Hungary showed that the Soviet leaders would in the last resort use force to maintain their grip on the satellites. Yet Russia's assertion of control over Hungary was made at a price; never again could its position in Eastern Europe be the same. The rigidity of the Stalin era has given way to a more flexible policy in Moscow's handling of the satellites.

Quite apart from the change of personalities (the importance of which is difficult to assess) there are a number of reasons why Soviet foreign policy should have been modified after the death of Stalin.

One is the development of nuclear weapons and the means of delivering them. It is vital to the Soviet Union as well as to the West to find a basis for co-existence instead of accepting an inevitable clash between the two systems, since nuclear war would destroy the civilized world. Another is Russia's new confidence arising from recent technological advances and the rising standard of living. This has lessened the genuine fear of the West which so obsessed Stalin. Russian truculence in the immediate post-war period was, to some extent at least, a bold front to hide a very real weakness (due to enormous losses in manpower and in the Russian economy generally as a result of the Second World War). The recent advances of Russia in space research and the achievement of its scientists are giving a new confidence today.

A third factor is the change of climate in Russian opinion since the death of Stalin. Although this, too, is difficult to assess, it is clear that Khrushchev was more concerned with public opinion in Russia and more subject to pressure groups than was Stalin in the heyday of his power; Brezhnev and Kosygin have been preoccupied with problems of technical development.

Nor must we overlook the effect of Western policy on Russia. Stalin's policy, especially in Eastern Europe and Germany, led to the build-up of NATO and the 'containment' of the Soviet Union. In short, Stalin's policy had ceased to pay dividends and Communist expansion through military occupation was no longer possible without war.

With a stalemate in Europe, the Cold War shifted at the end of the year 1955 to the 'uncommitted' areas of the Middle East and South-east Asia. The efforts of the Western Powers to build up security pacts had been limited in these areas by 'neutralism'. Bulganin and Khrushchev made a tour of India, Burma and Afghanistan in 1955 in which they attacked the West on several occasions and supported India and Afghanistan in their quarrels with Pakistan (which had joined anti-Communist pacts). In the Middle East the sale of arms to Egypt in 1955 was the first step in a new drive to secure a foothold in that region. There has been considerable increase in Russian influence in Syria and Iraq, and in the Mediterranean.

The rivalry with China has split the Communist world and modified Russia's criticisms of Western capitalism. Stalin never stirred outside the U.S.S.R., except to visit Teheran in 1943. Khrushchev, Bulganin and Kosygin have travelled widely. As a result, the Russians have come to see their rivalry with the West more than ever in terms of industrialization. The proclaimed aim of the Soviet leaders is to wrest from the United States the economic leadership of the world—'competitive co-existence'. This is why their technical achievements and space-flights are so important.

The Russian leaders are prepared for peaceful, competitive co-existence, but only under certain conditions. Long-term objectives have not changed. As Khrushchev said, 'We are in favour of a lessening of tension, but if anybody thinks that for this reason we shall forget about Marx, Engels and Lenin, he is mistaken. This will happen when shrimps learn to whistle.' Nor will the Russians give up any territory gained by Stalin in the immediate post-war period. In short, they are prepared, for an unspecified time, to co-exist on the basis of the existing territorial position while remaining free to pursue their long-term aims by propaganda and undermining of national morale.

Co-existence on these terms is unacceptable to the West, but the threat to the West is no longer primarily a military one. The West has therefore to transform its military alliance—NATO—into an Atlantic Community.

Western Europe since 1945

Since 1945 there has been co-operation (economic, military and political) between the countries of Western Europe, as never before in peace-time. It has been encouraged by the United States and stimulated by fear of the Soviet Union. There has also been the growth of a 'European' idea independent of both.

It was encouraged by the fact that Western (and Eastern) European economies had been almost totally destroyed, and needed a total rebuilding; there was as a result a most unusual willingness to think in European rather than in national terms. It was helped by the further chance that Adenauer (German Chancellor 1949–63), De Gasperi (once a member of the Viennese Diet but Prime Minister of Italy 1946–54) and Robert Schuman (born in Luxembourg but Prime Minister of France 1947 and 1948) were all in varying degrees internationalists; all three spoke German and all three were Catholics in religion.

Britain has taken a leading part in this development, although her Commonwealth ties and special relationship with the United States have hindered her so far from becoming too deeply committed to Western Europe.

Six Western European countries (Belgium, France, the German Federal Republic, Italy, Luxembourg and the Netherlands) have decided to go beyond co-operation towards some form of federation.

This co-operation has three aspects, economic, military and political.

Economic co-operation

The first step here was the decision to set up the O.E.E.C.

The Organization for European Economic Co-operation came into being on 16 April 1948 to develop economic co-operation between member countries and to assist the United States Government in carrying out its programme of aid to Europe.

This programme of aid had been announced by General George C. Marshall, the American Secretary of State, in a speech in June 1947. America would help Europe to recover from the devastation of the war, but the initiative and planning should, he said, come from Europe; the programme was to be a joint one for Europe as a whole. It was welcomed by Ernest Bevin, then British Foreign Secretary. Soviet Russia and her satellites refused to take part, and so did Finland and Spain. But sixteen nations drew up an analysis of Europe's needs and outlined a plan (the European Recovery Programme) for the next four years. The Organization for European Economic Co-operation was set up to administer the programme.

Members of O.E.E.C. are Austria, Belgium, Denmark, Eire, France, Greece, Iceland, Italy, Luxembourg, the Netherlands, Norway, Portugal, Sweden, Switzerland, Turkey, the United Kingdom (the original sixteen) and the German Federal Republic. Canada and the United States are associated with O.E.E.C.

Marshall Aid, as it came to be called, as such ceased in 1951, but O.E.E.C. continued to function as the chief organ of economic co-operation in Western Europe. It has been the main reason for the recovery of Europe since 1945. It has now been replaced by a new organization, the *Organization for European Co-operation and Development*, which will pay attention to the problem of the under-developed areas as well as of Europe.

The second step has been the growth among some European states of the idea of a Common Market. This began with *The European Coal and Steel Community* (E.C.S.C.) which was set up under a treaty signed in Paris on 18 April 1951 by Belgium, France, the German Federal Republic, Italy, Luxembourg and the Netherlands. In the summer of 1952, the treaty had been ratified by all six countries and the organization was established at Luxembourg on 10 August 1952.

A common market for coal, iron ore and scrap was established on 10 February 1953, for steel on 1 May 1953 and for special steels on 1 August 1954. The High Authority (the executive organ of E.C.S.C.) thus abolished frontier barriers in coal and steel trade between the member countries, doing away with customs duties, discriminating freight rates and currency restrictions. It created a single economic unit where coal and steel are concerned.

On 21 December 1954 an Agreement of Association was signed between the United Kingdom and E.C.S.C. This agreement sets up a permanent 'Council of Association' between the Community and the United Kingdom, and calls for joint consultation at the highest level on problems of mutual interest. It was, however, only in 1961, largely under American pressures, that Britain began seriously to discuss membership of the 'Six'.

At a conference at Messina in June 1955 the six E.C.S.C. Powers agreed that their goal was a European common market.

Treaties to establish both E.E.C. (*European Economic Community*) and *Euratom* were signed at Rome by the 'Six' on 25 March 1957. They began to reduce tariffs between each member state on 1 January 1959, and are now planning further reductions. They hope to abolish all tariffs by 1973 and in the end to set up an elected European Parliament with a single executive.

The European Free Trade Area. During 1956, with the plans of the 'Six' well advanced, the O.E.E.C. Council decided to examine the question of some European countries forming a Free Trade Area associated with the Common Market. By the end of the year, support for this had gained ground among members of O.E.E.C., including Britain. Members of the Free Trade Area would be able to retain tariffs with other countries at their present level while removing all tariffs on goods from the other member countries. Certain goods, e.g. agricultural products, could be excluded from the Free Trade Area. The scheme, however, failed largely because of French opposition, and in 1959 an 'Outer Seven' organization was set up (Britain, Austria, Switzerland, Portugal, Norway, Denmark and Sweden) which Finland joined in 1960.

Military co-operation

A number of important organizations have come into existence for West European defence. The most important are:

The *Brussels Treaty* was signed on 17 March 1948, by Britain, France, Belgium, the Netherlands and Luxembourg. It is a treaty, primarily for collective security, of 50 years' duration. Under its terms an organization known as Western Union was established. The potential enemy was still seen as Germany.

The *North Atlantic Treaty* was signed on 4 April 1949 by Britain, France, Belgium, the Netherlands, Luxembourg, the United States, Canada, Norway, Denmark, Italy, Portugal and Iceland. It is of 20 years' duration.

On 2 April 1951 an integrated command was set up for Europe and General Eisenhower took up his appointment as Supreme Commander Europe (SACEUR). Turkey and Greece were formally admitted into NATO on 18 February 1952, and the German Federal Republic on 9 May 1955.

A permanent organization, with Lord Ismay as Secretary-General, came into being on 4 April 1952. One of its main objects was to develop the non-military aspects of NATO, i.e. an Atlantic Community. Lord Ismay retired in 1957 and his successor was M. Spaak (Belgium). In 1961 he was succeeded by Dr Dirk Stikker of Holland.

Western European Union came into being under the Paris Agreement of 23 October 1954 (ratified by the following May). It is in fact the Brussels Treaty Organization with wider powers and including Western Germany and Italy. The 'enemy' was no longer Germany but Russia.

The German Federal Republic promised not to manufacture atomic weapons; and Britain pledged herself to maintain on the continent the equiva-

Countries	Organization for Economic Co-operation and Develop't (O.E.C.D.)	North Atlantic Treaty Organization (NATO)	Council of Europe	Western European Union (W.E.U.)	European Communities			European Free Trade Assoc'n (E.F.T.A.)
					European Coal and Steel Community (E.C.S.C.)	European Economic Community (Common Market)	European Atomic Energy Community (EURATOM)	
Belgium	*	*	*	*	*	*	*	
France	*	*	*	*	*	*	*	
German Fed. Republic	*	*	*	*	*	*	*	
Italy	*	*	*	*	*	*	*	
Luxembourg	*	*	*	*	*	*	*	
Netherlands	*	*	*	*	*	*	*	
Canada	*	*						
Denmark	*	*	*					*
Greece	*	*	*					
Iceland	*	*	*					
Norway	*	*	*					*
Portugal	*	*						*
Turkey	*	*	*					
United Kingdom	*	*	*	*	†		†	*
United States	*	*						
Austria	*		*					*
Irish Republic	*		*					
Sweden	*		*					*
Switzerland	*							*
Spain	*							

* Member.

† The United Kingdom has a special association with the E.C.S.C., and an agreement for co-operation with Euratom.

lent of four divisions and a tactical air force. There are now at least 12 divisions permanently on guard in Western Europe with 4,000 aircraft. No ground has been lost to Russia in Europe since 1949.

Political co-operation

The Council of Europe. The Statute of the Council of Europe came into effect on 3 August 1949. Members of the Council are Austria, Belgium, Denmark, Eire, France, Greece, Iceland, Italy, Luxembourg, the Netherlands, Norway, Sweden, Turkey, the United Kingdom and the German Federal Republic.

The aim of the Council is 'to achieve greater unity between its members for

Separate exposures of a film record how a Titan rocket is brought to launching position at Cape Kennedy.

the purpose of safeguarding and realizing the ideals and principles which are their common heritage and facilitating their economic progress '.

It has two component organs, the Council of Ministers and the Consultative Assembly.

But political co-operation has been much less impressive than economic and military. The Assembly is a debating body only, and it has no legislative or executive power. It does not discuss defence, and confines itself largely to cultural questions.

Britain and the Common Market

One of the major questions facing Britain in the last decade has been: On what conditions could it join the Common Market? There are many reasons why it should.

(*a*) The political and economic unity of Western Europe is a British interest. The Common Market is ending the possibility of war between Germany and its Western neighbours, and strengthening the West.

(*b*) Unlike armed alliances, union in Western Europe provides the sort of peaceful strength and stability which could make an understanding with Russia and Eastern Europe easier.

(*c*) Economically, joining the 'Six' would give British exporters a home market of between 210 and 250 million people, compared with 90 million in the 'Seven'.

(*d*) It would bring cheaper European goods into British shops and give British industry a valuable stimulus from competition.

(*e*) It would make our economy and incomes grow faster by stimulating investment and improving productivity.

(*f*) A united, wealthy Europe would be better placed for a joint effort to help the under-developed countries, including the Commonwealth.

(*g*) A European community which included both Britain and France could help the emerging states of Africa to form a strong community, too, which could protect them from poverty and political upheaval.

(*h*) All attempts to negotiate a loose association between Britain, together with its partners in the 'Seven', and the 'Six', have failed so far. Austria and Switzerland apart, members of the 'Seven' are scattered around the edges of Europe. They are neither strong enough economically nor near enough geographically to form an attractive market for businessmen.

(*i*) Only full membership of the European Economic Community could offer Britain the chance of political influence equal to the other members and a realistic possibility of negotiating an economic arrangement. This could give Britain access to the European market and provide some guarantee that opportunities for Commonwealth exporters in the markets of Europe, including Britain, would be preserved.

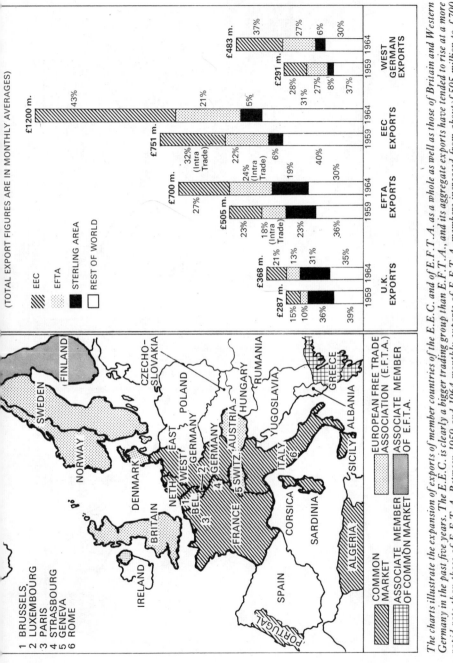

(TOTAL EXPORT FIGURES ARE IN MONTHLY AVERAGES)

EEC

EFTA

STERLING AREA

REST OF WORLD

WEST GERMAN EXPORTS

£483 m. — 37%, 27%, 6%, 30% (1964)
£291 m. — 28%, 31%, 27%, 8%, 37% (1959)

EEC EXPORTS

£1200 m. — 43%, 21%, 5% (1964)
£751 m. — 32% (Intra Trade), 22%, 6%, 40% (1959)

EFTA EXPORTS

£700 m. — 27%, 24% (Intra Trade), 19%, 30% (1964)
£505 m. — 23%, 18% (Intra Trade), 23%, 36% (1959)

U.K. EXPORTS

£368 m. — 21%, 13%, 31%, 35% (1964)
£287 m. — 15%, 10%, 36%, 39% (1959)

1 BRUSSELS,
  LUXEMBOURG
2 PARIS
3 STRASBOURG
4 GENEVA
5 ROME

FINLAND

SWEDEN

NORWAY

DENMARK

BRITAIN

IRELAND

NETH.
EAST
WEST GERMANY
GERMANY
BELG.
FRANCE
SWITZ. AUSTRIA
HUNGARY
ITALY
YUGOSLAVIA
CORSICA
SARDINIA
SICILY
ALGERIA
SPAIN
PORTUGAL
GREECE
ALBANIA
RUMANIA
POLAND
CZECHO-SLOVAKIA

EUROPEAN FREE TRADE
ASSOCIATION (E.F.T.A.)

ASSOCIATE MEMBER
OF E.F.T.A.

COMMON
MARKET

ASSOCIATE MEMBER
OF COMMON MARKET

The charts illustrate the expansion of exports of member countries of the E.E.C. and of E.F.T.A. as a whole as well as those of Britain and Western Germany in the past five years. The E.E.C. is clearly a bigger trading group than E.F.T.A., and its aggregate exports have tended to rise at a more rapid rate than those of E.F.T.A. Between 1959 and 1964 monthly exports of E.F.T.A. members increased from about £505 million to £700 million, while those of E.E.C. members rose from about £751 million to £1200 million a month. Intra-trade is also clearly greater within the E.E.C. than within E.F.T.A.—this accounts for about 43 per cent of the total exports of E.E.C. members, whereas the corresponding proportion for intra–E.F.T.A. exports is 24 per cent.

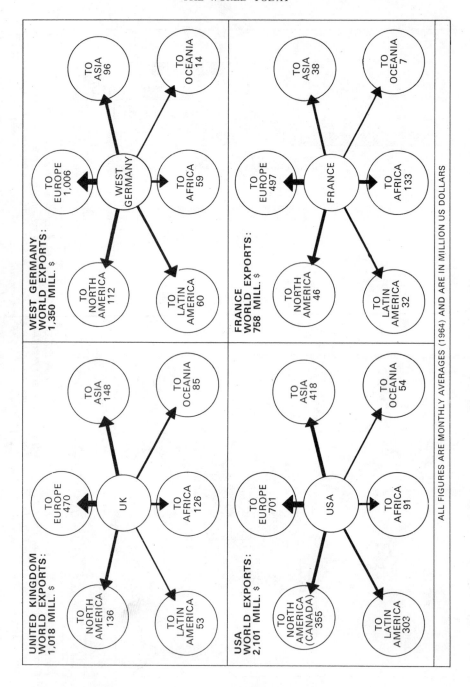

WEST GERMANY
WORLD EXPORTS:
1,350 MILL. $

TO EUROPE 1,006
TO ASIA 96
TO OCEANIA 14
WEST GERMANY
TO AFRICA 59
TO NORTH AMERICA 112
TO LATIN AMERICA 60

FRANCE
WORLD EXPORTS:
758 MILL. $

TO EUROPE 497
TO ASIA 38
TO OCEANIA 7
FRANCE
TO AFRICA 133
TO NORTH AMERICA 46
TO LATIN AMERICA 32

UNITED KINGDOM
WORLD EXPORTS:
1,018 MILL. $

TO EUROPE 470
TO ASIA 148
TO OCEANIA 85
UK
TO AFRICA 126
TO NORTH AMERICA 136
TO LATIN AMERICA 53

USA
WORLD EXPORTS:
2,101 MILL. $

TO EUROPE 701
TO ASIA 418
TO OCEANIA 54
USA
TO AFRICA 91
TO NORTH AMERICA (CANADA) 355
TO LATIN AMERICA 303

ALL FIGURES ARE MONTHLY AVERAGES (1964) AND ARE IN MILLION US DOLLARS (*j*) The gains so far in the economic resources of the 'Six' are too impressive to ignore. Economically, the 'Six' have already gained immensely, not only from the direct effect of their tariff reductions but perhaps to an even greater extent from the stimulus to trade that the establishment of the Common Market has created. The results of the opening of frontiers to competition have been much better than were hoped for. At the beginning of 1959 the first tariff reduction of 10 per cent came into effect, and in that year trade between the 'Six' showed an increase of 19 per cent over 1958. In the first six months of 1960 there was an increase of no less than 30 per cent over the corresponding period of 1959. Some American investment has been diverted from Britain to the 'Six'.

The performance of France has been more impressive than any of her Common Market partners. In 1959, French exports to other Common Market countries were 35 per cent higher than in 1958, and in the first half of 1960 they showed an increase of 42 per cent over the first six months of 1959. But the development of Western Germany and of Italy is almost equally striking.

Why, then, did Britain hesitate?

First, for political reasons. As a monarchy and as a member of the Commonwealth, its interests could suffer, especially if in the end a federal Europe emerged. What if a United States of Europe were set up at, say, Strasbourg? What of the effects on the British Monarchy, on British Trade Unions, on the Welfare State, or on British sovereignty?

Second, economics, especially concerning Commonwealth products. So far, New Zealand butter, Malayan pineapple or Australian fruit have received favoured treatment in Britain. With Britain inside a Common Market with a protective tariff against outside products, then the tariff on these Commonwealth goods could destroy their British market. And in return New Zealand or Malaya or Australia could raise protective tariffs against, for example, British motor-cars. Again, the guaranteed markets for some Commonwealth products could disappear.

Third, the British farmer. He has been heavily subsidized by over £200 million a year from the taxpayer. On entering the Common Market, cheaper food could come in from Europe; there would presumably be small need for subsidies; and although we could get cheaper food, some British farmers could be ruined. There are similar fears by British industry if, say, our motor-cars or shipyards were challenged by French or German products—even if such competition would be healthy.

British hesitation was marked under the Labour Government (1945–51) in part because its economy was stronger than Europe's at that time, and in part because it was embarking on a series of measures of nationalization which would be difficult to fit into a federal Europe; relations with a non-Socialist

Trends Towards European Unity?

	Military	Economic	Political
1948	*Brussels Treaty* for defence of Europe	**O.E.E.C.** set up to organize American aid (Marshall Plan) towards European recovery	
1949	**NATO.** Permanent British and American contributions to military defence of Europe		**COUNCIL OF EUROPE** meeting in **STRASBOURG**
1951	**SUPREME COMMANDER EUROPE (SACEUR)** appointed		
1952		**EUROPEAN COAL AND STEEL COMMUNITY** (beginning of the Common Market Plan)	
1955	**WESTERN EUROPEAN UNION** including German contribution to defence of West	*Messina Treaty*	
1957		*Treaty of Rome* sets up **COMMON MARKET**	
1959		**EUROPEAN FREE TRADE ASSOCIATION** is set up. The 'Six' begin to reduce tariffs	
?			A European Parliament for economic and political decisions?

(and 'Catholic') Europe worried the Labour Government. Mr Churchill, as Opposition Leader, made a number of 'European' speeches but on becoming Prime Minister in 1951 found himself more an Imperialist than a European. Undoubtedly had Britain in the first ten years after the War shown sympathy, it would now have been 'in' Europe.

From 1957—by which time the Treaty of Rome had been signed—Britain began to show a real interest. The reasons are clear.

(a) The Commonwealth was becoming increasingly centrifugal, diverse and 'African' in character. Burma left it in 1948, South Africa in 1961. There were wars in Cyprus between Greek and Turkish Cypriots, ugly disputes between India and Pakistan over Kashmir, tensions between Singapore and Malaysia, occasional riots in British Guiana, recurrent crises in the new African states. Pride in 'Empire' has slumped as its costs and problems have soared.

(b) It became increasingly clear that Britain could not in a military or political sense have a distinct 'Third Force' position between U.S.S.R. and U.S.; to stay 'independent' of Europe meant being, in fact, at best an ally, at worst a dependant of the United States.

(c) Suez 1956 revealed the weakness of Britain's role as an independent military power.

(d) The collapse of the Paris Peace Conference, 1960 (of U.S., U.S.S.R., France and Britain) because of the revelations of the use by the U.S. of high-flying reconnaissance planes (U.2) spying on U.S.S.R., was a blow to the role of British Prime Minister Harold Macmillan, who, until then, had tried to be 'the honest broker' between East and West.

(e) In 1960, too, Britain was compelled to abandon its own independent deterrent (Blue Streak) and to become dependent on U.S. carrier vehicles (Skybolt), and this in turn was abandoned two years later.

(f) The recurrence of British balance of payments problems, with French and Swiss banks often acting as supports.

(g) The prosperity of the Common Market itself.

Not until 1961 with the appointment of Edward Heath as Lord Privy Seal with special responsibility for Common Market affairs (in 1965 he was to become Leader of the Conservative Party) did Britain decide actively to seek membership. It took a further 16 months of debate in Britain while support was marshalled at home for this policy. By January 1963 the French economy was prosperous and the Algerian question settled; and French fears (after the Nassau Conference, 1962) that Britain was an American dependant seemed to be confirmed. In January 1963, because of French opposition, the British application for entry was refused, to the disappointment of Britain and of 'five' of the 'six'. In 1966 Mr Wilson announced that he intended to apply for entry also; but France again said 'No' in 1967.

In the long run it would seem that Britain must enter Europe, with whose

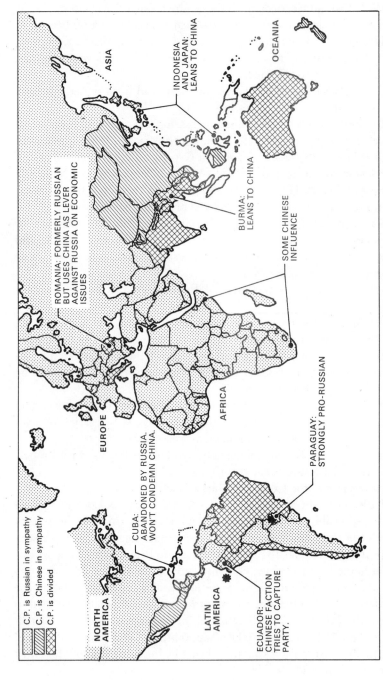

Here is the world of the Communist parties, whether large or small, showing their allegiance to the U.S.S.R. or to Communist China. Areas with pro-Russian parties are lightly shaded. Those with pro-Chinese ones appear diagonally shaded. Criss-cross shading indicates a party split by the existence of a pro-Chinese minority. Note that Africa takes the shading of Russia because China has captured no parties there, but parties are not yet highly organized in Africa.

fortunes we have for 2,000 years been involved. Neither Britain nor the U.S.A. can afford isolation today.

The split world of Communism

The split between Russia and China is the most striking development in the East since 1962, and transforms all calculations about the future of Communism. For the origins of the split, see ch. 6, p. 194.

Its possible consequences

If the break between Communist China and Soviet Russia becomes complete, what will its consequences be?

The first and most obvious result is that the world will have two Communist movements. Neither side will be willing to give up the name of Communist, and each side will, of course, claim to have a monopoly of orthodoxy. In short, there will be rival 'Popes' in Moscow and Peking, and two movements called Communist but in fact in each case Nationalist and Imperialist.

There will be a protracted struggle fought out in several areas. By far the most important of these will be the under-developed and 'uncommitted' countries of Asia, Africa and Latin America. It is this vast area that is the real subject of the Sino-Soviet ideological quarrel about the question: 'Is war between capitalism and socialism inevitable?'

The Chinese, in saying that war *is* inevitable, mean primarily that revolution will not come without a struggle, perhaps a war in the under-developed countries. The capitalist-imperialists, they say, are armed to protect their property, both in obvious cases like South Africa and in other countries where there is apparent freedom, but where European or North American capital is entrenched. Therefore, say the Chinese, there must be bloody revolutions. Algeria is their favourite example of a people who won their freedom only by being prepared to fight for it.

China versus Russia: Who supports Whom

Moscow is supported by:	Split:	Peking is supported by:
73 Communist parties— all the Communist parties of Western Europe and of Eastern Europe except Albania, which is violently pro-Chinese.	Cuban, Italian and many Latin American Communist parties are divided between the two camps.	13 Communist parties —mainly Asiatic: Burmese, Indian, Singhalese, Nepalese, North Korean, North Vietnamese, Indonesian.

The Russians claim to see a possibility of much more peaceful transition. They say that the existing military and economic strength of socialism in the world has made it possible for countries to free themselves without defeating the imperialists in pitched battle. Thus, allege the Russians, Soviet inter-continental missiles were the cause of the forced withdrawal of Britain, France and Israel at Suez. Egypt is free from imperialism without itself having had to fight. Further, state the Russians, socialism means the State ownership of industry and collective ownership of farms. This is impossible when there is no industry or when farming is too primitive to be usefully collectivized. Therefore, it is right and proper to co-operate with all governments of a generally progressive kind, whether they call themselves Marxist-Leninist or not. Technology must come first, and socialism afterwards.

China's attack on India

These differences of outlook have already had many important practical results. The most important was the Chinese invasion of India in September 1962. This is seen by the Soviet leadership as China's gravest sin so far. The Chinese attack, in Russian eyes, was a grave setback to the cause of socialism in India. Though Mr Nehru was no Marxist, the State industrial sector in India is growing with Soviet help. By means of trade with the socialist *bloc*, and by taking Soviet arms, India is becoming increasingly free from control by imperialists. All this progress was endangered by China's action, which the Russians called 'a clear-cut imperialist aggression'.

The reasons for the attack on India are clear. China has long been contemptuous of Indian civilization and recently of India's claims to be a rival 'model for Asia'. By exposing Indian weakness, while China demonstrated first its strength and then its forbearance, they may have hoped to destroy India's ability to compete with China for the respect of Asian neutrals.

It is possible, too, that a connection existed between the border campaign against India and the deterioration of China's relations with the Soviet Union. Sinkiang had become a strategically important region and the road through the disputed territory in Ladakh was a major route to Sinkiang. If China had negotiated an agreement with India, as seemed at one time likely, by which China was permitted passage over the road while acknowledging Indian sovereignty, the fear might have remained that in a Sino-Soviet crisis India would succumb to Soviet pressure to close the road. Another explanation for the sudden attack may have been the desire to boost the army's morale by a short victorious campaign. The victory on the Indian frontier showed what the Chinese army could do in a short and carefully prepared action against an unprepared enemy. In terms of manpower the Chinese armed forces are, of course, very large—the usual figure quoted is around 2,500,000–2,750,000, in addition to the militia. The modernization of these forces was severely handicapped by the withdrawal of Soviet military advisers in the summer of 1960 and the simultaneous decrease in supplies and equipment from the U.S.S.R. The air force is believed to have been especially severely affected by these steps. Nevertheless, the Chinese army has shown that, given the right circum-

Lance, a ballistic missile developed for the United States Army.

stances, it can be a formidable adversary which should not be underrated in conventional warfare.

Chinese troops stormed across the Himalayas and swept down into the poorly protected northern states. The border fighting shattered Prime Minister Jawaharlal Nehru's careful effort to depict China as peaceful and friendly. India was forced to seek arms in the West, putting its cherished neutrality in doubt. Ironically, India, although the victim of aggression, lost stature among Asian neutralists by turning to the West. And China remains more solidly than ever in control of disputed areas on the Indian–Chinese border.

Chinese influence in Africa

The Russians appear also to believe that the Chinese stirred up the mutinies in 1964 in Kenya, Uganda and Tanganyika, and thus actually helped to bring back British troops into these countries. Certainly China is bidding for the leadership of the Communist movement in Africa, as Chou En-lai's tour of

Asia confirmed. Similarly, the Russians see Chinese revolutionary activity behind the sailors' revolt in Brazil which led to a right-wing *coup d'état* there, and behind the recent crisis in Indonesia (1965–66).

If the Communist movement splits into two parts, the Russian part will continue to pursue its path of caution and of emphasis on economic progress in the under-developed world, while the Chinese will continue to foment revolution as the prerequisite for progress. There will probably be both pro-Russian and pro-Chinese parties in many if not most under-developed countries.

In the end, perhaps, the development of life in China itself will do much to determine the course of events in the Communist movement outside. For the most important fact about China is that the Communists there succeeded in 1949 in doing precisely what they are advising other Communists to do elsewhere. They rose in arms—against Russian advice—and defeated domestic capitalism and its American 'imperialist' backing, and relied upon a peasant movement in doing so. Their prestige on this account must be potentially very great in all other under-developed countries. Much depends on whether they make a success of their economic development and thus show that their way can work in the end.

The Chinese future

China is clearly not winning in the ideological war with Russia. Dr Castro of Cuba, early in 1966, complaining about a 50 per cent cut in Chinese rice deliveries to Cuba, accused the Chinese of 'exerting blackmail, extortion, pressure, aggression, and strangulation, and of the worst methods of piracy, oppression and filibustering'.

The most spectacular reverse for the Chinese recently has been in Indonesia. It was only in April 1965 that Chou En-lai, the Chinese Prime Minister, visited Jakarta to celebrate the tenth anniversary of the Bandung Afro-Asian Conference—an important landmark in the Chinese campaign to influence the non-aligned nations. Just six months after Chou's visit came Indonesia's attempted Communist *coup*, which failed and which resulted in the discrediting of the Chinese-orientated Communist party. Many Communists were arrested or shot, and the leader of the party has not been heard of since. Now the two countries are openly hostile.

The second half of 1965 was a particularly bad time for the Chinese in Africa, where until then they had been making good progress. Their setbacks started in June, when Chou En-lai had been invited to visit Tanzania, and he made it known he would be happy to visit other African countries while he was in the area. Not one country responded. In Tanzania itself the visit was very far from a spectacular success. Chou's often unreasoning anti-Western propaganda angered Tanzania's leaders, who pride themselves on their strictly literal interpretation of non-alignment. President Nyerere put it bluntly when he said at an official banquet: 'Neither our principles, our country, nor our freedom to determine our own future are for sale.' Later, a Chinese offer to build the projected railway linking Tanzania and Zambia was turned down in favour of a Western syndicate.

Later that month came another major African blow for China—the revolt in Algeria which resulted in the dismissal of President Ben Bella, who had been on good personal terms with Chou. The revolt had an important side-effect. It caused the cancellation of the conference of Afro-Asian leaders that was scheduled to take place in Algiers at the end of the month.

The Chinese had been looking forward to the conference as a forum for drumming up support in their squabble with the Russians. They had been working hard to have Russia excluded from the conference—on the grounds that it was not strictly an Asian country—but it was by no means certain that they would have succeeded even in this. The issue was still undecided when the conference was cancelled as a consequence of the revolt.

Other Chinese adventures were equally unsuccessful. The Kenya Government took strong exception to activities of members of the Chinese embassy, and action was taken to limit the number of its personnel. Attempts to land crates of arms, believed to have originated from China, were discovered and prevented. The technique of heavily over-staffing their embassies and using the surplus men for furthering their world revolutionary cause is a feature of China's ideological offensive in Africa. It has been particularly widely used in the former French colonies in West Africa, but here again there were two major setbacks in 1965 and 1966. In both the Central African Republic and Dahomey there were military *coups d'état*, and in both places all Chinese diplomats were expelled by the new régimes. In the Central African Republic, Colonel Bokassa, the leader of the *coup*, said he had discovered a Chinese plot to form a 'popular army' to overthrow the Government.

Western strategists would be wrong, however, to take over-much comfort from China's recent wave of tactical errors. Though discredited in a number of places, they are by no means defeated. Things are still going their way in Vietnam. And, in Africa, they maintain powerful influence in the Congo (Brazzaville) and to some extent in Tanzania. The Chinese doctrine of world revolution will continue to have an innate attraction for the poor, developing countries—at least so long as the terms of world trade under the capitalist system work against them as viciously as they do at present.

Much will depend on Mao, now over 75 years old and said to be a sick man. 'Chairman' Mao, as he is universally known, already enjoys almost god-like status in China. His ethical precepts, his views on class struggle, on self-sacrifice and the inevitable success of world revolution, Chinese-style, are a central part of the curriculum of every school pupil in the People's Republic. Most adults are obliged to attend twice-weekly ideology classes designed to ensure that when Mao steps down or dies his ideas will go marching on. The average age of the Politburo is 68, and if Mao were to be replaced today, someone from this select and closely-knit group would almost certainly step into his shoes. The most likely choice is now the Defence Minister, Lin Piao (b. 1907), a bitter critic of Soviet Communism and of the West. He was with Mao on the Long March in 1934, when he commanded the First Red Army group; he is the country's leading military strategist; he believes firmly that the poor nations in the world will isolate and overthrow the rich. He advocates a return to the pure and revolutionary discipline of the 1930s. Other major figures are Liu Shao-Chi, China's Head of State, a mild undemonstrative man with high capacity for leadership who, like Mao, comes from Hunan province, and is the author of a number of Chinese Marxist classics; and Chou En-lai, who knows the outside world better than any of his colleagues on the Politburo, and as Prime Minister is well known in the West.

QUESTIONS TO CONSIDER

1. Trace the stages between 1945 and 1949 of the outbreak of the Cold War.
2. What were the steps by which Europe came to co-operate after 1945 against Russia?
3. What are the reasons for the hesitation of Britain in joining the Common Market?
4. What are the main international problems facing the government of Britain today?

WORDS TO NOTE

Euratom: The European Atomic Energy Community set up in January 1958 by the 'Six', to plan the production of nuclear energy on a large scale in Europe.

Malenkov: Georgy Malenkov (b. 1902) succeeded Stalin in 1953 as Chairman of the Council of Ministers in the U.S.S.R. He resigned this post in February 1955, and was succeeded by Marshal Nicolai Bulganin. In 1958 Bulganin was in turn succeeded by Khrushchev, who, since shortly after Stalin's death had also been First Secretary of the Communist Party. Stalin had held this latter post for thirty years, and, from it, like Khrushchev, governed the Soviet State.

National Communist, National Deviationist: The Communist theory devised by Marx and Lenin was seen as being international. It could be applied to all countries; and in 1919 its target was world revolution. But it is now clear that national differences between states affect the application of the theory, that some, perhaps all, Communist leaders are also strong nationalists and that there are many roads to socialism. Yet Communist theory continues to believe that any markedly nationalist emphasis is a deviation or departure from the true path to socialism, to world revolution and a classless society. Leaders of such deviations are criticized and sometimes even assassinated. Tito of Yugoslavia, who had come to power between 1942 and 1945 and carried out the reorganization of his country after 1945, largely without Russian help, broke with Moscow in 1948. Russian Communists regard him as a deviationist, a national Communist. Critics of the 'party line' inside the party are also called 'deviationists'.

Party Line: It is the practice in 'the people's democracies' and in the democratic parties of the West for party policy to be discussed and voted on in mass meetings of the party—at the annual Soviet Congress in Russia or at the annual meetings of parties or of professional associations in the West. The policy thus agreed on becomes 'the party line' and is, at least in theory, binding on the party and its leaders until the next congress meets.

Puppet State: A régime or a state that has, like a puppet, to dance as it is directed by another more powerful régime or state. Such states are sometimes in more kindly terms called satellites, since their movements are influenced by more powerful bodies. Thus Hungary, Poland, East Germany or, today, Cuba are sometimes described by the West as 'puppets' or 'satellites' of Russia, and in Russian eyes the Chiang Government on Formosa is a 'puppet' of the West.

Summit: Name given to meetings of the Heads of State of the Great Powers.

Veto: The right to reject. At the Yalta Conference, February 1945, it was agreed that if any one of the five permanent members of the U.N. Security Council (U.S.A., U.S.S.R., Britain, France and non-Communist China) refused to agree to a major matter of policy, that policy was not to be carried out by the United Nations.

FOR FURTHER READING

Connell-Smith, Gordon: *Pattern of the Post-War World*, Penguin, 1957.
Crowley, D.: *The Background to Current Affairs*, Macmillan, 1958.
Kitzinger, Uwe: *The European Common Market and Community*, Routledge, 1967.
Mowat, R. C.: *Ruin and Resurgence, 1939–65*, Blatchford, 1965.
Boyd, A.: *The United Nations*, Penguin, 1964.

10. *The United Nations*

Despite the failure of the League of Nations, the ideal of a world ruled by law not force was one of the war aims of the Western Allies. In 1941, before the United States were at war, Roosevelt and Churchill had agreed, at a meeting on the battleship *Prince of Wales* off Newfoundland, on the principles they were fighting for (the Atlantic Charter). In January 1942, the 26 states then at war with Germany accepted the Atlantic Charter as their war aims, and for the first time called themselves 'The United Nations'.

At the Moscow Conference on 1 November 1943, the representatives of China, the U.K., the U.S.A. and the U.S.S.R. declared that they recognized 'the necessity of establishing at the earliest practicable date a general international organization based on the principle of the sovereign equality of all peace-loving states, and open to membership by all such states, large or small, for the maintenance of international peace and security'.

The Dumbarton Oaks Conference, October 1944, made proposals for the structure of the world organization. It provided that the key body in the United Nations for preserving world peace was to be the Security Council on which China, France, the U.K., the U.S.A. and the U.S.S.R. were to be permanently represented, and which was to be given much more power than the League Council. On the Security Council there would also be six non-permanent members, elected by the Assembly for two years. In January 1966, the number of non-permanent members of the Security Council was increased to ten. The question of how the Security Council was to vote was left unsettled until February 1945 when the Yalta Agreement, between the U.K., the U.S.A. and the U.S.S.R., established the principle of the 'veto'. Any single great power can, by using the veto, block the Council's decisions. All member states are represented in the General Assembly.

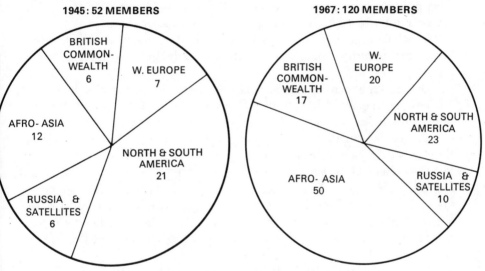

U.N. growth and distribution of members.

The United Nations

Delegates of 50 nations met at San Francisco between April and June 1945 to sign the United Nations Charter and the Statute of the International Court of Justice. The United Nations formally came into existence on 24 October 1945.

Membership of the United Nations is open to all peace-loving states which accept and, in the judgement of the organization, are able and willing to carry out the obligations of the Charter. New members are admitted upon the recommendations of the Security Council, but must receive a vote of at least two-thirds of the General Assembly. There have been disputes as to the admission of new members and several states are still excluded. But by December 1967, 120 states were members, the majority Afro-Asian. The United Nations Assembly is no longer a parliament of white men.

The framework of the United Nations is as follows. The *General Assembly* meets once a year, and in it every member state, whatever its size and power, has one vote. The more important matters require a majority of two-thirds.

The *Security Council* is the power-house and driving force.

The General Assembly elects 18 countries to sit on the *Economic and Social Council* for a period of three years each. This Council studies world problems and is aided by the specialized agencies such as the United Nations Educational, Scientific and Cultural Organization (UNESCO), the Food and Agricultural Organization (FAO) and the World Health Organization (WHO).

The *Trusteeship Council* administers all trust territories (those former mandates that are not yet independent).

The General Assembly and Security Council also elect the 15 judges, all from different states, who serve on the *International Court of Justice* at The Hague and try to arbitrate in disputes between member states.

The whole organization is administered by the *Secretariat* which brings before the Security Council any matters thought likely to threaten world peace.

The Secretariat consists of a Secretary-General and such staff as the United Nations may require. The Secretary-General is the chief administrative officer of the United Nations and is appointed for five years by the General Assembly on the recommendation of the Security Council. Dag Hammarskjold of Sweden was appointed as Secretary-General in 1953 in succession to the first Secretary-General, Trygve Lie. In September 1961 he was killed in an air crash in the Congo and succeeded by U Thant, a Burmese. The Secretary-General submits an annual report to the General Assembly on the work of the United Nations. The permanent headquarters of the United Nations is in New York City on land provided partly from money given by John D. Rockefeller, Jr., and partly by the City of New York.

The United Nations has had considerable success in settling disputes. In 1946 when Iran appealed to the Security Council about the continued Russian occupation of her northern territory, Russia was persuaded to withdraw her troops. The U.N. ended the bitter colonial war between Dutch and nationalists in Indonesia. In 1948 it helped to mediate between Israel and Jordan over Jerusalem and in 1949 between India and Pakistan over Kashmir. The war in Korea (1950–53) was fought by U.N. troops against North Korea, helped by Communist China. But in some areas, notably when Belgium hurriedly left the Congo in the summer of 1960, in Vietnam since 1964 and in the Middle East in 1967, U.N. forces and administrators have been less successful in keeping order or in maintaining the public services. The U.N., like the League of Nations, depends on the will of the member states. When Lord Cecil was asked, 'Will the League work?' he replied, 'Don't be silly. Does a spade work?'

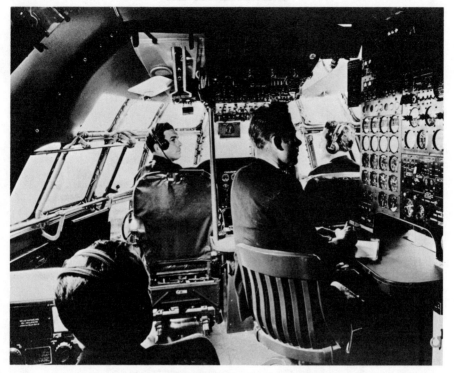

The control cabin of a Boeing Stratocruiser.

The problems before it

In the last few years the United Nations has increased its membership to 120 (December 1967) and it has attempted to deal with five particularly difficult problems—the Congo, Cyprus, South Africa, Rhodesia and Vietnam.

Congo. When Belgium granted complete independence to its former colony, the Congo, in 1960, there was a serious danger that the government of the new state would collapse and divide up into separate provinces; there was, in particular, a powerful movement for the secession of the rich mining area of Katanga—a movement led by Moise Tshombe but helped by Belgian business interests, especially the *Union Minière*, and mercenary troops. There was much rioting and tribal war, and there was serious danger of military intervention by the Great Powers. In July 1960, therefore, the United Nations sent an emergency force to the Congo to try to keep the peace, to preserve law and order, to run essential services and to stop civil war. There followed a period of great confusion, in the course of which the first Prime Minister of the Congolese Republic, Patrice Lumumba, was murdered (January 1961). It was widely believed that Tshombe was responsible for this murder. On 13 September

267

Rhodesia and its neighbours.

1961, U.N. forces entered Katanga and declared secession at an end, but in fact fighting continued intermittently. Five days later Dag Hammarskjold, who as U.N. Secretary-General had sought to act as arbitrator between the tribal armies, was killed in an air crash while visiting the Congo. Fighting did not stop until December 1962 when U.N. forces broke the Katangese resistance and established control of the principal towns. Unification of the country under the Central Congolese Government was finally achieved in January 1963, with the incorporation of the secessionist province of Katanga.

Withdrawal of the U.N. peace-keeping force was completed in July 1964, but the Congo's troubles were not over. Rebellions in several of the provinces have left a trail of death and destruction. It is believed that these rebellions were instigated by the 'National Liberation Committee' set up in Brazzaville (ex-French Congo).

In an effort to preserve unity, President Kasavubu invited Mr Tshombe to return from exile and form a new Cabinet; thus the former President of Katanga, the breakaway province, became Prime Minister in the Central Congolese Government. In 1965 he again went into exile, spent mainly in France. His plane was 'hijacked' in 1967 and he was imprisoned and tried in Algeria.

Cyprus. Cyprus—where 80 per cent of the 560,000 population is Greek-speaking or Greek Orthodox in religion—was a British responsibility from 1878 to 1959. The Greek Cypriots, led by Archbishop Makarios and the EOKA movement, demanded union with Greece (*enosis*) and this was the cause of a bitter guerrilla war from 1955 to 1959. In February 1959, following discussions in Zurich between Greek and Turkish Ministers, an agreement was

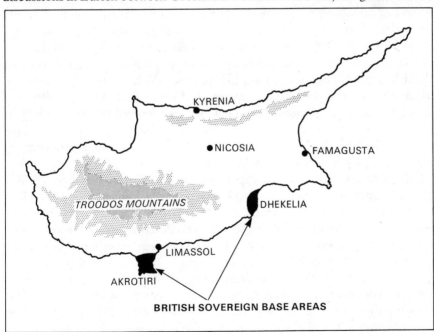

The Cypriot population of about 560,000 is divided into some 480,000 Greeks, some 80,000 Turks. The Greek Cypriots are Greek Orthodox in religion and look to Greece; the Turks are Moslem and look to Turkey. The President of the Republic is the Greek Orthodox Archbishop, Makarios. The Vice-President is Dr. Kuchuk, a Turk. The island lives in an uneasy peace, mainly the work of the U.N. Peace-keeping force of 4,500, of whom one-quarter are British. Britain retains two sovereign bases at Akrotiri and Dhekelia, 70 miles apart.

signed in London by the Prime Ministers of Great Britain, Greece and Turkey, and declared acceptable by the Greek and Turkish Cypriots. By this agreement Cyprus became not Greek but independent; Britain was to retain sovereignty over the area containing its military bases (Akrotiri and Dhekelia) and the right to use Nicosia airfield. On 14 December 1959, Archbishop Makarios was proclaimed President but Cyprus did not become a republic officially until 16 August 1960. In March 1961 its application for Commonwealth membership was accepted.

At the elections to the House of Representatives held on 31 July 1960, the Patriotic Front, supporting Archbishop Makarios, won 30 seats; the Akel Party (Communist-led), 5 seats; and the Turkish Nationalists, supporting the Vice-President, Dr Fazil Kuchuk, 15 seats.

Until the troubles between the Greek and Turkish communities revived in December 1963, the island had made considerable progress. Although Cyprus is not self-supporting, it produces wine, cereals, tobacco, fruit and copper. Under a five-year development plan, there has been a fall in unemployment and a boom in tourism. Relations with the British authorities in the bases were, on the whole, harmonious; indeed, for three and a half years after the signing of the London-Zurich agreements Makarios was genuinely friendly towards the British. He displayed considerable qualities of statesmanship, and in world affairs he contrived to keep Cyprus nominally neutralist while building up friendly links with the West. Despite this progress, clashes between Greek and Turkish Cypriots became open war in December 1963, and British forces were called in to try to separate the two sides. In February 1964 the problem was placed before the U.N. Security Council, which approved the formation of an international force and the appointment of a U.N. mediator. The U.N. Force in Cyprus (UNFICYP) was formed in March 1964, with military contingents from Britain, Canada, Sweden and Ireland.

Four facts are central to the explanation of the Cyprus problem. First, a difficult Constitution, with a 'Greek' President, a Turkish Vice-President and uneasy racial balance which, by the end of 1963, had broken down. Second, the deep animosity of Greek and Turkish Cypriots: the Greeks regard themselves as, morally and culturally, the superior race, inheritors of thousands of years of Western culture whose birthright is being usurped by an Asian 'barbaric' minority. Nothing embitters the Turks more than this sense of being regarded as second-class citizens; hence the fanatical pursuit of partition, to ensure that they will not be governed by the Greeks. Third, the apparent predominance in Greek-Cypriot circles of the hard-core Eoka men headed by General Grivas who led the struggle against Britain in 1955–59. The failure of Makarios to curb these men is seen by the Turks as a sign of weakness or insincerity. And fourth, Makarios's own attitude to the Communist-dominated Akel Party. The estimate that about two-fifths of the Greek electorate are

Communist is undoubtedly an exaggeration. But the possibility that the Greek-Cypriot right-wing might one day disintegrate into warring factions, allowing the Communists to seize power, is a considerable fear in the minds of not merely the Turkish-Cypriots but the Greek, Turkish and N.A.T.O. governments.

South Africa. The United Nations has been greatly concerned over the question of *apartheid*. The Afro-Asian group of member-states has campaigned actively against this policy. In August 1963 the Security Council rejected an Afro-Asian move calling for a boycott by member-states of all South African goods and an embargo on exports to South Africa of 'strategic materials of direct military value'. However, the Council did adopt an amended resolution calling upon all states to cease forthwith the sale and supply of arms, ammunition and military vehicles to that country. Britain and France abstained on this motion, while the other nine Security Council members voted for it.

The African group in the General Assembly is likely to continue to press for definite economic sanctions, including, perhaps, an embargo on oil supplies and a denial of shipping services to South Africa. Such measures, however, are not likely to command full support in the Security Council, and, failing such support, any motion calling for sanctions would not obtain the seven affirmative votes needed for its adoption. Furthermore, the Afro-Asian members of the United Nations argue that the South African delegation to the Assembly represents only the white minority and cannot speak or vote on behalf of all the people of SouthAfrica. In this issue Rhodesia has been linked. It was the African members of the Commonwealth who pressed for sanctions in the U.N. against Rhodesia in 1966; such sanctions are likely to be effective only if there is readiness to extend them, if necessary, against South Africa. This demands the support of U.S. and Britain. But, even without this the African *bloc* in the U.N. can wield influence: they can muster 38 African, 24 Asian, all 23 Latin American and 10 communist votes—95 in all.

Vietnam. The United Nations is helpless here, largely because neither North Vietnam nor China is a member. U Thant has made plain his belief that peace in Vietnam now depends primarily on American concessions. His plan is three fold: the end of American bombing of North Vietnam; the reduction by both sides of military activity in South Vietnam; and recognition of the Vietcong as party to the negotiation.

U.N. Weaknesses

On the death of Dag Hammarskjold in 1961, U Thant of Burma, who had served as Chairman of the U.N. Congo Conciliation Committee, became Acting Secretary-General and in November 1962 was elected Secretary-General. U Thant had been the permanent Burmese representative at the United Nations since 1957, and in 1959 he was Vice-President of the General Assembly.

The Post-war World

New Forces at work	General effects	Effects on United Nations	Long-term problems
COMMUNISM	(1) Growth in power of U.S.S.R. (2) Control of Central Europe by U.S.S.R. (3) Victory of Communism in China. (4) Pacts organized by West to oppose it: NATO, SEATO, CENTO.	(1) The use of the veto by the Great Powers has prevented effective action by the Security Council. (2) U.N. General Assembly has become a platform for speeches for or against. (3) But U.N. acted promptly in Korea (1950–53). (4) Vietnam war.	(1) Will West and U.S.S.R. be able to 'co-exist' indefinitely? (2) Russia–China split.
NATIONALISM	(1) Opposition to foreign control in former colonial territories. British withdrawal from Empire in India and Africa; French wars in Indo-China and North Africa. (2) Reform movements in many countries: Egypt, Turkey. (3) 'National Communism' in some countries, e.g., Yugoslavia, Cuba.	(1) Many are new members of U.N.—all in General Assembly. (2) Assembly-more Afro-Asian now than white. (3) Western bloc no longer sure of majority in U.N. debates.	(1) So strong a force that it will destroy all foreign political control—the day of 'empires' is over. (2) Many new nations, poor in resources and education, are run on dictatorial not democratic lines. (3) But some older nations—the 'Six' in Europe—are now looking to new forms of international action.
NEUTRALISM	(1) Strong in Middle East, S.E. Asia and Latin America. Leaders: Tito in Yugoslavia, Nasser in Egypt. (2) Organized into their own group at Bandung in Indonesia 1955.	(1) Neutralists seek economic help from specialized agencies of U.N. and are less sympathetic to military issues. (2) But some neutralist and small states help to police trouble spots—Irish and Ghana troops in Congo, Pakistani in Arab-Israel war.	(1) Neutralist states are on the whole poor. They need foreign capital for development. Can they accept it and stay neutral? (2) Neutralist states lack the military resources of the Big Powers.

There are four main reasons for United Nations weakness. First are the weaknesses caused by the machinery through which the U.N. has to operate: (*a*) the exercise of the veto by the five permanent members in the Security Council (China, France, the U.K., the U.S.A. and the U.S.S.R.: Russia has used the veto at least 100 times); (*b*) the absence of a permanent and strong international police force; (*c*) the absence of compulsory jurisdiction forcing states to submit disputes to the United Nations for adjudication; and (*d*) the acceptance of the 'one state one vote' doctrine in the General Assembly, whatever may be the difference in power and resources between the states.

Second are the avoidable human weaknesses of U.N. members: members do not pay subscriptions. Russia owes £19 million, and refuses to pay because it claims that the financial assessments for the Middle East and Congo operations were never approved by the Security Council. In all, there is a total unpaid bill (December 1964) of £48 million (Russia, the Soviet *bloc* countries, some Latin American countries and France). The United States already pays 32 per cent of any U.N. budget—more than twice the amount paid by any other country; to ask it to pay more is to stimulate criticism of the United Nations in the United States.

Third, the exclusion of Communist China from the U.N. This is largely because of the views and pressures of the U.S. Yet there is a growing feeling at the United Nations that the Chinese must somehow be brought in, even at the cost of the inevitable disruption this would create. Peking would have a veto in the Security Council. It would no doubt try to use the Assembly to propagate a revolutionary vision of the world. It would be certain to claim its quota of posts in the United Nations Secretariat. The balance so delicately contrived here over the past years would be shaken and a new one would have to be found. But to find such balances and to provide such a forum is in a sense part of what the United Nations is for. It is better that Peking should talk inside the United Nations than fight outside it. The United Nations survived the deepest freeze of the Soviet cold war. Mao could not do it much more damage than Stalin at his worst. Moreover, Mao is no more immortal than Stalin—and China, like Russia, may mellow into a more co-operative mood.

And fourth, the unusual environment in which the United Nations finds itself. While its record since 1954 is highly creditable, its work has been bedevilled by the Cold War and by the atmosphere of extreme nationalism and anticolonialism in which its deliberations take place.

Nevertheless, the future is hopeful. The above reasons for weakness are not new—the same explanations were given for the failures of the League of Nations. The success of the United Nations can be summarized very differently.

U.N. successes

First, its military and diplomatic achievements: military in Korea, Congo

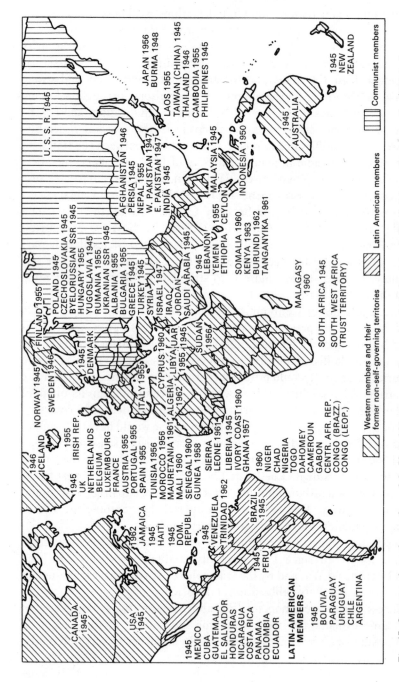

Fig. 47. Our map shows the members of the United Nations and the year in which they joined. Financial contributions to the U.N. budget are as follows: 'Western' bloc, 55 per cent; Communist bloc, 22 per cent; Africa, 2 per cent; Latin America, 5 per cent. The biggest contributor is the U.S. (32 per cent). Britain pays 7.5 per cent. The most important non-member is Communist China, but seven non-members participate in certain U.N. activities, such as the International Court. The U.N. faces a permanent financial crisis: of the total debt of £48 million on the Congo and Middle East operations, Russia owes £19 million and France has also refused to pay her share.

and Cyprus; diplomatic in New Guinea and Kashmir. It has halted some wars and averted others.

Second, in the eyes of the new nations, the United Nations has extraordinary importance. Membership in the organization is a symbol of nationhood, and participation in its councils a cherished opportunity. For many of the smaller nations, the United Nations provides an indispensable arena for contact with the outside world. In addition, the United Nations and its specialized agencies are an important source and channel for technical and economic assistance, preferred in many instances to assistance from individual nations. Far more than the Great Powers, the small nations look upon the United Nations as a shield against aggression. This 'deterrent potential' of the United Nations is doubtless more effective than we are apt to realize, in protecting some of the small new nations from the ambitions of less small neighbours.

It is true that the admission of the new nations, and the consequent doubling of membership, has created difficulties in the functioning of the U.N. Sixty-four new nations have come into being since 1945. The meeting rooms that were generously planned in 1950 are now cramped and will become more so. Again, a deliberative group of 120 is obviously more cumbersome than one of 50, and that applies not only to the General Assembly but to its seven main committees, which are composed of all member-states. Thus it has become more and more difficult for the General Assembly to finish its work in three months, because on many issues all the delegations feel they have to speak.

More significantly, the advent of the new nations has greatly increased the influence of the Afro-Asian group, which now comprises half the membership. Some 30 new African and 15 Asian nations have appeared since 1945. The influence, however, is less than it might otherwise be, because of the many different political orientations represented within the group—from Turkey, through many shades of non-alignment, to Mongolia. While the Afro-Asian group periodically meets and makes plans in an effort to arrive at agreed positions, it is often unable to achieve that result. However, the group has had striking effect on the United Nations. Many of these African and Asian states are former colonies of France and Britain, and thus are distinguished by a concern over 'colonialism'. They are particularly concerned with racial issues, with measures to eradicate *apartheid* in South Africa or with protection of the African majority in Rhodesia after U.D.I. Their problems are not of the Cold War but of development. So Afro-Asian solidarity is both a fight of the 'have nots' against the 'haves', and a geographical distinction. Some of these 'colonial' tensions are carried into U.N. debates. Many people in the West denounce the polarization of the United Nations into feuding power groups, but the Afro-Asians see this as a fulfilment. To them the value of the U.N. is precisely that it gives them admission to a world parliament. Secretary-General

U Thant of the Asian nation of Burma notes: 'The widening of membership has also brought the organization nearer to its goal of universality.'

The Afro-Asian nations are concentrating on what is important to them: more representation on councils and committees; an end to colonialism; elimination· of white discrimination against black in South Africa (though some themselves practise reverse discrimination). These small nations may well press these demands until the United Nations breaks; but until that happens, it offers to the new nations a platform, a political instrument and a safety-valve.

Third, it should be stressed that, on balance, the new nations in the General Assembly have usually come in on the Western side of the debate. The Soviet Union's proposals for the admission of Communist China, the exclusion of Nationalist China and advance approval for Communist China's ambitions against Formosa have been rejected emphatically by the Assembly. The new nations have given overwhelming support to Western initiatives, like the proposal for the 'Development Decade', for increased international co-operation in outer space and for an international surplus-food programme. The only issue on which the Western nations were several times out-voted was that of nuclear testing. But this was not a case of Soviet success. Part of the time the Soviet Union was in the minority, along with the United States. And on one occasion the Assembly, with Western support, voted to appeal to the Soviet Union not to explode its 50-megaton bomb—a resolution which the Russians fought bitterly.

Exercising in the Channel, Britain's first nuclear-powered submarine, Dreadnought.

And fourth, the United Nations must be judged not only as a debating body or as a military force but as the focus of a number of specialized agencies all working for progress.

The summing up

In the introduction to his report for 1956–57, the late Dag Hammarskjold offered as useful a balance sheet of U.N. success and failure as can be found:

'The Charter, read as a whole, does not endow the United Nations with any of the attributes of a super-state or of a body active outside the framework of decisions of member governments. The United Nations is, rather, an instrument for negotiating among, and to some extent for, governments. It is also an instrument added to the time-honoured means of diplomacy for concerting action by governments in support of the goals of the Charter.

'From time to time complaints are heard about the limitations upon the organization's power. . . . To turn aside from the United Nations now because it cannot be transformed into a world authority enforcing the law upon the nations would be to erase all the steady, though slow and painful, advances that have been made, and to close the door to hopes for the future of the world society, toward which present efforts and experiences should be at least a modest stepping-stone.

'We should, rather, recognize the United Nations for what it is—an admittedly imperfect but indispensable instrument of nations in working for a peaceful evolution toward a more just and secure world order. The dynamic forces at work in this stage of human history have made world organization necessary . . .

'Systems of alliance, maintained side by side with the United Nations in recognition of the prevailing balance of forces, may serve a useful purpose during the period through which we are passing. However, most of us agree that such systems of alliance, like other traditional means of diplomacy and defence of the national interest, are limited in their value as safeguards of the present and future security and welfare of our countries. Nations and groups of nations will never again be able to live and to arrogate judgement unto themselves in international affairs in ways which once were a matter of course.

'The greatest need today is to blunt the edges of conflict among the nations, not to sharpen them. If properly used, the United Nations can serve a diplomacy of reconciliation better than other instruments available to the member states.

'Conflicts may persist for long periods without an agreed solution, and groups of states may actively defend special and regional interests. Nevertheless, and in spite of temporary developments in the opposite direction under the influence of acute tension, the tendency in the United Nations is to wear away, or break down, differences, thus helping toward solutions which approach the common interest and application of the principles of the Charter.'

Index

THIS BOOK HAS BEEN SET IN MONOPHOTO EHRHARDT AND PRINTED
IN GREAT BRITAIN BY WILLIAM CLOWES AND SONS, LIMITED,
LONDON AND BECCLES